West Coast Bodybuilding Scene
The Golden Era

West Coast Bodybuilding Scene
The Golden Era

Dick Tyler

Foreword and captions
Dave Draper

On Target Publications
Santa Cruz, California

WEST COAST BODYBUILDING SCENE
The Golden Era

Dick Tyler

Foreword by Dave Draper
Captions by Dave Draper

First printing April 2004
ISBN: 1-931046-29-8

Published by
On Target Publications
P. O. Box 1335
Aptos, CA 95001 USA
(888) 466-9185
info@ontargetpublications.com
www.ontargetpublications.com

Library of Congress Cataloging-in-Publication Data

Tyler, Dick.
West Coast bodybuilding scene : the golden era / Dick Tyler ; foreword by Dave Draper ; [captions by Dave Draper].
p. cm.
Includes bibliographical references and index.
ISBN 1-931046-29-8 (trade paper)
1. Bodybuilding—California—History. 2. Bodybuilders—California—Interviews. I. Title.
GV546.5 .T95 2004
646.7'5'09794—dc22

2003022246

10 9 8 7 6 5 4 3 2 1

Contents

Foreword

Musclebuilding, I suspect, is as old as the hills. When man first realized women were attracted to a slick, muscular body and discovered that rocks, prey, mischievous cave dwellers and monsters were lifted more easily with a mighty back and strong arms, he put his genius to work, and thus his body, to improve his sinewy assets. The Dinosaur Championships held in 10,000 BC crowned the original Mr. World and records were established in rock snatches and boulder clean-and-jerks.

The movement had begun and the next thing you know John Grimek is Mr. America and Steve Reeves is making Hercules films. This muscle stuff is becoming popular; there's a subculture budding in the grungy YMCAs and garages across the states—it's spreading to the sunny beaches of California and before long it will be mainstream.

And so the stage is set for the West Coast Bodybuilding Scene, that time in the history of weightlifting when bodybuilding neared critical mass, swirled in its growing energy and attracted its grand external source of power, the spectators. It was the Golden Era of Bodybuilding, new, young, alive, untainted, unworn, unexploited... and adored. The spectators became fans.

West Coast Bodybuilding Scene is about a particular group of people with a special interest who inhabited a small region of California during a short period of time. Dick Tyler experienced, observed and recorded this golden stretch of bodybuilding history between '65 and '71 as a journalist, as a participant and as a weightlifting devotee. His eyes and ears were acute and his love for the sport was wrapped up in an affectionate sense of humor, the most accurate and appealing conduit of delivery for this unique physical expression.

You see, bodybuilding is a sport, an art form, a diversion, a hobby, an obsession, a competition, a love affair and a lifestyle.

Things heated up around the world in the '60s. Life became restless. Emotions and passions of the sensitive and few picked up the current, responded to the eddies and felt the vibe. Men looked for something to hold onto, to keep them ready and balanced, directed yet entertained—iron and steel, muscle and might. Muscle Beach, too wonderful to endure, sadly unraveled. Individuals surfaced in its place and what simmered for years was ready to erupt in slow motion.

Watch the passionate explosion of events from the lens of the cameras whose shutters were triggered at the most perfect moment by artists Russ Warner and Artie Zeller, Jimmy Caruso and Gene Mozee. Few photographers have witnessed in their viewfinders the vivid story which is about to unfold. Those same picture-takers engendered the events, stimulated bodybuilding's progress, universally popularized physical fitness and recorded the stunning occasions now known as history.

There were only a handful of weightlifters, powerlifters and bodybuilders during this natural period of bodybuilding development. And in the U.S. three men and their magazines—Peary Rader with *Ironman,* Bob Hoffman with *Strength and Health* and Joe Weider with *Mr. America* and *Muscle Builder*—sought to expand the sport and popularize its participants.

Popularize soon became known as capitalize. It was during the Golden Era when the machinery of competition and marketing magnified and amplified the activities of muscle and might, iron and steel, and went on to create the rather large pool of spectators and participants of all shapes and sizes we know today. Bodybuilding, once a puppy with a wagging tail, is now a monster. I do not say this without affection. Monsters can be cute.

My name is Dave Draper and I had the precious advantage (graced by God, actually) of being in the middle of it all. And I'm in the middle of it all again. The years have come and gone and tons of weights have moved up and down. I, as you, love this stuff and I can't, nor do I wish to, put it aside.

The story is accompanied by 160 pictures worth a thousand words, and I slip in my two cents to comment on the black and white portrayals and keep you apprised of names, dates, places and events.

As this is not a history from which to learn, but a memory to share and delight in, a stiff and factual account gives way to loose continuity. There was a marriage in minds and souls of Dick and Artie that cannot be duplicated and their synergy provides an insight into a beautiful past that no historian or scholar could ever understand.

Life happens once. Only here may it happen again. Have fun and God's speed.

Dave Draper
Santa Cruz, California

Preface

When I was fourteen years old I looked in the mirror and decided if I just had a bit more muscle the girls would be mad about me. Hmmm. Now just how could this be done?

About a month or so later I came across a magazine at a newsstand. Its name was *Muscle Power* and it had on the cover a photo of a man with the biggest set of muscles I had ever seen. Inside was an article about him with a picture of him flexing his incredible biceps. That was it! Here was the secret of eternal, everlasting, magnificent, all-powerful, triumphant, girl-catching manhood. How did he get that way? The magazine clearly stated the only way I could get massive biceps, turnip-shaped thighs, diamond-shaped calves, melon-shaped deltoids, granite pecs and washboard abs was to lift Weider weights and follow the Weider System of bodybuilding. I bought the magazine and carried it so the cover was showing—I hoped anyone looking at me would think I was a muscleman, too.

I got a set of weights and a training partner and set up the gym in my garage. This was in the 1940s and was the beginning of a way of life I follow to this day.

But things were a little different then. Bodybuilding had only a few hardcore disciples. The average person thought of a bodybuilder as some kind of musclebound freak who would have a difficult time trying to tie his shoelaces. Anytime I could talk someone into going to a physique contest they would end up laughing and making fun of the thing I took so seriously—all except my training partner, who was as nuts as I was.

After a few months, my friend and I felt we had cultivated enough turnips and melons to challenge a professional wrestler in the ring, but were gratefully saved from probable death by the ushers at the arena.

Things were so different—no two bodybuilders looked the same—you could tell who was who just by their shape. If all you saw was a silhouette, you could tell a John Grimek from an Alan Stephan or George Eiferman or Marvin Eder or Steve Reeves or Clarence Ross or Vince Gironda or Eric Pedersen. Everyone came with a different set of muscles and a different personality.

Try as I might, even training all day till eleven at night in my pajamas, I began to accept the fact that I could never be like those bodybuilders in the magazines. But this didn't end my desire to be muscular and strong. Even when friends dropped away to do other things, I kept lifting weights.

It wasn't until the late 1950s when Steve Reeves played Hercules in a movie that the public realized a muscular and powerful man was something to be admired. Soon people wanted to look like him and gyms began to spring up around the country. Physique contests were no longer relegated to the backend of weightlifting meets, always after midnight, and instead became premier events. Now the bodybuilding champions became heroes and in was ushered the Golden Era of bodybuilding. Champions like Larry Scott, Bill Pearl, Arnold Schwarzenegger, LeRoy Colbert, Dave Draper, Frank Zane, Rick Wayne and Franco Columbu became household names and by Joe Weider I was given the "job" of recording this exciting period. This, then, is what this book is all about.

I want to thank all the aforementioned bodybuilders, and those I have unintentionally forgotten to mention, for making this literary journey so interesting and so much fun. Thanks to writers like Armand Tanny, Gene Mozee and Rick Wayne for being so good at what they did. To Ron Haddad for putting music into contests to match the greatness of the athletes competing. To Russ Warner and Artie Zeller for looking through the lens of their cameras and creating images the world of bodybuilding will never forget. To Joe Weider for creating a new world of bodybuilding and allowing me to record it. To George Jowett, Eugen Sandow, the Saxon Trio, Hermann Goerner, Siegmund Klein and Louis Cyr, some of the strongmen of old, for being strong men. To Bert Elliott—Kraft Heil! To Vince Gironda and Joe Gold for developing the pots that boiled the biggest and best sets of muscles the world had ever seen. A very big nod of gratitude to Bill Keyes for his interest and skill in compiling the things I wrote. To Laree Draper for her support and editorial expertise. A special thanks to my friend Dave Draper for believing that my efforts might be something worth saving.

And finally, my gratitude to my friend and inspiration—the greatest writer in the history of strength and bodybuilding, Earle E. Liederman.

Dick Tyler
Rocklin, California

Dick Tyler's text was written during the Golden Era of bodybuilding and appeared in Joe Weider's magazines *Muscle Builder* and *Mr. America* from 1965-1971. The photo captions that follow were written by Dave Draper, current day, using the benefit of hindsight.

More than twenty photographers contributed to the material that follows, including casual shots taken by Dick Tyler during his outings with the photographers. Artie Zeller, Jimmy Caruso, Gene Mozee and Russ Warner top the list of notable West Coast Bodybuilding Scene photographers.

ZELLER

Arnold speaks, Katz and Draper listen. Gold's original gym one late summer evening, 1970, the peak of what later became known as the Golden Era of bodybuilding

STERN

ONE

1965

Journey into the Past—Bill Pearl's Sandow Display

The lamplighter has just placed his lighter into the ornate globe of the street lamp outside our window. You can hear the horses' hoofs and the clatter of the carriage over the wet cobblestones as they make their way to the theatres and cabarets of the city. I'll be ready as soon as I fasten this last button on my shoe.

There's a light rain outside so we'd better wear our overcoats. The timepiece over the mantel checks with my pocket watch, telling us we had better hurry if we want to make it to the Music Hall on time.

Ever since we read the notice in the evening paper a few weeks ago of the impending visit of the magnificent Sandow, we've been anxiously awaiting the event. At last the day has come and, of course, we are going to the very first night of his appearance. I can hardly wait. The excitement of seeing one of the greatest strongmen in the world has had the whole city buzzing and here we are with front row seats. If we don't find a carriage soon, we'll be late and it's cold standing out here. Everyone who passes looks like they're puffing steam with the light from the street lamp illuminating their condensed breath.

"Hey, cabbie!" Ah, at last we've got one. "To the Palace Music Hall, and in a hurry, please!"

As our carriage draws up to the Music Hall, there are still a few people entering; we still have time. What a mixture of people—there are those in furs and jewels with their escorts, while just entering the theatre are what looks like a family in somewhat threadbare clothing. Almost all are here out of either admiration or curiosity. All are here, however, to see the featured attraction of the evening, Sandow.

I can hear the orchestra playing as I hand our tickets to the attendant. Except for the light from the orchestra pit in front of the stage, the hall is dark. There are our seats, the third and fourth from the aisle in the front row. Looks like a packed house; people were standing in the back as we entered. Shhhh, the curtain's going up.

It starts off with a dog act—it's amazing what those little animals can do. Next is a song and dance man, followed by a troupe of acrobats. A comedy team is next and they leave everybody laughing. They're followed by a sensational juggling act.

Now, for the moment we've all been waiting for. The curtain is down as the orchestra starts to play the stirring strains from the Grand March of Aida. The curtain rises. The footlights are dim, revealing a stage littered with chromed and shiny weights placed in dramatic array. In the center of the stage is a large pedestal. On the back and to the rear of the pedestal is a gleaming white Roman column.

As the music rises, Sandow himself comes from a side of the stage. Slowly, he mounts the posing pedestal and begins a phenomenal display of artistic poses and muscle control. The audience is cheering. They have never seen anything like this before.

All the noise makes me blink and shake my head. I close my eyes hard.

As I open them, I look around and see the people around me dressed in the modern clothing of suits and sports clothes. The cheering is the same, only the man on the stage is not Sandow but another immortal—one of the present day: Bill Pearl. My imagination let me wander into the realm of the past. Now, I was seeing things as they were actually happening. Pearl is going through his posing routine to the thunderous applause of a delighted audience.

STERN

Bill Pearl's muscles were thickly and symmetrically mounded one upon the other as if by the hands of a sculptor. His physique exuded strength and few strongmen have matched his total body power. This is Bill as Sandow in the '60s.

After the posing, which is bathed in a flickering light to give the feeling of antiquity, Bill leaps from the pedestal and walks to an imposing globe barbell in the center of the stage. Placing his hands carefully on the bar, he cleans the weight to his shoulders. This is no ordinary clean, for the bar seemed to almost bend in half with the force of the initial pull. Now it's at the shoulders. After a moment's pause, Pearl rams the weight overhead, then lets it come crashing to the floor. It sounded like a ton had been lifted. Pearl steps to the footlights and tries to quiet the applause with his outstretched hand. Finally, it subsides.

"Anyone who feels he is able to duplicate the feat I have just performed is free to try."

A startled murmur goes through the audience. The auditorium is filled with big, strong men. Many, for fear they may fail, refuse to even try.

Then, from the rear of the hall can be heard, "Go on, go on, you can do it."

"Go ahead, try."

"Go ahead and do it."

In response to the urging, a monstrous man finally stands and hesitatingly makes his way down the aisle. As the audience becomes aware the challenge is being accepted, they start to applaud their encouragement.

A lot taller and heavier than Bill, he looks like an easy mark to win the defy Pearl has issued.

Time after time, the giant tries to lift the weight, but can get it no further than his midsection, sort of a high deadlift. More perplexed than disgusted, he gives up and goes back to his seat to the applause of everyone for his effort.

After the audience is settled again, the mighty Pearl picks up a pair of seventy-penny spikes, the biggest made. He clangs them together and hits them on the floor so the sound will attest to their content of metal. Placing his hands on either end of one of the spikes, he hunches forward. His mighty deltoids and arms bulge in the anticipation of what will be required of them.

Suddenly, there is an explosion of power and the spike submits to the force that was supplied. The spike, which is now bent into a "U" shape, is handed to the audience for their observation, with the challenge of anyone to unbend it. Bill then does this with several more spikes. No one, as yet, has been able to straighten the spikes or lift the barbell.

Pearl goes over to a standard car license plate. Placing it carefully in his hands, he braces it against his body. With a dramatic display of muscle and power, he tears the plate in half. The audience cheers this splendid display of strength. Without a pause, he picks up two more plates and places them together. With another mighty effort, the pair of plates are torn apart simultaneously. Now, we're really cheering.

Still displaying the strength of his hands, he tears a deck of cards in half almost with contempt for the ease it takes. It seems he has inexhaustible power. On he goes to a barbell brought to centerstage. This is no ordinary barbell, for in place of globes or plates there are chair-like seats on either end. Two lovelies are selected from the audience and placed in each of the seats. (The girls don't have to be lovely, it just makes work more enjoyable that way.) The girls, or should I say the bar, is then cleaned and jerked overhead.

Next, Bill places a chain around his chest. He pulls the heavy links tightly around his ribcage. For a moment he stands, concentrating. A hush falls over all. With a deep breath he lifts his shoulders. Suddenly, he flexes his lats and throws out his chest with a rush of power. A loud snap is heard and the chain falls to the floor, broken.

The cheering has hardly died down when we see this great strength athlete has a hot water bottle in his hands. Putting it against his mouth, he begins to blow into it as easily as most would blow into a balloon. The hot water bag begins to grow with each mighty puff from the Pearl lungs. With his massive chest heaving like a bellows, he forces more and more air into the bag until it is unable to resist the pressure from within. Wham! The bag explodes in testimony to Bill Pearl's powerful lungs.

With that explosion the act comes to an end.

STERN

A mighty man, hard-muscled, balanced and defined. Bill Pearl caused significant ripples in the pond of bodybuilding when he won his first Mr. America and Mr. Universe titles in 1953. He went on to cause floods and tidal waves when he won the professional Mr. Universe four times, '56, '61, '67, '71.

This unusual presentation came as no accident. It has been carefully developed over the years by both Pearl and his good friend and manager, Leo Stern. Leo is a fine athlete in his own right and owns one of the best gyms in the Southland.

It was back in 1957 the idea came into being. By then, Bill Pearl had already become justly famous for his physique. As a result of his renown, he was being constantly asked to give posing exhibitions. Bill and Leo decided that all Bill was doing was posing like any of the contestants in the actual contest. They wanted to do something different, something special. It was then they hit upon the idea of doing an oldtime strongman act.

They decided the act to copy was the most classic of them all, that of Eugen Sandow. With painstaking precision, they gathered photos of Sandow and tried to put into reasonable sequence the most artistic of the poses. After a great deal of study and work, the unique routine Pearl now uses was perfected.

But, was this enough? Not by a long shot. This proved to be only the beginning. To make the act as authentic as possible, they felt he should be surrounded by only those things that would complement the period of the turn of the century. Special Roman sandals like those worn by Sandow were commissioned and made in New York. During his act, Pearl wears a hairpiece, a posing outfit made out of animal skin and a mustache and the sandals. It creates quite a romantic picture of that era long ago. As time went by, the feats of strength were added until he now has the act as it stands today.

Since its inception in 1957, Bill's act has grown in popularity. Unfortunately, business commitments keep him from filling all but two or three engagements per year. Ah, but the places he goes when he can. Aside from having appeared around the United States, Bill has performed in Europe, Africa and India to thousands of enthralled fans.

If you are ever lucky enough to see Bill Pearl's strongman act, relax and let yourself be transported back to those glorious days of the past. You'll find it's an exciting journey.

•

The lives and feats of the old-time strongmen have always held a particular fascination for me. It is therefore quite natural that from time to time I would try my hand at some of their pet stunts myself. Now the bent press took too much style and time to learn; the back and hip lifts took too much weight and room, while supporting feats such as supporting a car with your feet took, well, aw c'mon already. Anyway, I hit upon "tearing" stunts. You know, telephone books, cards and stuff. I got so I was on a lost weekend with the cards. Drunk with power I ferreted out all I could find and tore them asunder with great gusto. My cure from that demon of deck-tearing came when I decided that I was ready to quarter a deck. For what seemed an eternity, I struggled with that little half-deck of cards. I must have worn them away, because after great sacrifice

I had a fourth of a deck of cards in each hand. In the process, however, my hands started to bleed. I ended my career with a little more wisdom and a little less of the red stuff.

BELLAS

Armand Tanny looks handsome and content as he denies the law of gravity in this one-arm clean and press. Can you imagine the stress and strain on the body and mind as the cold iron bar seeks a more logical resting place?

•

Behind the Weider Muscle Beach headquarters is an alley that leads to the back of the Santa Monica Post Office. Art Zeller, the well-known bodybuilder and Weider Publications photographer, works there and quite naturally comes to visit us often. The other day he dropped in to see about purchasing some weights and we got to talking about Zeller's old training partner, the phenomenal Marvin Eder. For those of you who might not know, Eder is not only one of the best-built men in the world, but also one of the strongest. His feats of strength are too numerous to mention except to say that pound for pound I don't know of any man who is stronger. All of his feats were done in slow and strict style. He only weighed around 198 pounds and did things that many of our super heavyweights of today couldn't even approach.

Zeller said that one of Eder's most impressive exercises, which was done as part of his regular workout, were sets of ten reps in the dipping movement using close to 400 pounds. That's right, I said 400 pounds, and those dips went all the way down and all the way up. Gene Mozee told me of the time he saw Eder down at the beach do a dip with Dom Juliano and Malcom Brenner hanging around his waist. The total poundage was estimated at around 420 pounds, not counting Eder's own bodyweight. Zeller claims that one of the secrets of his power was his heavy bone structure. Whatever the reason, Marvin Eder goes down in my book as one of the great strongmen in bodybuilding.

•

Reminds me of Muscle Beach and the old days—every weekend was like a three-ringed circus. The lifting pen was always busy with some of the best power and physique men of the time. The crowds were sometimes ten deep to see these physical wonders. It was commonplace to see such men as Farbotnik, Reeves, Hilligan, Tanny, Eiferman and many more hitting it hard under the Southern California sun. On the adagio platform you would see the likes of Les and Pudgy Stockton, Harold Zinkin, DeForrest "Moe" Most and Bruce Connors doing balancing and strength feats that would stretch the imagination. Scattered around the sands were some great ring and bar men such as Johnny Robinson executing stunts that would have the crowd gasping. Sounds like fun? Well, it sure was. 'Scuse, please, while I brush away a tear and blow the old bazoo.

CHARLES

Building totem poles at Muscle Beach when the building was good. Where have all the flowers gone, long time passing? Muscle Beach in Santa Monica, California, in the mid-'50s.

•

Those of you who watch the popular TV show "The Adventures of Ozzie and Harriet" probably noticed Rick Nelson has more than his share of muscles. This, dear reader, was not your imagination working overtime. Rick is probably one of the most dyed-in-the-wool weight trainers around. He has been known to train even in the early hours of the morning if this was the only time he could find in his busy schedule. One of the first things he asked me when I saw him recently was, "Just how big is this David, the Gladiator?" As you all know he was referring to our own Dave Draper who has one of the most popular programs on Los Angeles TV. My answer to that question was simply, "Mighty big, Rick, mighty big."

•

Near the back door of the office here at Muscle Beach headquarters is the wash room. There's a good mirror in said room, which more often than not serves as a great reference mirror for the poses of our leading California physique men. The sunlight streaming in through the back window gives us a great posing light, while the posing dais is a box full of Weider barbell plates and our audience is made up of the muscle men who happen to be visiting at the time. The only hitch is the washroom door has to be taken off its hinges, however this is something we've gotten quite proficient at.

This particular day Ray Raridon came in to purchase a pair of Reg Lewis posing trunks for a forthcoming contest. Ray put on the trunks and off came the door. Dave Draper, Chet Yorton and I all kitbitzed Ray's routine. Now Ray has great overall development. Good shoulders, chest and arms—but his legs, particularly his thighs, are absolutely amazing. In fact, I would say his thigh development is about the most spectacular I've ever seen. It must be seen to be believed. I have never seen so many striations and so much shape on any man's leg before. He has so many cuts it's like looking at a leg through a piece of broken glass.

•

Not long ago I had a talk with David "Deacon" Jones, one of the Los Angeles Rams' fearsome defensive line. He claims all the Rams are hooked on weight training. This was borne out on a television program that showed the extensive weight facilities at the Rams' training camp. According to the Deacon, Roosevelt Grier is the only member of the squad who refuses to train with the iron. You know they say you can't argue with success, however as great as Grier is now, I can't help but think how much greater he might be flexing his powerful muscles with weights attached to them.

•

When the warm weather comes around and I have the opportunity, I love to go into my backyard, put on the suntan lotion, turn on the portable radio and soak up the warm and relaxing rays of King Sol. My mind usually wanders back a few years to when a group of us hardy weight trainers used to get together for Sunday outings at State Beach.

Now if you don't know where State Beach is, it's about a mile or so up the coast from Muscle Beach. Let's see, our group consisted of Jerry Wagner, Don Houston, Skip Klassen, Roger Torrey (Roger is six-foot, five inches of the muscle you may have seen in the flicks or on TV) and me.

Oh, wait, I forgot, there was one more, his name was—now, let's see—oh, yes, Larry Scott. The lumps were just budding at the time, but even then I could tell Larry had a great future in bodybuilding.

Our day would be spent tossing around plastic flying saucers, lolling in the sun, running in the sand, tossing the shot, racing, jumping and most of all exercising our eyes looking at all the dolls.

On those long summer days we'd stay till almost seven or eight in the evening. The tide would be going out, leaving the wet sand like a gold and shiny sheet of glass. Ah, the smell of that salt air and the sound of the sea! Finally we would leave and get together later for something to eat and a show.

Sometimes we go through periods in our lives when great camaraderie abounds, then slowly it all passes and we go on our separate ways never to return.

•

MOZEE

It's not that Don Howorth has wide shoulders, but he's the only guy I know who had to turn sideways to enter a room. Barn doors were named after Howorth and he cast a shadow like a beach umbrella in the afternoon sun.

Stopped by Vince's Gironda's gym the other day and as usual the joint was jumping. There's so much wall-to-wall muscle at times you can get a pump just watching. While there I got talking to Don Howorth, who seems to be exploding with new muscle every time I see him. His entire training is being geared for just one thing—the upcoming IFBB Mr. America contest.

"This is it for me, Dick," said Don. "I'm going to be in the best shape of my life for this contest; I'm going to win it." Just looking at the colossus he has become, I find it hard to doubt this might be an infallible prediction.

•

Quiz time: What two bodybuilders are known as "The Surfboard" and "The Wall," respectively? Now you may have some pretty worthwhile ideas in mind, but around Vince's Gym "The Surfboard" is Larry Scott, while "The Wall" is Don Howorth. Me? Oh, I'm known as "The Flab."

•

During a recent visit to Marcy's Gym—hey, can you believe visiting gyms is my job?—I found two mighty behemoths struggling with the iron. Bob Bennell, the taller of the two, looks like he stands around six feet and must weigh a good 200 or more pounds. A great deal of this weight seems to be centered around his arms, chest and shoulders. The area is like a great nest of rocks.

Bob's training partner has to be seen to be properly appreciated. Let's just say he is a walking cannonball who answers to the name of Mickey Rubin. Mick stands around five-foot, five inches and weighs close to 200 pounds.

Both men are quite strong. They attribute a great deal of their power to a system of pauses between the reps of many of their exercises. Without releasing the weight, each rep is a complete test of continuing strength, for each repetition of most of the sets is started only after a pause of a couple of seconds. This means no jerking or bouncing movements. Try this for a full workout sometime, ye who think ye are strong.

•

Jack LaLanne was built to endure. He was also built to inspire, motivate and pull tug boats around Alcatraz every so often. He encompasses all periods of bodybuilding and we shared the Golden Era together, onstage, backstage and in the gym.

WARNER

Saw Jack LaLanne the other day. Here is one guy who not only seems to have stopped the process of aging, but has found a way to push it back. He looks younger every time I see him. Told me that seven days a week he gets up at five in the morning and works out till seven. He then goes to the TV studio where he does his well-known exercise show. If I know Jack, that two-hour workout of his would take the average weight trainer at least four hours.

Reminds me of the time I walked into the gym years ago to be greeted by Jack who ran to me (he hardly ever seems to walk) and brightly said, "Dick, let's take a workout together."

"Sure," said I innocently. Well-l-l-l-l, minutes later I couldn't even open or close my hands, they were so tired. I collapsed on a bench to watch in amazement as Jack leaped from one exercise to another.

If he asked me to work out with him today, I'd be smart and collapse before I got started.

•

Lou Degni, alias Mark Forest of those foreign muscle extravaganzas, is back in town. He and his good friend, Armand Tanny, were seen doing the strip recently. That's the Sunset Strip here in Hollywood, where some of the most famous nightspots in the world are. Lou looks in great shape; he's never one to let his lumps slip. The only thing that outshines his muscles is his personality.

STUDIO

Lou Degni, also known as Mark Forest, built his muscular body on the sands of Muscle Beach in time for the early hero films, those built on movie sets in Rome. Chains in hand, Lou plays Hercules as he tears down another castle wall.

•

Our main man. There is the eye of the beholder and the eye of the beheld. Dick Tyler possessed the eyes of both. He chronicled the days of Muscle Beach and the Golden Era, while himself immersed in the power of the iron and steel.

BELLAS

All this talk reminds me of a time that could have been pretty disastrous for yours truly. TV was young at the time and so was I. In fact TV was so young the biggest draw on the ten-inch screen was wrestling, while I was so young I believed it was all on the level. And, brother, that's young.

It was on the occasion of my birthday I decided it would be jolly good fun if I could hold my party at the wrestling arena. Now in those days, as at present, there were the heroes and the villains who fought it out till the bitter end. It seemed every week a villain would become so baited by the crowd he would issue a challenge to all who dare step in and try his might.

My training partner at the time was my good buddy, Mike Barrier. We had budding weight-trained bumps that were a lot larger in our minds than on our bodies. Armed with these unfortunate misconceptions, Mike and I made a pact that the first villain to offer a challenge would be met by our combined force, which would therefore destroy him. At the matches, the card had proceeded to a bout that featured "Gorgeous" Billy Darnell and "The French Clutch."

"The Clutch" won the first fall and was being harangued by the crowd when he had the downright gall to challenge the audience. Mike looked at me—I looked at Mike—this was it. Up we got and strutted down the aisle with lats spread (naturally). I had one foot in the ring when an usher, who is trained to be on the lookout for nuts like us, pulled us back. Had he not, maybe you wouldn't be reading this kooky stuff right now.

•

At the recent Mr. California contest, the audience was treated to an event that may never be repeated. On the stage of the Embassy Auditorium were undoubtedly three of the greatest bench pressers in the world—the youngest and best in the person of the amazing eighteen-year-old, 181-pound John Kojigian; the eldest and best represented by the seventy-four-year-old Karl Norberg and the just-plain best by that colossus, Pat Casey.

Norberg, who started training when he was sixty-eight, made "only" 430 pounds because of an injured shoulder. There was a friendly contest between Kojigian and Casey with Casey betting he could beat Kojigian by one hundred pounds. When Kojigian pressed an amazing 450 pounds, it set the stage for a showdown in the form of a world-record performance by Casey, who went up to 570 pounds and barely missed 580. The official best is 540 pounds. Now all of this was done in strict form, but none of these lifts could be considered for a record. Reason? They didn't compete in the squat and the deadlift. C'mon, AAU, wise up. Strength is strength and the best is the best; why all this jazz combining other lifts?

•

CARUSO

I can tell by the smile this is Zabo, also known as the "Chief." He answers to Irwin Koszewski, but only if it's time to eat. I call him Zabe.

More than anyone I know, Zabe epitomizes Muscle Beach with his natural lifestyle, Zen attitude and peaceful philosophy. After leaving the army in the mid-'40s, he's seldom been more than a mile from its sand and allure.

For some inexplicable reason he's famed for his abdominal development. Go figure.

Okay, okay, I'll get off the contest, but one more thing: Irvin "Zabo" Koszewski gave a surprise posing routine that was amazing. Amazing not just because he's in his forties, but equally because he looked so great for any age. His muscular separation seems better than when I first saw him pose some fifteen years ago. In fact, he might well have won the Mr. California title had he been eligible to enter. With the Mr. America, Mr. Universe and Mr. Olympic crowns up for grabs this September, I hope Zabo gives 'em a try.

•

Reg Lewis has recently opened a swank figure salon in Toluca Lake. When I visited his establishment recently, I expected to see Reg greet me in white tie and tails, his place is so plush. Let's just say I doubt if he furnished it from the gift coupons found on the back of a pack of cigarettes. It must have cost him a small fortune, but brother, it was worth it.

Reg was hitting a short workout. He had his shirt off and he went through a short posing routine for me. What a lat spread! In fact, his entire upper body looked in contest condition.

First come, first served. Reg Lewis was first when they were handing out lats. "I'll take a pair of double-XL, please." Thus, his V-shape out V'd the V of everyone else. He stands onstage at the Opera House in NY after winning Mr. America in 1963. He eventually won his final competition, the Masters Natural Mr. America, in 1982.

CARUSO

"I'm going to enter the Mr. Universe this year, Dick," he said while spreading his back until I thought his lats would touch in front. "If I'm lucky enough to win, I'll enter the Mr. Olympia."

With lats like Reg's and a strong wind, he should be able to sail to any heights he aims for. Ain't that awful?

Mr. America 1965—The Blond Bomber Emerges Victorious in a Hotly Contested Event

The pilot has just announced we are 35,000 feet above the surface of the earth winging our way to California. Looking through the window, I can see below the gold of the setting sun shining on the almost glassy smooth surface of the clouds. Every now and then this serene plain is broken up by dramatic formations that seem to erupt into billowing puffs and cones. All of this is splashed with hues of gold and contrasting lines of shadow. It is a scene that could be a setting for the golden chariots of Die Valkyrie or a playground for the gods of Mt. Olympus. To complement this visual grandeur the airlines supply a stereophonic sound system through headphones that complete a dazzling assault upon the senses.

With my eyes lingering on these scenes, my mind tugs on my memory and lets me know I must get to the task to which I have been assigned, that of relating to you the events of the evening before. This is not difficult, for the memory of last night illuminates the shadows of forgetfulness and turns my hand to the joyful retelling of a great event.

It was only a few days earlier that I arrived in New York, a little lonely, but anxious to see the big IFBB show for which I had traveled some 3,000 miles to witness. It wasn't long, however, before this loneliness was swept away with the activities of the contest.

At the New Jersey Weider headquarters everyone was scurrying about in the happy confusion that comes from anticipation. One of the favorite topics of conversation was Dave Draper. Since no one on the East Coast had seen Dave for a couple years, their curiosity quite naturally was high.

"I know he looks great in the pictures, but film is one thing, flesh is another. To me, he's still just big smooth Dave Draper." This seemed to be the general consensus. All liked Dave for the nice guy he is, but he was always just big and smooth; he'd never had any cuts. Most seemed to wonder why Joe Weider has stuck his neck out for a guy who had only won the title of Mr. New Jersey. Since that time Joe has publicized Dave as one of the coming greats of the bodybuilding world.

Even I wondered why Joe would go so far. Covers almost every other month and a steady flow of articles had made big Dave famous without even being seen by a vast majority of the bodybuilding public. Joe explained to me he felt when he first met Dave he had the potential to become a great champion.

"He possessed a great bone structure and splendid muscle shape and size. The only thing lacking was muscle separation and definition. At one time there might have been little hope for someone like Dave, but with the modern methods I have developed, my continually improving equipment, and new nutritional aids like Crash Cut, Dave could do what others wouldn't begin to try. You also have to have dedication and bomb your body every day. Dave has this quality; that's one of the reasons he should reach the top. Dick, I'm staking a great deal of my reputation as a trainer on whether Draper makes a good showing." Joe's eyes were narrowed and his jaw was set. I could tell how much this meant to him.

One evening before the contest we had dinner with two of the foreign contestants. On several occasions they made remarks about "fat" Dave Draper. To these men Draper was a joke. On leaving the restaurant they accidentally bumped into a fat man who was entering. "Oh, hello, Dave," they said laughingly.

"Just wait till you see." I snapped back at them. "You're all in for a big surprise. You'll eat your words before the night of the contest is over." They paid no attention. Joe just looked at me in a resigned way as if he had been through this many times.

Now came the day of the big show. This was not a place for weak hearts. It takes courage to stand up for your beliefs when all about you think you are wrong. No one was about to back down.

I was standing at the stage door as the entrants began to arrive. You can always tell the California boys by their great tans. There was Nista looking better than ever, followed by Zabo Koszewski and Chet Yorton.

When Dave Draper arrived he came over to me and said, "Well, Dick, I guess this is it." He looked like he was on his way to an execution. He opened his traveling bag and took out a beautiful pair of light blue trunks that were interwoven with silver. "Bill Pearl gave me this pair of trunks for the contest. He said it was the only time he had ever done that."

I told Joe about it. All he would say was, "Great, now if he has the muscle to stuff into them he might do well."

During the prejudging you could see it was going to be close. Nista looked in top shape, Koszewski was in the best shape of his life. Mike Ferraro was sensational and a host of others looked like they could take the title. When Draper posed you could see the looks of surprise on everyone's face. Chet Yorton, with blood in his eye, looked like one of the very best, although I thought he looked a little heavy. Time would tell. After the prejudging was over, all that was left to do was to wait until the band started to play and the curtains parted.

At exactly eight o'clock the strains of the Star Spangled Banner filled the huge Brooklyn Academy of Music. It was standing room only—the balconies were filled, as were the boxes. People were even standing in the aisles. The tension was terrific, like we were all waiting for something great to happen.

Bud Parker went to the microphone and the curtains parted again. One by one the greatest physiques in America took their place on the posing dais. Bernie Booth, while not tall, had such excellent proportions his physique would have worn well at any height. My good friend Zabo Koszewski delighted the huge crowd by giving one of the best displays of the night.

"Now, that shows what a real pro can do," said Joe Weider, who was sitting in the next seat.

CARUSO

Standing room only and the voltage rising. A privileged photographer with his back to the stage snapped this sensational picture of the Opera House audience. The energy and excitement was electric, the experience and emotions unchartered and the backstage action was a controlled frenzy.

Would the real LeRoy Colbert stand up and take a bow?

On and on they came, some of the best-built men I have ever seen.

Johnny Maldonado was another of the smaller fellows with muscles he knows just what to do with. Mike Ferraro was a surprise entry. With a little more work on his deltoids and arms, Mike will be unbeatable. His lats erupt like two giant crescents of muscle from the rib cage. His pecs balloon out like two enormous fists. His legs are powerful and shapely; his arms and deltoids have splendid separation and shape, all they lack is size. Mike's going to be a real world-beater soon.

Joe Nista won the short man's class. Joe has perfect proportions. The only thing that Joe has chiseled in his life is the muscles onto his body. His great muscles, personality and that great California tan make him a winner every time.

By now the audience was getting muscle-logged with the great array they had seen. Bud Parker announced the name Chet Yorton. Pandemonium broke loose. Whatever my doubts might have been during the prejudging, they vanished as Chet started his routine. For Herculean mass, Chet is second to none. With each pose he looked better until I thought those assembled to watch would go wild. Clearly he was the one to beat.

Finally, after a few more contestants, out came big Dave Draper. When his name was announced the crowd let loose with a burst of cheers. As he stepped under the posing light another cheer went up for before them was a bronzed colossus the likes of which they hadn't thought possible. Words alone cannot do justice to Dave's physique. His is probably one of the most dramatic combinations of size, shape and definition I have ever seen.

"I want him!" yelled a beautiful girl sitting behind us.

"Who me?" I said hopefully.

"No, stupid, that blond giant on the stage."

"Oh."

Win, lose or draw, Joe had proven his point. Weider methods had won again, and in a magnificent way. Since only the judges knew the decision until the winners were announced, Joe had to sit there biting his nails along with all the rest of us.

The emcee stepped once again to the microphone. The winner of Best Arms—Dave Draper; Best Chest—Tommy Aybar; Best Back—Chet Yorton; Best Abdominals—you guessed it, the abdominal sandman from Venice Beach, Zabo Koszewski; and Best Legs—Chet Yorton. The winner of the title Most Muscular Man in America was Chet Yorton.

All right! Who won the Mr. America title? The emcee stepped to the microphone. The winner of the title Mr. America for 1965 is...Dave Draper. What a wild scene followed!

CARUSO

When I thought no one was looking I held my breath, closed my eyes and leaped onto the posing dais, hit a few shots and miraculously disappeared. I later discovered the place was packed with screaming fans—"They were hanging off the chandeliers, Draper"—and I'd won the 1965 Mr. America title.

•

New York used to be my home, but since I was there last I've grown older while the city has grown younger. The city is glass, steel and flesh. Me. I'm nothing but flesh.

Early arrivals for the contest were NABBA Mr. Universe 1964, Earl Maynard, and the former Mr. Great Britain, Rick Wayne; two more fun-loving or personable men you've never met.

"I'm going to win the title, Dick, m'boy," remarked Earl. "I didn't come all this way to lose."

"Okay, then let's see that arm I've heard so much about," sez I, full of curiosity. He flexed his arm showing a full, well-rounded inner biceps. Without saying a word, he brought down his arm and showed its outer surfaces. It was an incredible sight, filled with those lines that make an extraordinary arm!

"You know, Earl, you've got a great overall arm development, but the view of the outer surface is better than the inside."

With a twinkle in his eye, he looked at me and said, "Ah, but Dick, I know; that's why I always save the best and show it last."

When he was wasn't lifting weights and competing in physique contests, Earl Maynard leaped into the ring and wrestled giants professionally. I'd rather leap onto a posing dais or over tall buildings.. "Say uncle, Earl. Louder."

•

Joe Weider should win the title of best host. I was treated like visiting royalty. Every night we went to a different place to eat. One night I ended up having two dinners. This got me pretty upset, however. Here was Joe, the most knowledgeable authority on bodybuilding in the world, allowing—no, forcing—my Adonis-like body to become a bag of heaving fat. I'll admit I didn't fight the process.

Maybe I should have, for during the Mr. America prejudging in the afternoon, I went out in the audience of the theatre to get a better look. There sitting in one row were Earl Maynard, Harold Poole and Larry Scott. Being so big, they had to allow a seat between them. When I joined them, I found that I was two seats away from Scott because I was so fat. They were all pretty nice about it though, and tried to convince me they were leaving more room for me because of my bad breath. And who said that your friends won't tell you?

•

Random impression of the East Coast office: Jon Twichell is a lot bigger than I had imagined...The office seemed like a bookie joint with all the bets that were flying around as to who would win the contest...It was great to see all the natural enthusiasm around; it was like being at a meat market listening to all the bodyparts being discussed.

Random impression from the show: The many languages used in interpreting the judges' instructions to the contestants made the Mr. Universe contest even more exciting...It was great to see the contestants encouraging and helping one another...Some of the trophies were so heavy that you had to be a weightlifter to take them home...A room was set up backstage as a gym. If you stood too close to the gym doorway during the pumping process, you took a chance of being sucked inside by the heavy breathing.

KAYE

Jimmy Caruso is a meticulous man, wiry and patient and focused. He was designed to create great physique photography and I have had the privilege to stand before his grand arrangement of cameras, tripods, lights, shadow boxes, umbrellas and backdrops. It's the numerous knotted strings attached to the various strobes and lenses that Jimmy nimbly uses to measure exact distances to achieve photographic perfection that'll drive you nuts. Ah, but the concoction works incredibly well and we call the man brilliant.

Here he kills time amid piles of iron with the inimitable Ricky Wayne, priceless characters of the Golden Era of Bodybuilding.

•

Larry Scott, Bill McArdle, Dave Draper, Joe Weider and I were heading out the stage door to look for a place to have dinner. Not so, said Dame Fortune. The audience had literally moved en masse from the theatre to the street outside, blocking our exit and the traffic in the street. Even the specially hired security guards couldn't guarantee our protection from the excited throng. The doors were bolted closed just in time, for they started pounding away on them. Amidt the din, we were secreted out another exit.

Looks like a crowd of enthusiastic bodybuilding fans surrounding Joe Weider as he exits the Opera House after an emotional evening. When New Yorkers displayed their uncontrollable appreciation for the ripped and oiled bodies posing dramatically to the pulsing music, we thought it was the march upon Jericho and the walls would come tumbling down.

•

After the show we all went to dinner at a steak house. While there, in came Rock Stonewall and LeRoy Colbert and their wives.

At my table were Dave Draper, Larry Scott, Bill McArdle and Joe Weider. We all had a great time talking over the events of the evening and hashing over old times. Joe told us next year the Mr. Olympia winner will get an additional prize of one-thousand dollars.

During the course of the conversation Joe said, "Dick, you can write anything about me in your column and I won't censor or change a word of it, I promise."

"Now, Joe, I'm a witness," piped in our current Mr. America, Dave Draper.

Okay, Joe, I take you at your word. Joe, thanks for letting me get that off my chest.

•

With all the awards presented on the night of the contest, there were still a few that I feel should be given. While no trophies will be presented, it should go on record that the men to be listed were duly recognized for their achievements.

Most Popular with the Girls in the Audience—a tie...Dave Draper and Bill McArdle

Most Popular with the Miss Americana Contestants—Chet Yorton

Best Announcer at the Show—Bud Parker. Bud was the only announcer, but I can't imagine one who could have run things better.

Most Surprising on the Posing Dais—Earl Maynard. He looked great in the prejudging and sensational under the lights. Newcomers could take a lesson from him.

Most Personable—Earl Maynard

Best Sportsman—Harold Poole. When Harold lost to Scott you could see the disappointment mirrored in his face, all those hours of training wiped away in the heartbreak of a moment. He was one of the first to congratulate Larry on his well-deserved victory.

Wisest Words Heard at the Contest—Harold Poole to Larry Scott..."Wait till next year."

Most Water Consumed Due to Nervousness—Larry Scott

Most Modest—a tie...Dave Draper and Harold Poole

Most Enthusiastic Spectator—Joe Weider

Most Stars Seen that Night—Thousands, by me when Joe Weider and I bumped heads in the aisle

Finally, the Most Intelligent Move Anybody Could Make Award—All those who plan to attend next year

Tom Sansone, between sets, has the honor of holding LeRoy Colbert from toppling as he knocks off a set of 85-pound seated dumbbell alternate curls. If you're taking notes, this is the exercise that built the very first 20½-inch muscular arms in the universe. These brutes dominated the New York muscle scene in the '50s.

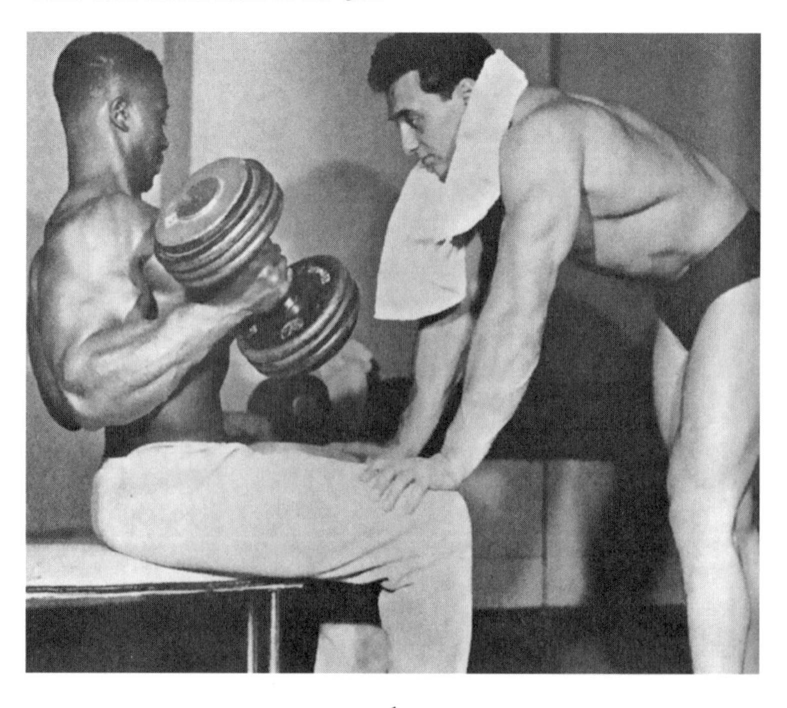

Around nine in the morning I hop in the wreck I fondly call my car and head for the Ventura Freeway that takes me through the dew-glistening Los Angeles suburbs in a matter of minutes. The Ventura Freeway winds into the San Diego Freeway going South through the rolling green hills to the Wilshire Boulevard West cut-off. With the Pacific Ocean still a few miles away you can see the silver band of water on the horizon. A short ride and I'm at work, but a few more blocks and the Muscle Beach office of the Weider Barbell Company would be on a raft floating out to sea. It's great working so close to the golden sands and the blue water. Our office is a beautiful red brick building serving as the nerve center of the bodybuilding and strength world on the West Coast. What a great place to work and what a great ride getting there. Guess I'm just lucky. Anyway, I thought you all would like to take the trip. Ain't it poetic?

•

Things have been jumping around here lately. Reason: Joe Weider is back in town. His enthusiasm is contagious—like a cold, but instead of sneezing, it leads to talking about bodybuilding. Looking over at Dave Draper early one recent morning Joe said, "Dave, your arms look bigger than I've ever seen them. Roll up your sleeve so I can take a look."

"Sure, Joe." Dave replied optimistically.

Little Dave unbuttoned his sleeve as we waited with breathless anticipation. We waited and waited and waited. Last I saw, Dave was still working on getting the sleeve over that massive forearm. I don't think Joe ever got to look at the entire arm. On my way home I began thinking of how many matches Dave must use to burn his shirts off his body. How else could he get them off?

•

Joe Gold, the well-known California muscle builder, is busy these days looking all over town for heavy pieces of scrap metal. The purpose of all this is to construct training equipment heavy enough to enable the giant strongman Pat Casey to handle the weights he's used to. I'm thinking if Joe has any leftover metal he better entertain the idea of building a cage while he's at it. That or hope Pat's always in a good mood.

•

Stumbling down memory lane reminds me of the time I used to have my most enjoyable, and I would say most productive, workouts. My partner at the time was the Tarzan of the movies, Gordon Scott. He was then married to a lovely actress by the name of Vera Miles. They had a beautiful home in the San Fernando Valley; the bathhouse, which was but a few steps from the pool, was converted into the greatest gym you ever saw. We had it loaded with the works: mirrors, benches of all types, fixed-weight dumbbells going to well over a hundred pounds and all types of barbells and pulley weights. It was quite a set-up.

Three times a week we'd start a workout at around eight-thirty in the morning. Gordon, who had been a training partner of Steve Reeves, carried over the Reeves quick-workout principle. As a result we trained as if our clothes were on fire. By ten we had blasted through and were ready for a swim. After a fifteen-minute dip, it was up to the showers and then a good health drink Gord would mix. By noon I was on top of the world. Ah, them was the days. Like all good things, it ended too soon as ole Tarzan swung over to Rome, leaving his ape-like buddy to train for himself.

Gordon Scott at play. The guy has a way of gaining your attention and persuading you to agree with him. When he played Tarzan ,even the apes listened to the man. Muscles speak a universal language we all understand.

I was talking with Chet Yorton here in Weider cave at Muscle Beach awhile back and Chet told me he could now prone press 435 pounds, squat with 540 pounds and do strict curls of 225 pounds, which goes to prove that with desire and Weider training principles you get a big, strong man.

•

The other day Russ Warner, another great Weider photographer, and yours truly decided to test our strength on one of those ordinary bathroom scales by seeing who could squeeze out the greatest poundage with our hands. After much eye popping and gnashing of our tusks, we couldn't seem to break our tie, which wasn't for too much poundage at that.

You'd think by now I would have learned, but I asked Dave Draper, who was standing nearby watching with amusement, if he thought he could do better. For a moment I thought he had broken the scale. Then Bill McArdle squeezed it as far as it could go. Even Chet Yorton, who was nursing a bum hand, pushed as far as it would go with ease. In disgust Russ shuffled into his office and closed the door and I went back to squeezing the keys of my typewriter.

•

CARUSO

This man, who looked like a pile of rocks and lifted steel like a crane and shredded and crumpled anything he got his hands on, was a gentleman, a peacemaker and an artist. He insisted you go first while he carried your load; he counseled troubled young men in the California state penal system and created with brush and oils on large canvas incredible old west paintings in marvelous detail. Chuck Sipes was a mighty good man.

Mr. America and Mr. Universe winner Chuck Sipes dropped by our Muscle Beach office the other day to say hello. When you shake his hand, it's like holding onto a steel claw. He's not like those morons who try to prove their power by attempting to make mashed potatoes of your hooks. He doesn't need to squeeze to let you know how strong he is, you can sense it. Glad he's a friend.

•

It's getting to sound almost like an old-time western just to hear Larry Scott talk. Seems there was this hombre whom Larry had a showdown with a few years back. Now this here dirty dog beat our hero in a fair and square match. Ever since that time Larry has been improving until now he's just itching to mix it up again to prove once and for all who's top dog.

MOZEE

Larry Scott off-season in the mid-'60s with maximum mass, no fat and enough power to generate electricity for a small town.

In case you haven't guessed it by now, the dirty dog in Larry's story is the sensational Harold Poole. The battleground has been offered by Joe Weider and accepted by Poole and Scott. This real-life showdown will probably settle in many people's minds who is the greatest bodybuilder of our time, with the winner being crowned Mr. Olympia. When the dust settles, only one will remain standing. I hope to be there watching the fireworks.

Popping Questions at Actor Brad Harris

Most of the time we try to publish stories that inspire our readers, stories that tell of a man's struggle to overcome great odds. Unfortunately I feel it's only fair to tell you right from the start that if you're looking for a rags-to-riches epic you'd better flip the pages cause you're at the wrong place. The story of Brad Harris is one of a success who has become even more successful.

I can well remember first meeting Brad at the beach around six or seven years ago.

"Good grief," was the first thing I could think of saying. Everywhere Brad went he'd get the big stare. He had size, shape and definition. Others may have had as much, but it wasn't all put together in just the same way. Brad had one of the most rugged physiques I had ever seen. He left an impression at Muscle Beach that still lingers. This was several years ago. Now Brad is a movie star of international importance. He travels all over the world making films, many that he produces and directs himself.

For a man who's on the go as much as Brad, one has to be a sharpshooter to stop him long enough to get a story. While I'm no Wyatt Earp, I get lucky once in a while. One such lucky day happened not long ago. I was in Vince's gym to get a story on one of his members when who should come up to me but Brad Harris. He was on one of his rare trips to the States and told me he planned to head back to Europe within the next few days. This was my chance, so I made arrangements to get a story for our magazines; we set up another meeting for a few days later.

Unsuspecting, I waited out in front of Vince's at the appointed time. With no warning Brad came plummeting at me from across the street and leapt with all 185 pounds on top of me. It was a miracle that I didn't go splat on my face. As I staggered under the load Brad said, "Carry me into the gym."

What I won't do for a story. We got inside and sat in a corner so we wouldn't be trampled by the marauding muscle men who were hitting the weights.

In a scene from one of his many European-made action flicks we catch Brad Harris in one of his lousy moods.

STUDIO

Dick: Brad, let's start from the top. When did you get started in weight training?

Brad: Well, I've always been a natural athlete. I was on a football scholarship to the University of Southern California and while I was training to go out there I had a bad accident and I hurt one of my knees. I busted the cartilage and I had to have my knee operated on. The doctor I had at the time suggested I go into a gym to strengthen my knee with weight training.

D: How old were you at the time?

B: I was eighteen years old. When I got to the gym I saw all these weights lying around and began to think I wanted to build more than just a muscular kneecap. I also happened to be, and this is a theory of mine, in a growth period. You know there's a period between seventeen and something like twenty-five when you grow. I think that coincided with my training because I just blew up like a balloon over that summer. Since then I haven't had much trouble maintaining those initial gains I made when I was eighteen.

D: I know you got started in weight training to correct an injury, but did you ever think of bodybuilding just for the sake of bodybuilding?

B: Well, naturally I think most people—even ninety-nine percent—of the male population at some time are interested in their physiques. I found while I was in the gym and made such easy gains in such a short time, why naturally I became very enthusiastic. So I became dedicated to bodybuilding because it made me feel good to develop that way and I also noticed I got a lot of respect. People would inquire how I achieved my development so quickly and easily.

D: I remember down at the beach years ago, it used to amaze the rest of us how someone could be in the condition you were in. We'd ask what you did and you'd tell us you'd train just off and on whenever you felt like it. This was accompanied by the rest of us gnashing our teeth in envy.

B: Well, that's the way it's been. I'll admit, however, that I trained fairly hard for the first two or three years. I mean hard for me. Which was to hit the weights for about two hours, three times a week. I finally got to the point where I didn't want to get any bigger since I felt I would be out of proportion if I did.

D: So you just cut out training all together for a while?

B: No, but when I did reach that point where I wanted to go no further, I started to cut down on my routines and found I could maintain what I had with only an hour, three times a week. Say, it's pretty noisy in here, why don't we go to my place?

(That sounded like a pretty good idea. So, with Brad in the lead in his sports car we went into the hills to the house where he was staying.)

STUDIO

Brad Harris is an actor who loves muscle building, is certain to visit the gym regularly, but he doesn't need to slave, beg, bleed, suffer or cry over the proposition. He's a natural crisp-muscled athlete free of the millstone to which many of us are bound.

B: This is the home of a good friend of mine. Let's sit out here by the pool and soak in some sun.

D: In your training, did you ever have any inspirations?

B: Well, at the time when I first became enthusiastic, why naturally I was reading the magazines and had to go to Muscle Beach to see all the big men. It was there where I first saw Steve Reeves. I couldn't believe my eyes.

STUDIO

A bloodied Hercules, played by Steve Reeves, reviews the battlefield from his chariot. Now look at the mess I've gotten us into.

D: Reeves must have inspired more bodybuilders than any other single champion. I've always thought of Grimek as the best.

B: Oh yes, Grimek is great, but I had never seen him in person. With Reeves it was different. I got to know him a little and, of course, when you have a personal contact with someone you have more interest in them.

D: What about your diet?

B: Well, I guess you might say I just eat food, period.

D: You mean you don't take any supplements of any sort?

B: No, I just...

D: I know, you just never found the need.

B: I'm afraid not. I just seem to be able to keep in condition pretty easily, without any nutritional help.

D: What are some of your favorite sports?

B: I was always a natural athlete.

D: Figures.

B: My favorite sport, however, was football, in which I played fullback. My knee injury cut my football plans short, however.

D: How much do you weigh?

B: Right now I weigh between 185 and 190 pounds. I can hardly remember not being at that weight.

D: How tall are you?

B: I'm five-foot, eleven inches.

D: Do you know what your measurements are or do you ever take them?

B: No, I really don't. Once in a while I check them out just out of curiosity.

D: Have you been curious lately?

B: I taped my arm the other day and it was a solid eighteen inches cold. When I got back home around four or five weeks ago the arm taped seventeen and one-half inches. That was after a year and a half without being able to get to a gym.

D: In other words you packed on a good haf-inch.

B: Yes, that's how easy it is for me to put on muscle. My chest is around forty-eight or forty-nine inches and my waist is thirty-one.

D: You're a lucky guy.

B: I can't believe it myself. People ask me what I do and I tell them, but they always think I must follow some secret routine. The more surprised they seem, the luckier I feel.

D: Yeah, Vince tells me you never practice any posing and said that just taking off your shirt is something. He also says you take the wildest workout he's ever seen.

B: I don't follow any special routine. Speaking in generalities, I'd say that I just lift moderate weights with fairly high reps.

D: Do you have any hobbies?

B: I like horseback riding and motorcycling.

D: It's a wonder you have time for that with all your film work. How did it all get started?

B: I'd have to go back to Steve Reeves. He opened the doors as far as bodybuilders being in the films. If it wasn't for him I don't feel I'd be where I am today. As we all know, he went over to Italy and made "Hercules," which opened the doors for all of us.

D: How did you personally get your start?

B: I was over in Rome to see the Olympic Games and while I was there I went to see an agent. As a direct result of the furor that Reeves had created and my bodybuilding activities, I got the job.

D: I personally think that you're one of the best naturally gifted actors of all the bodybuilders to make it big in films. Why don't you do more work in Hollywood?

B: I suppose it's because I got my start in Europe and working there has gotten to be a habit. In the last seven years, I've starred in twenty-one films.

D: I didn't know you made that many.

B: Only four of these were physique films. The rest were all action adventure films or foreign intrigue, or westerns. At the end of this year I'll be producing, along with another fellow, my first film. This and the fact that I've got a great career in Europe and other parts of the world make it needless for me to come to Hollywood. I can work straight through the next five years without ten days' break if I want to. Now when I want time off, I have to make time off. I also have a great deal more freedom in doing what I want with a production. I have my hand in directing a film, I check over the editing and now I'll be producing. I could never do that in Hollywood. I don't think I could ever be happy just acting. I have to be more involved. That's the kind of person I am.

D: Is there any film we can look for here at home?

B: Just before I came home this time I finished a film with Dana Andrews called "The Seven Million Dollar Grab."

D: That was made in Europe?

B: Yes, we filmed in London, Italy, Monte Carlo, Cannes...

D: You've had a fabulous life, haven't you? You've been everywhere.

B: Yes, I've been very lucky in so many ways. Right now I am going back to do the sixth in a series of German spy thrillers in Yugoslavia. They've been very well accepted. I play a sort of a James Bond type. The next one will be done in Canada later this year. After that we'll be doing one of the series in Rangoon.

D: How do you get in any training?

B: I always manage to get in some training every day when I'm on the road. Even if it's just some chins and dips. No matter what, I never seem to go down.

I couldn't stand it any more. The guy has everything: looks, physique, talent, the whole ball of wax. I had heard enough. I went home and solemnly swore I would never touch another weight—until my next workout the following morning.

CHARLES

Three Muscle Beach guys who don't have a mean bone in their muscular bodies, Armand Tanny, Glenn Sundby and George Eiferman, line up in the desert sun in Las Vegas a half a century ago. I'll bet Mae West wasn't far away.

My first visit in the summer of '63 to the area once known as Muscle Beach. I'm the butterball kneeling on the precious sand between John Tristram, on my right, and Hugo Labra, Don Peters and Mike Bondura on my left. We represent the instant brotherhood of bodybuilders.

TWO

1966

The Great Bear Fight

Just about an hour before quitting time in the Weider West Coast office in Santa Monica, into the office burst our good friend, Ray Raridon.

"Hey!" he blurted breathlessly. "You guys want to win a car free?"

"Er...like what else is new, champ?" asked big Dave Draper.

"Naw, Tiny, (that's 234-pound Dave's nickname), I'm serious. It was on the radio just a few minutes ago."

"Okay, what's the gimmick?" I asked sarcastically.

"Oh, forget it," said Ray, picking up a magazine. Well, you know by this time we were curious. Ray naturally knew this better than anyone as he hummed to himself. I broke the silence.

"All right," I said, "what do we have to do?"

"Just fight a bear," said Ray simply.

"A what?" we said in unison.

"A bear," Ray repeated.

"You mean one of those furry things with the fangs and claws and stuff?" asked Dave.

"Yeah, yeah, but it's not that bad—honest," Ray continued. "All you have to do is wrestle the bear and pin his shoulders and you win a brand new car from this car dealer who's sponsoring the whole deal. And don't worry, the bear has a muzzle and the claws have been removed." There was a silence, but you could almost hear us thinking.

"How much does this bear weigh?" I asked.

"Around 450 pounds." There was another silence.

"We should have someone really big and strong to fight it," said Ray innocently. There was another silence, this one longer than the others.

"Oh, no!" said Dave emphatically. "Not me."

"Why not?" I chimed in. "Surely you can do it if anyone can."

And so, half stumbling into it, we pressured Dave to what was to be quite a contest. Like a jerk I began coaching Dave on how to fight a bear. Ya see, I had this Teddy bear once—but we were to find out that a Teddy bear and the real thing are not quite the same. We made our battle plans quite seriously.

"First thing you hafta do is to catch him off guard," I said pompously.

"How the devil are you gonna catch a seven-foot bear that's staring down your throat off guard?" asked Dave.

"Lissen, Dave," Ray interjected, "speed is the secret."

"Yeah, to run away!" said Dave. The more we talked about it, the bigger the bear became until King Kong was but an insect by comparison. You could almost smell the adrenaline.

"I can't do it, you guys," Dave said, pleading. But no one by this time paid any attention to him. I was too busy thinking what a great story this would make.

Finally, it was time to close the office. Ray went on ahead; we were to meet him at his house and go from there to the battleground. (Driving over the freeway from our Muscle Beach headquarters to the San Fernando Valley made me wonder what could be more dangerous than that.) At Ray's place we piled into my vintage car and went excitedly on our way.

"Lissen," said Ray, "I hear you get a hundred dollars for every minute you're able to stay in the ring with this bear." For once I began to feel interested in fighting the bear; the feeling didn't last long, however.

It was around seven o'clock when we pulled up in front of the dealer's lot. It was quite easy to find where the bear was by spotting the crowd. With mixed feelings of excitement we got out of the car to see Dave's adversary. It turned out to be a bear all right, but not the monster we had created in our imaginations. The bear looked to be around six feet tall on its hind legs. It was "wrestling" with a young man who was working himself into a sweat while our animal friend just shuffled around.

The bear had been at work for several hours by the time we got there, and still there were people waiting in line to wrestle it. The funny part of the whole thing is that there was no car or money to be gained by wrestling this bear. It seems the whole thing was just an overgrown rumor. To top it all off, you had to pay a dollar for the privilege of playing around for three minutes.

A bunch of young high school boys were trying to impress their girlfriends by beating the bear. What a joke that was. The poor bear just looked like it was about to go to sleep.

"Aw, the poor little bear," said Dave.

The bear's trainer overheard him and came over to where we were standing, a sly glint in his eye.

"Don't kid yourself, big boy. This bear has been trained to wrestle with professional wrestlers. He puts out only enough to keep going. When someone big and strong like you appear to be tries to challenge his strength, he's in for a big surprise."

This almost sounded like a challenge. By this time, some of the spectators had begun to recognize Dave as their local TV favorite—the Gladiator. Now you could feel the air of expectancy as the crowd moved in closer.

STUDIO

A fearsome picture of David the Gladiator as he takes on Hollywood from the soundstage of KHJ-TV. The year was 1963 and I hosted the airing of action-hero films every Saturday night from 8 to 10 until the foreign film pantry was bare, about a year. It was my Jersey accent that got me the part.

"Okay," said Dave, "here's my buck." Dave slipped off his shoes and entered the ring.

Slowly he circled the bear, who now stood on its hind legs and seemed bigger than before. Dave's mighty muscles made him look like he was wearing a suit of armor under his sweatshirt. Suddenly with the speed of a jungle cat Dave leaped at the bear's neck and clamped on such a vicious headlock it seemed you could hear it crack the big animal's bones.

The hair on the bear's neck seemed to bristle for a second. Then, like a big dog shaking off excess water, it sent Dave flying into the air and into the prettiest one-point landing I've ever seen. You've never seen such a surprised look on anyone's face as on Dave's. Stunned but still determined, Dave again clamped on a headlock that could have scrambled the brains of a gorilla. What a sight it was, man against beast in an age-old struggle. With a mighty swipe of bear paw, Dave went flying again.

After it was over the trainer came over. "I've seldom seen my bear put out against a man the way he did with you. Bears have phenomenal tendon strength that even the strongest of men cannot master. All I can say is that you must be as strong as you look."

And all I can say is I'm glad I wasn't that animal. And if you're big and strong and fast don't go looking for bears.

•

I was talking to Zabo the other day at Joe Gold's muscle pit in Venice. We were on the subject of strength stunts when Zabo looks at me and sez, "Dick, see if you can hold this broom parallel to the floor with your arm at your side."

I looked at the broom for it moment. It was a long one all right and all you could use to keep the broom parallel was the strength of your wrist. I took hold of the handle of the broom and seemed to have no trouble in holding it level to the ground.

Zabo just smiled, "No, Dick, not yet—I mean with a two-and-a-half-pound plate on the end."

I checked myself in the mirror. Gosh, your forearms look powerful, Dick ole boy, I was thinking. A minute or so passed.

"Go ahead, Dick, try it," said Zabo.

He didn't know it (or maybe he did), but for that last minute I had been straining my guts out. The blasted thing hadn't moved an inch off the floor. I strained again, but the end of the broom lay there like a rock. Zabo said, "Here, I'll show you what I mean." And proceeded to lift the thing off the floor and parallel.

"Ah, ha," I said like a big rear end, "you had your elbow bent a little."

"Uh, yeah," was Zabo's only reply as he handed the broom back to me. Well, to end this little drama, let me just say try as I might, I couldn't lift that broom with its plate weight so much as an inch off the ground. I left the gym a pretty disgruntled guy.

As life is composed of extraordinary moments, its cast is comprised of unforgettable characters. In the middle of the Twentieth Century in the middle of Muscle Beach, Zabo Koszewski and Big Steve Merjanian roamed, rustled and raged. Here we see Zabe, the grand daddy of muscle building, taunting Big Steve, the world's strongest man hauling the world's thickest shoulders, with a banana. Steve is lodged between the rails of the multi-pulley system in Joe Gold's original gym in Venice, the scene of the feeding frenzy.

RARIDON

•

It's with reluctance that I must admit that I don't like Rick Wayne. I mean how could anyone? Here's a guy with enough talent for ten men. He's good looking, has one of the most muscular physiques in the world, is an excellent singer and entertainer, is strong and intelligent, and to make things worse he's one of the most exciting writers in the muscle business. As if this wasn't enough, he's now joined the Weider staff as editor of the magazine you're now reading. I know most of you are now probably thinking I'm some kind of stupid, jealous jerk. You probably think I wish I had his physique, or that I could sing like he does, or was as powerful. Well, you're wrong. Why, I'll bet you even think I wish I had Rick's brains and writing ability. Are you kidding? Why dat didn't even make me tink twicte. I knows dat Joe Weider, my grate boss, won't never let no one tink I ain't got no brains or dat I can't tink as good as no one else.

So who cares about Rick Wayne and how good a writer Joe thinks he is? I do. Aside from all his other attributes, Rick is one heck of a nice guy and it's great to have him on our side.

•

Several years ago they were casting for the part of Tarzan. (It seems that they're always casting that part.) Anyway the producers were in the process of seeing all of Hollywood's musclemen.

Well, they finally saw six-foot, four-inch Danny Vafiadis who, with his athletic physique, was the very picture of Tarzan himself. They had him strip down so they could see his muscles.

"What on earth are those things growing out of your shoulders?" one asked. Danny gave them a baleful look. "My traps," he said.

The producers decided that he looked too unusual. Tarzan had to be someone the audience could identify themselves with—a flabby old man, I guess. Danny went on to become a star of many of those Italian muscle films, proving the Hollywood moguls had something growing out of their ears.

STUDIO

The fastest gun in the west, Bill Smith, was also famous for taking men down in mean arm wrestling contests. I remember Bill from TV's "Laredo," and as a friend who would back me up if I was down. Tough as nails, loved the iron.

Popping Questions at Bill Smith, TV Star of "Laredo"

Now I've always been a fan of good westerns and TV has more than its share. One of the best of this, or any other, season has been the one called "Laredo." This is due, in no small part, to the acting of Bill Smith.

If you've seen the show, you couldn't very well have missed the rugged good looks, superior acting ability or the great set of muscles owned by big Bill. On a number of occasions Bill is called upon to have his shirt off; he looks so unbelievably muscular he seems almost ready to take on Larry Scott for the Mr. Olympia crown.

I used to train with Bill several years ago. He was one of the group that included Larry Scott who went every week down to the beach together. Aside from his great musculature, Bill had an arm like a steel vise that was virtually unbeatable when it came to arm wrestling.

After seeing the show one night, I began to think back on the mighty Smith arm. It wasn't too long before the mighty Tyler skull began to wonder if Bill would like to put his arm to a test at our upcoming Mr. and Miss Western America show. As part of the show I was going to have an arm wrestling match for the world title. Why not, I thought, have Bill defend a title as the Champion Arm Wrestler of the Motion Picture and TV industry? The contest would be open to all those connected with movies or television in any way. This, my friend, takes in some pretty powerful men.

Excited by the idea, I gave Bill a call, and to my delight he seemed eager to enter the battle. During our conversation I suggested we do a story on him for *Mr. America* magazine and we set up a date for the following weekend. Luckily it was one of those beautiful days that Southern California likes to claim are eternal. The sun was cracking through the air at high speed as our ace photographer, Russ Warner, strongman Bert Elliot and I headed for Bill Smith's castle.

A castle is literally what Bill lives in. It's located in the Hollywood hills in a beautiful rustic canyon with turrets and all. There are so many stairs leading up to the Smith front door I felt I'd pumped a gallon of blood into the calves by the time I reached it.

Russ whipped out his camera while I whipped out my tape recorder. Russ was quicker on the draw, so I had to be content to follow around and grab Bill between shots.

Dick: How long have you been training, Bill?

Bill: I started working out about fourteen years ago.

D: Did you have a specific reason for starting with the weights?

B: Well, yeah, Dick, I did. I had always been very thin when I was a kid. I had rheumatic fever and asthma. As a result, when I got out of high school I was six-foot, one, weighed 129 pounds and was very weak. I always wanted to be strong and admired strength and had always wanted to play football. So the reason I really started was for football and I figured weights were the quickest, easiest way to get big and strong.

D: Did you have any bodybuilding goals when you started?

B. Just to be strong and healthy, but I remember the one thing I wanted to do was to have fifteen-inch arms. I felt if I got a fifteen-inch arm it would be the most colossal thing in the world.

(I didn't think to ask what Bill's arm measured now, but it looked like a good eighteen inches. On top of its obvious size, it had some of the most dramatic cuts and striations you could find on the arm of any of the leading bodybuilders today.)

D: Did you have any early inspiration?

B: Well, I think back in those days almost everyone thought of Grimek as the best. I was no different. Of course, I was tall and thin and wasn't structurally like Grimek at all, so a few years later Steve Reeves became my inspiration.

D: Did you...(Just then Russ Warner came over to us.)

Russ: Bill, how about you standing over here on this ledge? It's got just the background we need.

(Bill stood on the ledge Russ showed him.)

R: Can you put on some more oil?

(Bill put on a little more oil and then started going through some poses. This guy has a truly remarkable physique. His arms, in particular, are amazing. The outer head of his triceps looks like a roll of lead pipe, while his biceps take on the appearance of a sixteen-pound shot. Soon Russ had to reload. Now was my chance to continue the interview.)

D: Did you ever participate in any sports, Bill?

B: Yeah. Played high school football and junior college football and four years of football in the service. I also boxed in the service and threw the discus quite successfully.

D: What was your best in the discus?

B: I threw it 151 feet and that year the AAU event was won with 150 feet, six inches. This I did after only three weeks in training.

D: That's pretty incredible.

B: My coach felt I had a natural aptitude for it. I have long arms and they sort of whipped it out. For a long time I tried the shot, then one day I stayed out in the field and I was asked to throw back a discus that landed at my feet. I threw it back further than they had thrown to reach me.

D: Have you won any awards for your athletic endeavors?

B: I won the light-heavy German-Austrian boxing title while I was in the service.

D: I never knew that.

B: It wasn't that I was so good. It's that I was in good condition. After the first round my opponents would usually begin to fade and by the second or third round I could have them for lunch.

(Bill was being modest. With those arms and their demonstrated power, I'll bet there were a lot of men who wished they had tired in the first instead of the second round.)

D: How about eating?

B: When I'm in really good training I try to follow a sensible high-fat protein diet with low carbohydrates. When I'm working, however, and on location, I virtually have to eat what we're fed. They don't always have the diet concepts you and I have. Of course, I burn off a lot of the carbohydrates I take in through work. I like fats, and I really don't think they make you fat. I think the body uses them and they have a useful purpose. I think if you stick with protein and fats and stay away from the carbohydrates, you can have cuts and strength and not be smooth.

WARNER

Bert Elliot and his mustache are in a world of their own as I congratulate Bill Smith for his arm wrestling prowess and admire his championship awards. Shortly after this photo was taken by Russ Warner, I beat Bill in two out of three brutal rounds with both arms tied behind my back.

D: When did you get started on your acting career?

B: It was around 1959 and I was planning on working for the government. I'd spent a number of years studying languages with this purpose in mind.

D: That reminds me, I remember you used to speak, read and write Russian fluently. How many languages do you speak?

B: Five.

D: And I have trouble with one. Why didn't you go into government service?

B: My wife is French and you can't work in any classified capacity if your wife is foreign-born. So then someone suggested acting, and I will admit when I first went into it, it was kind of a lark. But something about it grabs hold of you and you become an impassioned actor. I'm very serious about my craft now.

D: Where did you first start working?

B: I first went with MGM and was under contract there four years. During that time I appeared in some feature films and did thirteen weeks in a series called "The Asphalt Jungle." After the show was canceled I just sat around.

D: What would you call your biggest break?

B: I really think, Dick, my big break is right now, in "Laredo."

D: Yeah. With big shows canceled almost every week, you're lucky to be in one so popular. Of course, one of the reasons it's so popular is because of the work you do on it.

B: I appreciate your saying that, but as they say in sports, it's a team effort, believe me. I'd like to say one thing about working out and movies. I think it's always an asset for a guy to be in good shape. I think it's great if you can make it as an actor and then someday have to take off your shirt and be in tremendously good shape. And I think today the stigma that has been on bodybuilding—the fact that if you have a few muscles you have to be some sort of a nitwit, which everyone concerned with bodybuilding knows is not the truth, is beginning to vanish. There are many, many actors today who work out and who stay in shape and think it's an absolute necessity. It's also great to see weight training being so readily accepted in sports now after so many years of prejudice.

D: Do you have any lifts you're particularly proud of?

B: Yes, Dick, I do. I did a reverse curl of 163 pounds once at a bodyweight of 171 pounds.

D: I don't know if they keep records on that lift, but I have never heard anything as good as that, especially at that bodyweight. What do you weigh now?

B: I weigh 198 pounds.

D: Why did you stick with the reverse curl so much?

B: Well, I've always loved arm wrestling and I found the reverse was very good for this activity.

(The mention of arm wrestling made Bert Elliot's mustache quiver and bristle.)

Bert: Did someone say arm wrestle?

D: Not now, Bert. Wait for the night of the contest.

B: It's been so long since my arm has been pinned I can't imagine it going in but one direction.

(Bert grinned.)

Bert: On the night of the contest, I'm going to break your arm, Bill. You'd better take out insurance.

D: Yeah, Bert works in films so he is eligible to try for your title. Getting back to your acting, what are your future plans?

B: I want to do some feature films. I suppose every actor in TV does, due to the wider latitude of that medium. I'd also like to do some theater work if time allows.

D: Do you have any prospects?

B: Yes, but it's all controlled by the scheduling of the TV series. I've lost parts because of this, so I just have to hope for the best. It takes around ten months out of every year to shoot thirty-four shows and we're never quite sure when that ten months will begin or end.

D: Do you have any words of advice for the young bodybuilder?

B: I think the greatest thing you must do to succeed when you train is to stick with it and be consistent. Have patience and don't let your enthusiasm burn you out. Work slowly and build and let training become a part of your life.

D: Who do you think are the greatest bodybuilders around today?

B: Larry Scott or Harold Poole. The Frenchman Paul Wynter is also pretty great. I also have been a big fan of Bill Pearl's, although I haven't seen him recently.

Since he didn't mention my name I realized it was time to go. As we were leaving I almost got knifed by the daggers that were flying between Bill and Bert Elliot. Guess they were already trying to psych each other out for the big arm wrestling match. As we were going down the stairs to the car, I could hear Bert mumbling, "I'm gonna break his arm."

Where arms are crashing to the table you can be sure ole' Bert will be loitering in the background. Bill splinters the wrestling platform as he engages a fierce competitor.

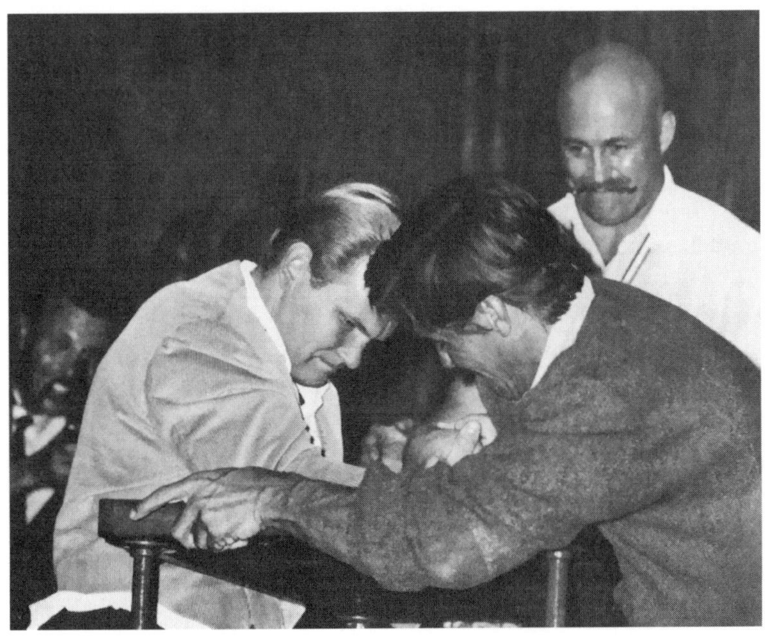

LEOMAZZI

•

I have an unusual announcement to make. I have found a man with twenty-four rows of abdominal muscles! I didn't count 'em, but it sure looked like twenty-four rows. Maybe it was twenty-three.

It all took place at Joe Gold's gym in Venice Beach. I went there to take some photos for some articles that Bill McArdle had written. I had never seen Bill look so cut up before.

"What have you been doing?" I asked.

"Fasting," was Bill's reply. "I've just come off of a four-day fast where I took nothing but vitamins and water."

He got on the scale and checked out his weight.

"Hm-mm-m," says the mighty Chet Yorton, who was peering over Bill's shoulder. "You haven't lost too much weight. You just can't lose muscle when you've trained properly."

"Who wants to?" said Bill as he hopped off the scale.

After the exercise photos, McArdle stood under the skylight, which makes for very dramatic lighting effects and I snapped some impromptu physique shots.

Just as I ran out of film, Bill decided to do some controls. Suddenly he does a vacuum and his midsection disappears. I did a double-take. Others in the gym stopped their training to see the phenomenal sight. I stooped down to see if my eyes were playing tricks. There in the dark cavernous recesses under his rib box was what was eft of his stomach. There it was, pressed against his backbone.

"Look," cried one of the onlookers. "You can see his spine!"

Well, that may not have been the case, but if someone would have bet on it, he wouldn't have had too many takers. It looked like you could see almost all the twenty-four vertebrae. It takes some fortitude to go on a fast; the most I've been on is a slow.

•

When we first begin in bodybuilding, it is usually with a picture of some great champion we admire as a beacon to training goals. Mine were Steve Reeves and Eric Pedersen.

URBAN

Eric Pedersen is wedged into the Golden Era of bodybuilding in that he was one of those before us whose muscular development we could not believe. Big, ripped and vascular muscles scarcely covered with tissue-paper skin. He inspired the brave souls who would construct and mount the launching pad of modern bodybuilding and man the heavily fueled rocket for its fiery take-off. Zoom. Zoom. Zoom.

And, gad, if I could just get muscles the size of Reeves! How I'd pore over the photos thinking of how great I'd look in a suit of muscles like some of the men in *Muscle Power* or *Your Physique,* the former names of *Muscle Builder* and *Mr. America.*

It wasn't long before I started looking at the printed words that accompanied the pictures, and it wasn't long before I was reading first and looking afterward. These words were written in a style that excited, amused and inspired all at the same time. They were not just ordinary words turned out by some hack writer. They seemed borne on the wings of a soaring spirit.

To this day I can still quote some of the editorials. The writer was surely no ordinary man. He seemed to have the power to draw the reader into that glorious world of strength and virile manhood by weaving the tales that fired the imagination. It would take 10,000 pictures to equal just one of his words.

No sooner would I get my copy of *Muscle Power* than I would be on the phone to my training partner reading some of those great bits of gossip or quoting from some of the articles. I don't believe any writer in physical culture reached and influenced more people than this man. His name—Earle Liederman.

For almost fifteen years his agile mind and wit kept the pages of Weider publications alive with the excitement of the iron game. He helped set the course that has led our magazines to become the largest-selling muscle publications in the world. Even before Liederman came to the Weider organization, he carved an immortal name for himself as a strength athlete and mail order instructor. Ten years ago, Liederman and Weider Enterprises separated. Now, after all that time, the firm hand of Earle E. Liederman will once again be pounding out those words in the style he made famous for *Mr. America* and *Muscle Builder*. Be careful or you might fall under his spell and become a champion. Welcome back, Mr. Liederman, or should I say welcome home?

The Cloak and Dagger Abdominal Exercise

I was using my old typewriter (it's even older than my car) the other evening, when the phone rang. It was a young bodybuilding newcomer who many think has great promise. I had just done a story on him, and he was curious about how the exercise photos had come out.

During the course of our conversation we got on the science of bodybuilding. Bet you didn't expect that! Anyway, it got involved, so I suggested he check with Vince Gironda, who owns the gym where he trained.

"Why Vince?" said my friend.

"Are you kidding?" I replied in dismay. "Vince happens to be one of the best technicians in the science of bodybuilding."

"Science of bodybuilding?"

"What did you think bodybuilding was, just a recreational pastime? That's okay for the man who just wants to keep trim, but for the bodybuilder who wants to become a champion it's a science. It has to be. After all, your body is the most miraculous machine ever created. It's a miracle of engineering and chemistry; if you plan to develop it and control it you must approach it with scientifically developed principles."

I was so thrilled with what I had just said I felt like crying.

There was a pause on the other end of the line. "Yeah?" My friend was doing a good job of controlling himself. "But," he continued, "I didn't know Vince was that great a scientist."

"I'd say his gym has more of the greats training in it than any other gym I know of at the present time."

"Yeah, I guess so."

"Why do you think that is?" I asked.

"Oh, I suppose the equipment and all." I didn't answer. "Vince?" he said finally.

MOZEE

The interior of Vince's gym as it appeared off-hours during the Golden Era. Wooden benches, barbells of steel and an atmosphere as thick as the muscles it developed.

"Sure," I said, "after all, a gym is a gym. If it was just weights and equipment you needed, you could get the best in the professional home-type through the Weider Space Age Exercisers. You can't get better anywhere. You can't get better training principles than those found in *Mr. America* and *Muscle Builder* magazines either. But it's the application of sound training principles that counts. You should only go to a gym that advocates and uses the most advanced and scientific training methods."

There was a silence and I thought my young friend had fallen asleep. (I have a tendency to lecture.) Finally he said, "Yeah."

"So, study bodybuilding by reading the teachings of Joe Weider and the champions in the magazines and learn first-hand from such greats as Vince Gironda. Right?"

"Right," he said as he hung up.

To heck with him. Some guys never learn without being clubbed with a commonsense stick anyway. Maybe you got the message. Just think of all the great training secrets that are printed in Weider magazines. Ever since I can remember—my memory doesn't go back to B.T. (Before Training)—I have been getting programs for my routines from the magazines.

Of course, when I first started the magazines were called *Muscle Power* and *Your Physique*. They were, as they are now, filled with many of the secrets of the greats. It's almost like having a personal instructor at your side while you train. How many things are really secret? I mean, like there's nothing new under the sun. Everything is just variation of something already done. Weider Research was formed with the idea of gathering and giving all forms of training information, plus discovering new—and improving old—training methods.

Sometimes the task of ferreting out training secrets of some of the champs can be harder than you might realize. Some of them jealously guard their favorite theories. It's rare when an established star volunteers anything but his name, rank and serial number. You can imagine my surprise when just a few moments after talking to that young bodybuilder, the phone should ring again and it was Vince. Honest.

We talked small talk for a while. All the time I knew Vince had something on his mind. It was just a matter of waiting.

"Say, Dick," he said finally. "I've got a secret."

"You mean the TV show? I like it, too."

"No, no, I mean I've got a secret. A training secret. One that I have never told anyone."

I sat there stunned for a moment. "Yes?" I asked, not knowing what to expect. I couldn't believe he was going to voluntarily give really secret information.

"It has nothing to do with diet or anything like that. It's an exercise for the abdominal region. One that I've been doing for some time now. It's the greatest result producer in the book."

"And you want to tell it to me?" I said hopefully.

"That's right. I thought it was about time I shared it with someone else."

With the phone held to my ear by my shoulder, I fumbled for a pencil and paper. "Okay, shoot," I said enthusiastically.

"Not now. Not over the phone"

I gulped, "N-n-not over the phone?"

"No," said Vince, "here at the gym."

I cleared my throat. "I'll be right over."

"No," said Vince, "not now."

"Not now?" I thought he was going to change his mind. "When?"

"How about the day after tomorrow?"

"Okay," I said eagerly.

I could hardly wait till the appointed time. Here was a training secret that had never been told before, much less published. I felt like the cub reporter, Jimmy Olsen, about to interview Superman. I must have been at the gym an hour early.

I let him finish his workout, just barely, before I pounced.

"Now, look here, old man," I said, unable to control myself any longer. "How about this here secret?"

Vince wiped off the sweat that was pouring from his body. "It's about the abdominals."

"I know, Vince, but I just finished an article on your complete abdominal routine. You mean it's no good now?"

"No, publish the article. It's one of the best routines available, one that I've worked on and given to others with great results."

"Then what's all this 'secret' stuff about?" I asked.

"About one exercise that I've never given anyone."

"What, never?"

"No, never."

It sounded like we were doing a Gilbert and Sullivan operetta.

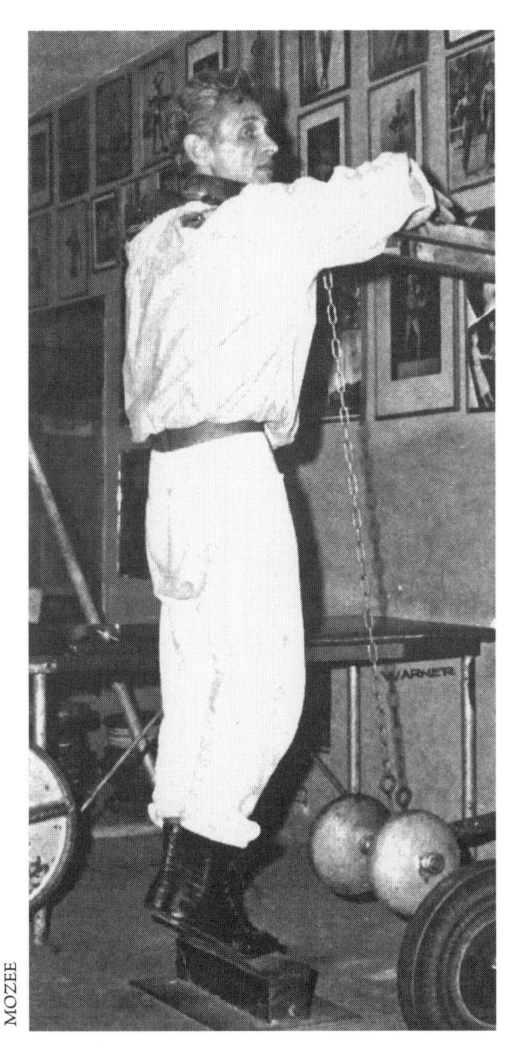

MOZEE

A knarly bucket of bolts, rusty and indestructible, Vince Gironda ran the North Hollywood Gym like a cowboy runs a saloon. Leave your guns at the door, lift weights, grow and get on with your life. Symmetry before size. Train hard, eat right, stay honest and don't let the swinging doors hit you on the butt on your way out.

"First," said Vince, "let's examine the anatomical considerations of the abdominal area. The primary function of the abdominal rectus is to act as a shield for the viscera in the abdominal cavity."

"Viscera in the abdominal cavity?" I asked a little confused.

"Okay, organs inside your gut."

"Yeah, yeah," I said, "now I dig, go ahead."

"The best way to build and strengthen this area is by contracting the abdominals. Right?"

"You bet your life," I answered. "But I know all this."

"Most people," continued Vince, "think of a full situp as the best way to reach this area. Actually a full situp is just a waste of time. You always see pictures of someone doing a situp with someone else holding their ankles. It makes me sick to see it. The only time the abdominals work is at the very beginning of the situp. They help get your shoulders off the floor and that's about it."

"That's why you never do full situps, isn't it?" I asked.

"That's right, I just do concentrations. That flopping back and forth stuff is for the birds."

"I agree, but what's new?"

"Obviously the best way to concentrate on a single muscle group is to isolate it. Contractions start to do that, but you still get assistance from the Psoas Major, Illiacus and Quadratus Lumborum."

"Aw, c'mon now, Vince. This is a clean magazine."

"Those," said Vince patiently, "are some of the muscles that assist in the situp movement. They have nothing to do with the abdominals."

"What is a guy supposed to do with them, cut them off? Ha, ha." Only I laughed.

"No," said the great Italian sage, "just don't exercise them."

"If even a simple contraction brings them into play, how can you keep from exercising them?" I asked.

He looked at me with a glint in his eye. "That's the secret." Vince turned from me and called over one of the gym members.

He had him lay on the flat abdominal board.

"Now, whenever the legs are stretched out, they not only act as an unwanted counter-balance, but activate that unmentionable muscle group we talked about earlier."

"I know! You fold your legs under you," I said in a flash of brilliance.

"You're on the right track. However, when you fold them under, the body still has a tendency to use other muscle groups besides the abdominals."

I was going to suggest cutting off the legs, but no one laughed at my earlier remarks so I kept my trap shut.

"Since you can't cut the legs off," said Vince—naturally people chuckled—you strap the hips down, thus negating all but the action of the abdominals."

So that was it. It seemed so simple, yet no one I knew had ever done abdominal work just that way.

"I do eight sets of eight reps. When you do an exercise correctly, you don't need to do more. In fact, I'm thinking of cutting down to six sets of six reps."

Before I left Vince took off his shirt and started posing under the skylight. Vince showed more muscle than I thought the human body possessed. Believe me, if you saw what I did, you'd be falling on the floor to do those Gironda abdominal iso-squeezes.

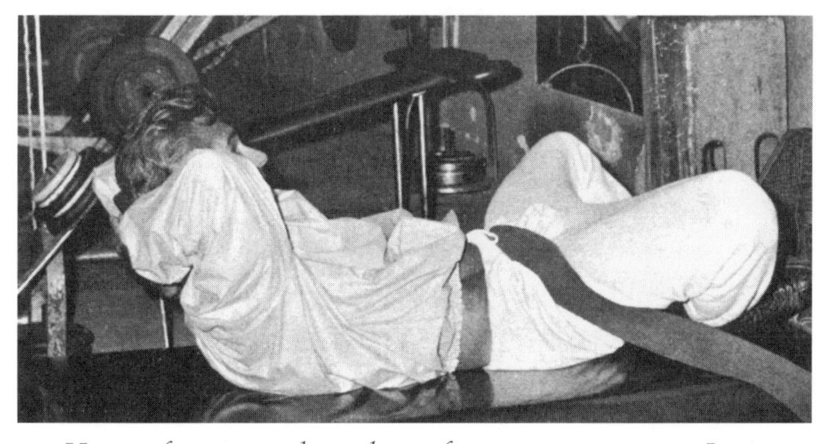

MOZEE

Vince performing crunches: isolation, focus, intense contraction. Listen when he speaks. "It's in the lines, muscle continuity and balance. The body is a poem and you're the poet. Let it flow."

ZELLER

Gone are the physiques that were unique and distinguishable. Don Howorth in his Mr. America days, mid-'60s, when muscle was forged by the hammer of guts and the fire of passion.

THREE

1967

1 2 3 Strikes...You're in a Howorth Photo Shoot

"Look, I'm telling you it just has to shine today. It's been sunny all week long," said the excited voice of photographer Art Zeller.

I squinted out my window. "Sorry, Art, but it looks as if the fates have conspired against us this time."

"No, no," insisted Zeller, "I tell you the sun will burn off all the clouds."

There was a silence. "Well, okay," I said at last, "I'll pick up Howorth and we'll meet you in front of the Weider office in Santa Monica."

At nine that morning I pulled up in front of Vince's Gym. When Howorth saw me he started shaking his head. I opened the door. "Get in, we're late."

Don looked at me in disbelief. "Are you kidding?"

"I know, I know," I said, "but Zeller promised the sun will shine."

"I see," said Don, "Zeller promised, eh?"

"Yeah, and he seems to know about these things."

On blind faith, Don and I drove out to Santa Monica.

It's a funny thing about the weather out here. It can be sunny in the valley and cloudy at the beaches and vice versa. With this in mind, we held a glimmer of hope for the day. After all, Zeller was right about one thing—the sun had been shining brightly for weeks; fate wouldn't deal us such a lousy blow. As we turned from the San Diego freeway to Santa Monica we came to the conclusion that fate, indeed, was only too glad to spoil the day. It was not only cloudy, but cold.

"I tell you the sun will shine," were Art's first words when he saw us. "We must have faith."

We went to a nearby restaurant for breakfast and waited for the ever-loving sun to break through. After an hour or so, we got in Art's car and journeyed several miles up the coast highway to the Malibu area.

"Look at all the surfers," said Art. "They have faith that the sun will come out."

"Are you serious?" said Don. "Surfers aren't looking for sun, just waves. They'd go in a typhoon if the surf was up."

Art just shrugged, "Well, it'll burn off anyway."

At this point we turned off the main highway and onto a road that led into the rustic inland canyons. Zeller is an artist in every sense of word. He spends literally days scouting for locations that will be good backgrounds for the subjects he photographs. Up into the hills we went to a secret location only Art knew of. The scenery was spectacular and several times I felt we should stop. "No," Art would say, "I've found a better place than this." So on we drove.

At last we pulled off another side road and came to a stop.

"This is it," said Zeller.

"This is what?" asked Don.

"The place of places," replied Art eagerly. We looked around at this so-called place of places. We were parked right next to the road. A few feet from us was a sheer facing of rock and bushes. Across the road was a little bluff that led to what looked like a plateau. Not too impressive, and I guess our faces showed our disappointment.

"Before you say anything," said Artie to stem the flow of criticism before it began, "let me show you something."

We climbed out of the car and nearly jumped back in.

"Y-y-you've gotta be kidding," said Don. "It's freezing out there."

"Yeah," I joined in. "Where's the sun you promised?"

"Patience, patience," muttered Art as he led us with his equipment.

We went across the road to the bluff. It was pretty steep and while Art and I were trying to negotiate the climb, Howorth zipped by us like we were standing still. Ahh, youth. On second thought we were standing still, trying to catch our breath.

At last we were on the plateau. We could now see an explosion of dramatic rock formations a few yards way.

"Looks pretty good," I said.

"Just wait," said Art as we approached the rocks.

As we climbed to where the rocks were, the view began to unfold. With each rock we scrambled over, a new vista presented itself. The only word for what we saw is breathtaking. There below us was a beautiful valley, like that of a Swiss Alps travelog. Everywhere we turned a new canopy of colors was revealed. We could even see the ocean in one direction, like a ribbon of shimmering blue. At the next moment we turned to see rugged cliffs and yawning valleys.

"You've done it, Art!" I exclaimed. "You've found the perfect place."

Art smiled and nodded. "Don, isn't this great?"

There was no answer. I turned around, "Don?"

He had vanished.

"Maybe he's gone back to the car."

"He couldn't have," I said. "He was just here a minute ago."

Art and I looked at each other and then down in the valley below. "You don't suppose..." I looked back at Zeller.

"Naw."

Just the same we renewed our efforts to find the missing Mr. America. In and out and around the rocks we crawled. Suddenly I heard Art exclaim he found the elusive Mr. Howorth.

Lo and behold, there he was, inside the rock. Time and the weather had worn holes and pits into the boulders with the result that they made pretty great refuges from the wind.

"I'm staying here until it warms up. If you think I'm going to get into posing trunks on a day like today, you're nuts."

"But it's gonna clear," pleaded Art.

Artie, about as spiritual as the rock upon which he kneels, insists on sun from the sun goddess. We have the physique, we have the camera and we have no sun, no shadows, no muscle contrasts, no warmth, no pump, no show, no good...nuts. Wrong. Artie had the sun in his heart and magic in his eye.

TYLER

Well, it didn't clear and after several hours of waiting and listening to Zeller chanting something about a sun god, we decided to leave and try again the following week.

The following day the sun came out in all its glory and proceeded to bake us for the next week until...yeah, Saturday when I again picked up Howorth. As if on signal, the curtain of clouds descended.

The following day the sun came out once again to taunt us. This time it lasted until we were able to go back to what we had now fondly labeled Howorth Rocks. Then the master began a field day with his camera.

In the middle of the session we heard a shrill voice echo around the rocks, "Hey, look at Tarzan!"

Wouldn't you know it? Some high school teenagers were on a class outing. They couldn't get to us fast enough. They crawled over the rocks like ants.

In spite of this we kept going. Stiff upper biceps and all that. The kids, of course, were flabbergasted. They had never seen anything like Mr. America before. When told who he was, one of the girls asked to interview him for the school newspaper.

In spite of the weather and all the interruptions, Zeller produced some masterpieces that must rank as some of the all-time great physique photos, classics that will live forever as long as people admire examples of rugged manhood dramatically presented.

If you ever meet Zeller don't ask him anything about the weather. Just look at his photos—that's where he reigns supreme. A truly great artist, but as a weatherman he'd do better photographing storm fronts than predicting them.

ZELLER

You can get lost in the Vasquez rocks, but you can't hide from the press. A cute on-the-spot teen reporter asks dreamy Don his plans for the future now that he's a star. She'll run it on tomorrow's front page in her high school newspaper. Extra. Extra. Read all about it.

•

There ain't no more Muscle Beach. Oh, the sand is there but as you know, the lifting apparatus, the weights and the muscle that made them move have been legislated off the beach to not contaminate the unsuspecting public with the benefits of weights. This was done by some eager-beaver politician who wanted to make a name for himself as some sort of clean-up crusader. Seems some of the boys of Muscle Beach got into trouble so this meant everyone had to pay. Last I heard Crusader Rabbit was mounted on a white horse, carrying a lance and washing people's clothes.

Oh, well, that's all water under the barbell as they say out here.

Who in their right mind would willingly, premeditatedly affect the end to such a magnificent and magical period of man's creation and creativity? Muscle Beach in the middle of the last century, a grand and inspired demonstration of skill and talent, strength and health, nature and goodness for an audience of delighted humanity. Beats spring break in Daytona.

The important thing is the spirit of Muscle Beach is still very much alive. The boys of Lump Landing just moved their equipment (tons of it) indoors and they moved faster than a man with a hot foot. It looked for a while like they were planning their own production of The Gypsy Baron. Now, and for the past few years, the sturdy Muscle Beachers have been holding strong and I do mean strong in the pit. The pit is one of the better names given to the old Tanny Gym. Let's just say it's a bit rundown.

Personally I dig this kind of setting over the chrome and carpet palaces. The Muscle Beach Gym has no fancy prices or guarantees.

You go there to train and get strong. Recently they kept a long-standing tradition alive by holding the modern version of the Mr. Muscle Beach contest. Believe me, this is a tradition and an honor to the winner. To be chosen Mr. Muscle Beach is like being chosen Mr. America to many. The one who wins this world-famous title should feel justly proud. This year it was our own Dr. Andy Burpee who won the marbles. Congrats, Doc! Remember your friends while looking at us from your throne.

•

Chet Yorton looks better than ever.

"I've got cuts I've never had before."

From the looks of it, he does. With his massiveness defined, he could be unbeatable.

While he was talking, along came Freddy Ortiz. The Freddy Ortiz. Every quivering pound of muscle of him. Seems to paralyze the traffic when he goes for a stroll. I heard one of the bigger men talking to his girl nearby. She said "Aw, go ahead," and he sez, "I will; I just gotta get his autograph."

This fantastic ball of lumps has taken Muscle Beach by storm. He's literally the talk of the sand dunes. In fact every time I walk into Vince's muscle-building palace where he trains, I hear talk like, "Did you see Freddy work out last night?"

"Yeah, what a sight."

"Have you ever seen anything like that in your life?"

"Yeah, in science fiction."

One of the area's biggest attractions now is seeing the fabulous one pump his bumps.

Looking at Freddy, Chet turned to me and said, "Now that's unbelievable. I made the mistake of standing near the guy while taking a workout recently and for the first time I couldn't concentrate on my own exercise. I kept looking at those arms of Ortiz. I finally had to quit before I got a complex."

•

MOZEE

Look closely. Larry Scott with his 20¼-inch arms outside Vince's Gym around mid-afternoon, 1965.

Arm wrestling is pretty popular right now, so I must tell you about some of the great stories my friend Bert Elliot throws at me. Bert is an arm-bending enthusiast from way back. This champion strong man has had many a barroom struggle.

One such time, he gets a kick out of recalling, happened a few years ago. He was visiting the bar Mac Batchelor governs when in comes this man who wants to challenge Big Mac. For twenty-five years mighty Mac reigned undefeated as the world-champion arm wrestler. He's retired and has been for many years, but this doesn't keep the would-be champs from trying to goad the genial giant into a match. All of them come in with tales of their great prowess; this occasion was no different.

"I've never been beaten and I've come here to prove it to you," said this one fellow as Mac just patiently smiled.

Mac Batchelor, a strongman from Oakland, fondly engaging his monster machine for developing arm-wrestling prowess. If the knarly brute wasn't pinning men's arms to the bar top in his tavern for beers, he might bend a quarter for twenty-five cents. He didn't make much money, but he was a very rich man.

"I don't arm wrestle any longer, but my friend Mr. Elliot here will be glad to oblige you."

Now Bert just loves wind bags because they look so funny when they deflate, so he seized upon the opportunity. While he knew he could beat the loud mouth, he also knew through experience never to underestimate his opponent. They went to one of the booths and prepared for battle. They clasped hands and Bert won. It was so easy that for a minute Bert thought perhaps he had forgotten to take hold of his opponent's hand after all. He lifted his mitt and lo and behold there it was.

"Wait," protested the astonished loser. "Let's do this fairly."

"Like how?" asked Bert.

"Put the hand that isn't wrestling in the air."

"What would that do?"

"Equalize things," said the jerk with a straight face.

Well, these results were even faster, which goes to show wind resistance won't change the results, or something like that. I'm not a scientist, so you figure it.

•

Powerhouse Bill "Peanuts" West is a level-headed guy and an honest one. I asked him recently how he liked our arm-wrestling tournament.

"No good."

I was a little set back.

"What do you mean? Everyone I've talked to said the arm wrestling was great."

"Sure," said West, "it was exciting and interesting. It just wasn't a true test of strength."

"How come?"

"Too many tricks."

"Tricks?"

"Yeah, those arm wrestlers use all sorts of tricks, like holding the table with the other hand for extra pull."

"That just helps equalize the bodyweight factor."

"Speaking of bodyweight," West continued, "they really lay into it when they start. They almost lever their opponents with their bodies."

"What would you suggest?" I inquired.

"Well, for one thing, the contestants should face in opposite directions with their bodies restricted."

He demonstrated what he had in mind.

"In this way," said West, "you would have a true test of arm strength."

I personally think arm wrestling is a great combination of strength, coordination, style and guts, but Peanuts came up with some provocative ideas that have definite worth.

•

George Eifferman enjoyed his muscles more than anyone I've known. There's the crowd, there's the sand, sun and sea and there's ole' George, pressing a 135-pound barbell over his head while playing a tune on his trumpet...and in his skivvies, yet. Oh, my.

Just got a letter from the great Mr. America, Mr. Universe, George Eiferman. He's in Kansas doing presentations for the state Board of Education. For years this man has been spreading the virtues of weight training to the young people of our country.

George operates a booming gym in Vista, California, but in spite of all the responsibilities entailed in such an enterprise, he makes the time to help young men and women wherever he goes. I keep asking myself why all of us in the physical culture world can't have the same devotion to a worthy cause as this gentleman. Just imagine all the good he does. Ever since I can remember Eiferman has been touring the country on behalf of our sport.

You lucky people around the Vista area should avail yourselves of the opportunity of training in the finest facilities and receiving instruction from one of the masters of the iron game. Regardless, do yourself a favor—just give yourself the opportunity to meet one of the finest human beings to grace this old mud ball in many a year. He must have the best-defined heart muscle in the world.

Bodybuilders on the Rocks

My wife leaned into the car window.

"Dear, (that's what she calls me when she isn't mad), I'm sure you've got the wrong address."

"I've got the right address," I said. "I wrote it down just as Joe told it to me."

"But..."

"Now, don't worry." With that assurance I backed out of my driveway and on toward a great adventure. After miles of traveling down strange roads and on faraway highways, I stumbled into a phone booth.

"Okay, okay," I said in my most charming manner, "where do I go? To pick up Joe, I mean."

At last I got the correct address and within five minutes I was at Joe Weider's doorstep.

"Uh, Joe, I'm late but you see..." I was about to blame my poor wife, like a dirty rat.

"That's okay, Dick, but let's get started or we'll really be late."

We hopped in my car and headed back to my house where by this time it should be filled with people.

For several weeks I had been planning to get Joe Nista and Larry Scott together with Russ Warner for some shots at a dramatic setting called Vasquez Rocks. We decided to make a day of it since Joe Weider was in town, and have breakfast before we all hit the road.

Sure enough the house was bulging with muscle when Joe and I arrived. Joe brought the latest issues of *Mr. America* and *Muscle Builder* with him and we had a ball looking through them.

"Good grief, Charlie Brown!" exclaimed Larry Scott. "Ortiz looks fantastic."

We all gathered around the copy of *Muscle Builder* to grab a look.

"That arm should be cut off and mounted," I said in disbelief.

"Breakfast is ready," said my wife. Actually she got no further than "Brea..." and I had gobbled down half-a-dozen eggs. I was working on a second plate when Russ said we should leave before the sun was in the wrong position for photos.

Reluctantly, I got in my car. I was to take Nista and his wife and my oldest daughter, who is eight years old. She prevailed upon me to let her go because she has a crush on Larry.

"Well, all right, but don't get in the way," I said to her, "and no smart remarks. That's what Daddy gets paid for."

Russ took Joe and Larry. Before we left I made sure Russ understood I didn't know where we were going and that my new car (already several years old when I got it) couldn't keep up with his Cadillac even if we were rolling downhill. It's not that my Falcon wagon doesn't have power, but we call it a sparrow.

Away they went in a cloud of dust. After the dust settled, my car started to move, so I held out hope that we all might make it. Russ every now and then forgot I was following him and started to go over thirty miles an hour. A quick honk of my horn set him straight.

The countryside was great. The rolling hills were bathed in the California sunshine.

"This is the kind of weather that makes me feel great," said Nista.

"There's no place like California," the lovely Joan Nista observed.

I've got to give the Nistas a lot of credit for guts. For forty-five minutes they endured my little girl's constant chatter (she's at that age) and my bad jokes (I'm always at that age). I must say they did seem happy when we arrived at our destination.

TYLER

An impressive gathering at the base of the Vasquez Rocks in the San Fernando Valley. It's the Weider Undercover Task Force headed up by Joe himself on the far left. In disguise are Larry Scott and Joe Nista to right of the legendary Trainer of Champs; off to the far right is Russ Warner with his Wonder Camera secretly taking a picture of the trio. And, of course, behind the camera that's before the camera is Dick Tyler. Say "Hi," Dick.

Vasquez Rocks is great rock, giant boulders and rock formations seem to erupt from the ground in an agony of strength—a perfect place for photos of men who match the mountains. The place is a state park and it costs fifty cents per car to enter, a bargain at any price. Being a Sunday, it was filled with people on family outings. For a while we didn't know if the crowds would get in the way. Scouting around, we decided the best and most dramatic formations were the rocks near where we parked. I took a blanket and a pillow for the girls to sit on.

We started to climb. I would have had an easier time of it if I hadn't been hampered by having to carry a heavy pillow. I also felt Joe could have helped if he had only yelled, "Charge!" In spite of it all, I made the top. The whole valley was stretched out below us in a startling panorama of green valleys and wild rocks.

"Boy," said Joe, "did you ever see such a view?"

In all honesty, I hadn't. It now seemed well worth the climb.

Soon Nista and Scott were going through their poses. It was an awesome display of rugged musculature as Mr. America and Mr. Olympia dazzled the people who were beginning to gather. Soon the cracks, crevices and boulders were swarming with the curious. Never before had an audience been treated to such a show. If you didn't like the view from above, just hop down a few ledges. Best of all, the whole show was free.

"How could anyone get such muscle?" asked one awestruck man.

By now the word seemed to have reached the whole park and from our vantage point we could see people heading our way up the pathways below.

One teenage girl near me said to her friend, "Ohhh, isn't all that muscle just terrible; I can't look," and she left.

A few minutes later I saw the same girl climbing to another vantage point to get a better view of what was so terrible. I have never seen so many flabbergasted people in my life.

Having removed his disguise it's plain to see that Larry, along with Joe are...wait...what are they looking at? And who are those suspicious people in the background? And where's the photographer?

WARNER

After all, even I could hardly believe that as much muscle could be put on a man's frame as these men found capable of doing. Nista started throwing some arm and chest shots that were great. A hush fell over the people watching as Russ and Joe scurried over the rocks to get better views. Then Larry started to pose again.

WARNER

Larry Scott at his thickest. He's packed with dynamite muscle and those arms are about to explode. For this reason Russ Warner carefully transported him to a remote and rocky area before allowing him to flex.

"Just look at that!" exclaimed Joe Weider.

Russ just looked down in the reflex finder of his camera and muttered, "It's hard to believe."

It was hard to stop taking pictures. Every time Larry or Joe would get ready to leave, we'd find a new rock formation or a new pose. We finally had to stop when Russ ran out of film.

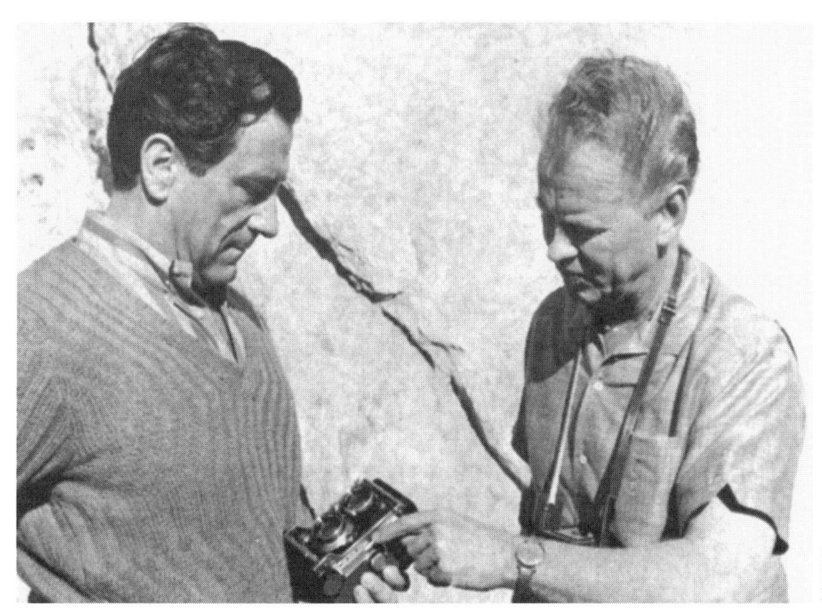

TYLER

These two men have conspired and conferred often and produced the best exhibits of muscle photography the world has ever seen. Joe Weider and Russ Warner brought into focus the original bodybuilding heroes (Reeves, Park, Gironda, Clancy Ross, Jack Delinger, Zabo, Eifferman, LaLanne...dem bums) and thereby provided the inspiration upon which we have glided. Thanks, guys.

On our way home, Joe Weider treated us to supper at a wonderful roadside inn. We sat and talked bodybuilding.

When we got back home, everyone went their separate ways. Joe Weider came in the house and we talked for a few minutes.

"I've got to be on my way," said Joe, "Betty (that's Joe's beautiful wife) is holding a late dinner for me."

"Dear," my wife called out as we were getting into the car, "are you sure you know how to get there?"

"Of course," I replied.

I dropped Joe off. A few minutes later I was in the phone booth calling home again.

"Honey," I said as if it were her fault. "What freeway is the best one to take to get home?"

She hung up. Ya know, it's getting pretty cramped writing this in a lousy phone booth. Hope she calls back soon.

•

Mr. America Dave Draper has always supported lone wolf training sessions, but in recent months has been hitting some hard workouts with surfing giant Rick Josephson. Rick, a mere nineteen-year-older, is a regular Baby Huey of six-foot, four inches, 235-pound proportions who throws the weights around like they were paper-mache. Training for only two years, he's made prodigious gains, which Rick claims helps him with his surfing also.

"This is all well and good," Rick mentions, "but each year I have to buy a bigger surfboard to keep me bouyant."

Rick's "before" nickname, by the way, was Spider, so you can get some idea of how skinny he once was.

•

It gets pretty chilly out here. I know, Southern California and all that, but today in Peanuts' gym it was downright cold; I think I read the temperature at seventy-eight degrees. In spite of this, the men pressed on, and I do mean pressed. I arrived just in time to witness the end of the bench presses. If you ever want to feel small and insignificant, just walk into this gym. I got so small I almost got lost in my clothes. I suppose after a while you get used to it, but today was something else again.

For a moment I thought Peanuts had erected a monument to a gorilla. Suddenly I noticed it moved—and talked—and called itself Steve Merjanian. In all honesty I can say I have never seen that much muscle mass and such shape combined on one set of bones.

At this point some of the men went on to squats, but big Steve and Joe DeMarco chose to do incline presses. Now, for the uninformed, Steve Merjanian is probably the greatest incline bench presser in the world. At present he can push up close to 480 pounds.

"I plan to hit 500 pounds pretty soon," said Steve. "I like nice round figures."

Yeah, but can he dance? Steve Merjanian, who is as tall when lying on his side as when he is standing up, once had his deltoids described by Oliver Sacks as having the size and consistency of two ripe watermelons.. Ollie, Muscle Beach strongman with whom I shared early morning Dungeon training and many a meal at the Little Inn Smorgy, went on to become a world-famous neurologist and author of many fiction and non-fiction books, including Awakenings, which became the movie starring Robin Williams.. What does he know about watermelons? Incidentally, that's big Steve pressing 440 on what appears to be an incline bench. Peanuts West has his back to the camera as he spots the man from Mars.

MOZEE

Steve is muscularly enormous, but has small bones, which gives that great mass such great shape. It's like looking at a muscular bull. He radiates sheer, terrifying power. He doesn't even need to lift the weight of his hand and you're convinced he could break yours just by looking at it. One of the best things about Steve is that he is one of the nicest and best-liked men you would care to meet. He's always encouraging his fellow conspirators to lift more.

Steve started warming up with 350 pounds. Now, when this guy takes hold of a weight—one that would break the average man's arms—and treats it like a toy, it makes you wonder if he's really human. Those eleven warm-up reps went so fast it looked as if he were trying to take off and fly.

"Good grief," said Bill Thurber, "who wound it up?"

After what seemed like hundreds of reps, Merjanian put the bar back in the rack. The only trouble with this whole thing is that some of these men do these things with such ease you fail to get properly impressed. You get to thinking nothing could be that hard if it goes up so easily. The man-mountain worked up to an easy 450 pounds and decided to stop. It looked like he could make that quarter-ton right then. As you read this, he may have already lifted it. I hope I witnessed it.

•

People are always asking me about the secrets of the champions..

"How did Dave Draper really build those arms?"

I simply answer, "Plastic."

"C'mon, tell me the special secret of Chet Yorton's legs."

I think for a moment (that's all I can take at a stretch) and answer, "Foam rubber."

Of course, the truth of the matter is there are few, if any, secrets. We aren't in business to keep secrets; we're in business to inform.

With this in mind, I feel obligated to let you in on one of these secrets. This one concerns powerlifting and one of its mighty men—Bill Thurber.

One of Bill's favorite lifts is the bench press and now I know one of the reasons he's able to lift so much: Growls. That's right. Growls. He psychs up, gets under the bar and as he presses the weight, he gets so mad at it that he literally growls. Imagine what it would be like if everyone did that. The humane society would be raiding all the gyms.

•

The men at the gym are great recordkeepers as well as record breakers. They seem to be writing almost as much as lifting. Almost all of them have little black books. The most exciting items in these books concern sets, reps and weight. Actually this is a very good idea. By examining the past, you can judge how much progress you were making under which training program. From that you can chart a better course in the future.

No man would touch another's little book—that's if he wants his arm left attached to his body. It is my sad duty, then, to report there's a mad scribbler in the group. I think they call him The Midnight Scrawler. Mysteriously, one of the men will find a little note in his diary such as, "Dear Diary, this guy is a liar. He can't lift all that weight, but don't tell him 'cause I hate to see a grown man cry."

Peanuts tells me they plan to rig up some kind of a trap where a weight will accidentally break his leg. Hope they catch that foul fiend before he scrawls again. I mean, I'd hate to be walking around with my leg in a cast.

•

George Frenn once squatted 730 pounds at a bodyweight of 242. Peanuts West is right behind the man during his training in case dear George decides to take a snooze or break for afternoon tea. Stay tight, George, look up...you can do this...

Speaking of injuries reminds me of the Beast, George Frenn. George is one of the world's greatest hammer throwers and certainly one of the world's strongest powerlifters. Recently George did a full squat with 730 pounds while weighing 242. One of the things that makes him so great is his incredible drive. Once he gets started on something, trying to stop him is like trying to stop the Super Chief with a thread. It can't be done. You'd think fate would have learned by now that road blocks don't mean a thing to this powerhouse.

I can well remember seeing George competing in a power meet, squats and all, with a cast on his lower leg. It hurt me just to watch. The other day it happened again. This time George was in an auto accident. Ahhh, but it was also time for a workout. Could lacerations and loss of blood slow down this juggernaut of power? Not on your life. He pushed aside the twisted metal, stepped over the broken glass, slashed his way through the Ben Caseys and Dr. Kildares, knocked aside half a dozen nurses, got to the gym a few minutes late and acted as if nothing had happened. Ho, hum. And you wonder about how a man becomes a champion. No, not car wrecks—determination.

Popping Questions at Bill McArdle

I was in the middle of dinner when the phone rang.

"Hi, Russ, what can I do for ya?"

"Dick, I thought I'd let you know the proofs are ready for the Nista article," replied Russ.

"Good," I said, "I'll drop over and get them."

"Not tonight," said Russ, "I have to go over to Larry Scott and Bill McArdle's apartment. Bill's going to do a story on the apartment while I'm going to do the photo layout."

"Wait a minute, Russ, how about me tagging along? I've heard a lot about their pad and thought I'd do a "Popping Questions" at Bill soon anyway; this might be just the chance."

About an hour later we were on our way. The apartment is a beauty. It's on a hill overlooking the lights of the San Fernando Valley. The door was slightly open when we arrived, so we just barged in. Russ and I got hardly a step in when we were stopped and informed by Larry Scott that we must remove our shoes.

MOZEE

From the shadows of Vince's North Hollywood gym emerged a bodybuilder's rat pack, starring Don Howorth, Bill McArdle, Larry Scott and a few lesser known, yet equally devoted muscleheads.

Much later, after Russ had gotten the photos out of the way, I corralled Bill for this interview.

Dick: Okay, I think we're ready. Bill, where were you born?

Bill: I was born in Aurora, Illinois.

D: I thought you were born in Texas.

B: No, I lived in Texas, but I was born in Illinois.

D: When did you move to Texas?

B: When I was five. Then I lived in Texas for seventeen or eighteen years.

D: How long have you been here in the Muscle Beach area?

B: For around a year and half now.

D: Why?

B: Why what?

D: Why did you decide to move out here?

B: I was interested in bodybuilding and I knew the best in the world were out here. I also heard at lot about the climate and I was interested in an acting career. This just seemed like the place to be.

D: What are your favorite sports?

B: Diving, gymnastics and karate.

D: Did you win any awards?

B: Yes, a couple for my diving.

D: What about karate? Have you been at that long?

B: No, just a couple of months, but I love it.

D: Now, Bill, you must have some reason for training.

B: Yes, I was weak and underdeveloped.

D: How old were you when you started?

B: Around nine years old. You see, I developed a complex about such things at an early age. I had an appendix operation when I was two and that left me abnormally weak for years. I first used some dumbbells my sister had.

D: Did you have any early inspiration?

B: My dad.

D: That's nice to hear. Too many kids today don't look up to their parents the way they should.

B: Well, I mean it. Oh, he wasn't a Mr. America or anything like that, but he looked strong and was strong and I admired him as a person as well.

Just then Russ got some ideas for some more photos. We went upstairs to where the bedroom, bathroom and sundeck are located. The bedroom has a giant picture window that gives a magnificent view of the valley. Near the window are some of the trophies that have been garnered by both Bill and Larry. Goldfinger would have been in heaven with all that hardware around. Also, in the bedroom was a large painting that was obviously still being worked on.

D: Who's the artist?

B: I am.

D: Where did you learn to paint like that?

B: Art and sociology were my majors when I went to college. I'm basically a creative person and I find it quite relaxing to sit by this window with this view laid before me and paint when I have the time.

D: Talking about being creative, didn't you say earlier that you were interested in becoming an actor?

B: Yes, but I'm also being realistic. Acting is a competitive business. Almost everyone who comes out here seems to want to enter the acting trade. That's why I'm studying hard at a drama school.

D: What type of parts would you like to do?

B: You may think this is funny, but I'm trying very hard to get into commercials. There's a great deal of money in commercials. Then I want to play it by ear.

D: You're taking it quite seriously, aren't you?

B: I'm this way in everything I do. That's the only way to progress.

(Russ, by this time, had finished taking the pictures he wanted and we clumped downstairs.)

D: What about your diet? What types of food do you eat and what type of supplements do you take?

B: I just eat meat, fish and dairy products. I supplement that with Weider vitamin E chewables, Vitamin C, wheat germ oil and plenty of Super Pro 101. And speaking of Super Pro 101, come here for a second.

(We went over to the refrigerator and Bill took out a tray of what I thought were ice cubes. To my suprise they were little squares of Super Pro 101. Honest. He offered me a spoon and I dug in, and in, and in.)

B: Hey, that's enough. Leave some for the rest of us.

(After a mighty struggle, he wrenched it from my hand.)

D: What are some of your best lifts?

MOZEE

Bill McArdle made his way from Texas in the mid-'60s to train at Vince's Gym, win Mr. California, gaze at Hollywood and eventually pose on this rock in the Malibu Canyon. Beyond being an integral force in the physique world, Bill McArdle was an incredible artist who painted in the tradition of the great masters.

B: Let's see, well, there's getting out of bed in the morning.

D: Hey, now that's a great exercise.

B: And I've push-pressed 310 pounds for two reps.

D: I think I'll stick with the getting out of bed in the morning. What was your heaviest bodyweight?

B: About 228.

D: What is your best contest bodyweight?

B: I like to come in at around 195 pounds.

D: Bill, you know that idea of freezing the Super Pro is great. I should take one more taste, so I can give a proper evaluation to Joe. (Bill looked at me for a second with an all-knowing eye.)

B: Aw, go ahead and finish it off.

D: Hmmmm?

B: Go ahead, I don't care.

D: Well, if you insist, okay.

WARNER

As iron sharpens iron, so one man sharpens another. The '60s unwound and Larry Scott and Bill McArdle became a powerful combination of personality, friendship and wisdom. The three of us serendipitously joined forces regularly to investigate life in the Hollywood hills, on the sunny beaches and among the strawberry fields.

B: You were supposed to be interviewing me.

D: Of course, of course. What is your favorite recreational activity?

B: I love to play chess. Larry and I will spend hours at the board. I consider it a form of mental gymnastics.

D: What have been the easiest bodyparts for you to develop?

B : The ones I started working on last, my legs.

D: Okay, and what have been the hardest to develop?

B: Actually, arms. They've seemed like my best bodyparts to many who have observed them, but that's only because I've worked them so hard.

D: Do you have any exercises that you get the best results from?

B: Yes, but it's one I don't like: breathing squats. They're really non-lock squats.

D: What kind?

B: Non-lock. You just don't lock out. This puts constant exertion on the thighs so they don't get a chance to rest until you've finished the exercise.

D: I see why you don't like them.

D: Who do you think are the best bodybuilders in the world today?

B: I can think of four: Reeves, Park, Scott and my girl.

With that, Bill's date, and she was a beauty, came over to Bill and started getting comfortable. I thought I'd talk to Larry for a while, but he was similarly occupied. Russ and I looked at one another and decided to leave. I still don't think they know we left.

•

"Biggest Dope I Know" department...Leading the home stretch for the title would be me. Now try to picture this: A truck rolls up to the back of the warehouse here at the Weider West Coast headquarters with a couple o' thousand pounds of weights in boxes to be unloaded and stored. Along comes our shipping department manager, big (six feet and 240 pounds), Dave Draper, to me (five-foot, eight and 180 pounds), who asks for assistance in the unloading scene.

"Okay," sez I.

Soon, however, the unloading develops into a contest to see who can unload the most, which I seem to be mysteriously winning. There I am dripping buckets and busting my back with little Dave just standing there shaking his head in wonder. Slowly it begins to seep into the insulated walls of my skull that this is turning into a one-man contest—me vs. me with Dave winning. I have since won several more of these competitions. Guess I'll never learn. Okay, I'll walk to the winner's circle.

A Future Mr. America—Don Peters

I make the fearless prediction that Don Peters will be one of the greatest in a few years if he continues to train with the same desire and purpose he has now. All too many bodybuilders with great potential peter out whenever things don't come their way with the speed they want. Suddenly they stop training, chuck all they've worked for, and drop off the earth as if gravity vanished on the spot they were standing. What a pity and what a lousy waste.

Don Peters is not this type of person. He's one of those whose purpose is fixed and whose potential won't be denied.

I first remember seeing Don a year ago at one of the local contests. At the time I was impressed with his size and shape, but not enough to notice his name.

Last week I stopped by Vince's for my weekly lesson on bodybuilding from the spaghetti king himself. After listening to a few of the gems of wisdom he periodically imparts, I came up with a brilliant, "What's new?"

"Why don't you do a story on Don Peters?" was Vince's answer. There was that name again.

"Look, Vince, who is Don Peters?"

"One of the best newcomers around."

Now, I had to see who the guy was.

"When does he train?"

Vince looked at the clock. "In about half an hour. Why don't you stick around?"

I didn't need the invitation; I wanted to see who could be that good. I didn't have long to wait, for a few minutes later Vince interrupted our conversation.

"Hey, Don," he said to a man who had just entered, "I want you to meet Dick Tyler; he wants to do a story on you."

As Don walked over, I remembered having seen him in some earlier contests. I didn't want to do a story on him, however. We exchanged pleasantries and he went into the dressing room to get ready for his workout. I talked with Vince for a few minutes more and was about to leave when out on the floor of the gym came Don Peters, ready to take his turn at the iron.

He was wearing a pair of trunks and a Gironda gym shirt. As he passed under the skylight he seemed to burst with muscle. I looked over at Vince, who was just smiling.

"What did I tell you?" I could hear him say as I headed to where Don was standing.

"Before you get started, Don," I said, "how about making arrangements for me to do an article on you?"

"You name the time and place, Dick, and I'll be there."

The man was as good as his word and a few days later we were sitting in Vince's with me scribbling notes.

Don started training when he was a sixteen-year-old high school kid. He had always been thin and figured that bodybuilding with weights would be the answer. He found his inspiration in the pages of *Mr. America* and *Muscle Builder* and the photos and training routines of such champions as Steve Reeves, Dick DuBois, Lynn Lyman, Vince Gironda and Bill Pearl. He had to go it alone, for his track coaches were dead-set against his training with weights.

Fortunately, the unenlightened cannot hold back the progress of those who want to better themselves. Don continued to train in secret and continued to make gains. Not only did he begin to make great muscular gains, but his progress in sports matched the size of his budding lumps. He lettered in football and track; he broke the high school record in the high jump and pole vault.

Inspired by his success, he dove into his training with a vengeance. The more he read the magazines and heard about Muscle Beach and heard about Vince Gironda, the more he felt he had to move out this way. Now a firmly planted Muscle Beach man, Don works as a film technician at MGM studios. He is studying acting with the hope that success in this field might come his way. If his face looks familiar, it's no surprise. You might have seen him in such films as "Beyond the Time Barrier" and "The World by Night."

This is what I meant by Don Peters being a man who seeks success. He just isn't interested in the status quo. Progress to Don means moving ahead. Not only does he want to achieve success as an actor, but would like to one day wear the Mr. America crown. I've got a hunch he'll get both.

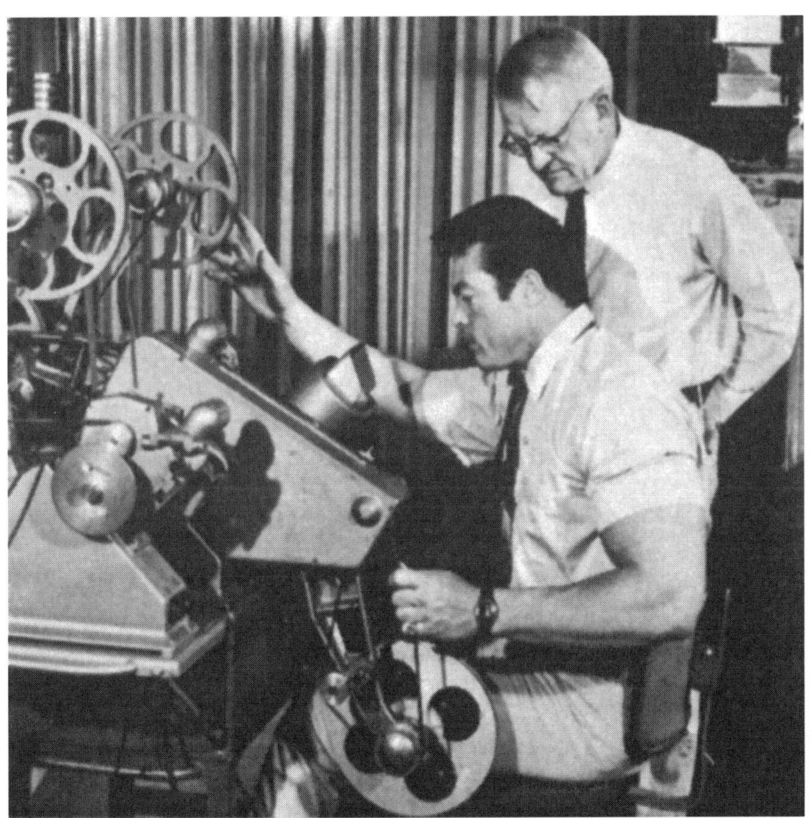
DOWNS

Wherever Don Peters was, a camera was sure to follow, and vice versa. When the camera came out, I hid behind a tree, a rock, a car if it wasn't moving. Don leaped out of nowhere drenched in oil and fully pumped. Scared me! This is the attitude one needed to make it as a physique star, make life bearable for the cameraman and please Joe Weider who was producing the shoot...kept the rest of us on our toes.

DOWNS

Mr. Olympia, AKA Larry Scott, under the powerful skylight of Vince's Gym. The man is like a structure of I-beams and razor wire.

FOUR

1968

We Want Scott

"Scott! We want Scott!" was the yell that rose from the throats of thousands of bodybuilding fans at the latest Mr. Olympia contest. The only trouble was, there was no Scott to be had. At the previous Mr. Olympia Larry told those who had just seen him win his second consecutive Olympia crown that he was retiring. Funny thing about people, they don't believe what they don't want to believe. They wanted to see Larry go on forever, so as far as they were concerned Scott would compete again.

"Scott, Scott, we want Scott!" went the chanting. Finally Bud Parker stepped to the microphone to tell them what they already knew—Larry Scott had retired. Luckily the splendor of the physiques present soon made everyone's attention center on the contests at hand.

Sure Scott wasn't there, but where was he? What was he doing? Those and many more questions were on the mind of Joe Weider as he came up to me backstage.

"What's Larry doing now?" asked Joe.

"Well, I talked to him on the phone last week and he said he'd cut down on his training and had dropped down to about 170 pounds."

Joe's mouth dropped open.

"I know," I said. "It doesn't sound possible, but several people have told me it's so."

"Good grief, what does he look like?"

After winning the first Mr. Olympia title at the Brooklyn Academy of Music, Larry warmed up the already blazing crowd with his bright and infectious demeanor and intelligent words of gratitude over the emcee's mike.

CARUSO

"I dunno," I shrugged. "The last time I saw him in person was at a posing exhibition he gave around six months ago."

"What did he look like?" asked Joe.

"Better than I've ever seen him. He had cuts, size and shape. It's hard to believe that he's lost all the weight."

Joe thought for a minute. "I want you to see Larry when you get back to Muscle Beach."

"Sure," I replied. "That's easy enough, then what?"

"I want you to do a human interest story on what he's doing now."

"But if he isn't training hard or competing, do you think the readers will be interested?"

Joe smiled, "Dick, the only reason I'm in business is to give our readers what they want and you heard them out there, they want Scott. So, okay, let's give them Larry Scott as he is today."

As soon as I got back to California I called Larry at work and lined up a day when Art Zeller and I could visit him at home. It was an overcast Sunday morning when Art and his cameras pulled into my driveway.

"Well, here we go," he said cheerfully. I got in his car and we were on our way. Art smiled as he looked at me out of the corner of his eye. "170 pounds. Who are you kidding?"

"Well, that's just what I heard, but you can't prove it by me." In a few minutes we were in front of Scott's home in Van Nuys.

Now we'd be able to see for ourselves what Larry Scott really looked like.

We went in the backyard and there was Larry, all 168 pounds of him, digging trenches for his sprinklers. His shirt was off, revealing the greatest set of 168 pounds I've ever seen. I can't believe that's all he weighs. I'll bet he could enter a contest right now and win against the best. It just shows you that once you've built quality muscles with quality methods, they stay even if you try to beat them away.

When I first knew Larry he weighed just a little less than 168, but he didn't look like that, even though he was quite muscular at the time. Now, at the same bodyweight he looked incredible, so bodyweight means less than you think. Quality is the thing to strive for.

The backyard looks like a small football field. In fact, it's so large the previous owners fenced off a full half of it because it was too big to take care of properly.

"Where's the team?" I asked.

"What team?"

"The one that plays football."

Larry smiled, "Yeah, I guess it is pretty large, but I like a lot of room to move around."

Art looked up from the camera he was adjusting. "Why don't you put in a pool?"

Suddenly, in the midst of our conversation, a giant bear (well, it looked like a bear) leapt at Larry. A struggle ensued as we stood transfixed by the sight. Over and over the struggling forms rolled. At last we could see that it wasn't a bear but a dog as big as a bear.

"How do you like our pup?" said Larry at last.

Art turned white. "You mean it gets larger?"

I laughed bravely...from inside the house. The minute I saw the beast I hit the trail to safety.

"Larry," I said, "is it true that you've given up all training?"

"Of course not, I'll train as long as I live. It's just that I've cut down a great deal on my workouts."

"How often do you train now?"

Larry shrugged. "Whenever I feel like it."

"Well, how often do you feel like it?"

"One, two, or three times a week."

"Why did you decide to lose all that weight?" asked Art.

"The weight? Because I want to go into acting."

ZELLER

Life is Mr. Olympia, his dog and his bike in sunny California.

"You mean you've given up bodybuilding?" I asked.

"For competition, yes. In fact, I'll go so far as to say I'll probably never even give an exhibition again. It takes too much time and energy to get in top shape."

"You've won everything anyway," I said.

"Yes. For a long time I was consumed with the desire to be the best bodybuilder in the world. More than anything I wanted to win. My first Mr. Olympia victory was quite a thrill. When I won the second—the night I announced my retirement—I was happy, but I felt a little hollow. The kicks were gone. The great challenge had been answered."

"Now, you have another challenge?"

"Yes, acting."

"Well, why not?" said Art. "After all, look at all the musclemen who have made it big in films."

"I don't want to do just a muscleman in films. I want to be an actor. I've found that it takes every bit as much concentration to master the emotional techniques of acting as it does the physical ones of bodybuilding. Right now I'm ready to test the water."

"And the loss of weight helps?"

"Yes. If muscle is too large it must be explained by the part you're doing. This, of course, limits you in your choice of roles."

"Then you don't believe a good physique helps?"

"Sure it does, but it must be a bonus that can be used when needed. I've had a background in gymnastics and bodybuilding that will help me if I'm ever called upon to do my own stunts. I also practice on the trampoline I have in the backyard so that I can keep supple."

The hours went by and before we knew it, it was time to go. Before we left I took one last look at Scott's trophy room which was filled with plaques, trophies, scrolls and crowns, testimonies to his immortality in bodybuilding. I couldn't help but wonder what an Oscar on the shelf would look like.

•

The other day I was driving along when I see this face towering above me. I drove a few blocks and tried to clear my head. "Did I see what I just saw?" I mumbled to myself.

"Yeah," I answered.

"Well, what are you gonna do about it?" I asked again.

"Go back for another look?" I asked.

"Right!" I said.

As you can tell I have some great conversations with myself, and no argument that I can't win. So I rode back to the spot where I first saw this enormous face to see if I hadn't been too close to a banana or something. Well, there it was again, a billboard ad for a stamp company with none other than Bert Elliott's shining dome and waxed lip hair staring at the world. The billboard was proclaiming one of the things you could redeem for the stamps was this electric razor that was flirting with Bert's mustachio. Now, it didn't actually say whether it was Bert or the razor that could be redeemed. Come to think of it, I haven't heard from him in a while. Maybe someone got Bert for a couple of stamp books.

LEOMAZZI

"I'd recognize myself anywhere," says Bert Elliott, "but I had to get a closer look to make sure. Yeah, that's me okay. I can tell by the manicure."

•

In sports the most exciting part of any contest is the actual competition—or is it? When you're lucky enough to be backstage during and before the battle, you'll find that some of your greatest memories will be honed from the drama of great athletes preparing for the test. It's actually a study of men under pressure.

Like drinking, all men react differently. Some are great kidders and release their tensions with laughter while others take their pent-up concerns out on the weights. Some do better in the warmups when nothing is up for grabs than they do when everything counts on the way they lift and how much. Call it jitters or pressure, but the bigger the contest the greater the excitement. Of course, I can just sit back and enjoy it all, 'cause all I gotta do is rest on my gluteus maximus and take in the sights and sounds.

From Where I Sat

Most often I start writing contest reports on my way home from them. This time things were different. Joe asked me not only to watch the contest, but to act as one of the judges. Ordinarily that's no hassle, but on a panel of ten I was to be the only judge from the West Coast. I got the feeling all eyes would be on me when it came to voting for the contestants who entered from the Muscle Beach area. It was like being under a microscope. I didn't want to vote for certain men because they were my friends. At the same time, I didn't want to vote against anyone for the same reason. Even up to the day of the contest I tried to pull up the stakes of my tent and silently steal away. The gears were already meshed, however, so I had to accept my fate. As I winged my way to New York, I wondered how I could write about my friends winning or losing, much less judging them.

Before I go any further, let me say this account of the contest is just one man's opinion. I hope my thoughts come out on paper just the way I have them stored in my head. The most important thing to remember is the judging was an honest representation of the opinions of the judges who held them. Sure, emotions for or against someone can unconsciously sway opinions, but I had the feeling this was a group of men too dedicated to the sport of bodybuilding to taint any decision with personal feelings. We were all there to judge the physiques of the contestants and nothing more.

When we arrived at the Brooklyn Academy of Music it was still early in the afternoon. One of the greatest things to see is the enthusiasm of the fans in the east. Already a crowd had gathered in front of the hall and at the stage door. They were waiting to catch a glimpse of the stars as they arrived for the prejudging. Everywhere I went people ran up asking for autographs—not mine, but Elliott's who had come to the show with me. You can spot that shiny dome and waxed spikes he wears on his upper lip a mile away.

At last we were seated on the stage. The lighting was flat and cold as one by one the contestants filed out in front of us to be judged by height division. The first group was the short class of the Mr. America contest. I won't attempt to give you all the contestants who competed, for that would take up too much space.

Right away it was apparent it would be a two-way contest between Joe Nista and Rock Stonewall. Joe Nista, our current Mr. Western America, had trained harder than ever for this contest—and it showed. He was a razor blade's dream. But it was Rock Stonewall who seemed to be the class of the division. He not only had definition, but the size and shape to go with it. Another thing often overlooked is muscle balance. He seemed perfectly proportioned. His upper body seemed to match his legs. He was balanced from top to bottom, a harmonious blend of quantity and quality that made him the unanimous choice of the short man's class.

The next class was the medium height. Again some men just stuck out like sore biceps. This time it was Zabo Koszewski and Frank Zane. Zabo looked incredible. There he stood with forty-five-year-old muscle on his bones, looking more muscular and fit than men who weren't even born when he started training. Mouths drop open; it's almost unbelievable.

As for Zane I can run out of adjectives. He has undoubtedly the best of everything. He's one of the handful of men who can truly be considered a Mr. America in every sense of the word.

ZELLER

Frank Zane with elegance and might reaches for the skies above the canyons. Actually, he just landed from a precision skydiving exhibition. If you look closely you'll notice his hands are clenching almost-invisible filament parachute leads. The very next photo taken showed the chute engulfing Frank and nearly knocking the camera off its tripod. Fun stuff...shoulda been there.

At this point I wished there wasn't a tall man's class. After all, the choice was hard enough as it was. But sure enough there was a tall man's class and after I saw Don Howorth, I knew who Mr. America had to be. One of the judges leaned across to me and said Howorth looked better than ever and that he was literally amazing. This made me feel good because I didn't want to be accused of favoritism.

The judges adjourned to the side of the stage to ballot. To my surprise the voting favored Rock Stonewall as the winner. Rock is excellent, but I really thought Howorth was better. Then the arguments started. We all gave reasons for our picks. It was stimulating to hear the opinions, as diverse as they may have been. Here were some of the leading bodybuilders and bodybuilding authorities of our time discussing the pros and cons of what they had seen. It was like being allowed to observe a session of the Joint Chiefs of Staff. As it turned out, everyone stuck to their guns and going into the show that night—if things remained as they were—Rock Stonewall would be the new Mr. America.

At promptly eight o'clock, the National Anthem was played and the greatest show on earth—bar none—began. After Ben Weider gave his welcome to the standing-room-only house, we were treated to rock 'n' roll singing by Rick Wayne. That's right. That heaving mass of muscle also heaves a great song, which had him back for encores.

Next on the program was Ed Jubinville, who spent the next ten minutes proving to everyone why he is considered the greatest muscle-control artist in the world. Some of his controls are unbelievable. I like to think I know something about anatomy, but I saw Jubinville move muscles that just aren't there. He should be captured and placed somewhere so science can study this phenomenon.

Other acts came and went, but we were all waiting for the Mr. America contest. At last the stage darkened as the murmur of excitement passed through the crowd. The music began to play as the contestants took their place one by one upon the lighted dais. For sheer excitement, nothing beats the feeling generated by a New York audience. They just about climb on the posing platform.

I was backstage, organizing the coming arm wrestling event when a loud roar was heard. I ran to the wings to see what had happened. It was Zabo that happened; he brought down the house with the first ovation of the night.

CARUSO

Zabo Koszewski, Ken McCord and Joe Nista waiting for a cab on a crowded corner in New York. It's no wonder they can't get a ride dressed like that in a sophisticated city. California is casual and these boys...wait, my mistake, they are backstage at the Brooklyn Academy of Music in line to use the men's room. No, no...a closer look tells me they are onstage hitting poses to the wild cheers of the crazy fans...crazy...and wonderful.

Back to the arm wrestling, once again the frenzied screaming of the fans brought me to the side for a look. The yelling wouldn't stop. Then I saw why. Howorth was standing on the dais. Just standing. He hadn't even done a single pose. They just kept cheering. It reminded me of the ovations given to Larry Scott. Finally a surprised Don Howorth waved his thanks to the fans. Only then did he start to pose. It was a moment I won't soon forget. It seemed such a short time ago that I saw Don walking down the hall after losing to Chet Yorton the previous year. He was the picture of a man alone. But Don had the stuff of champions. For a solid year he dedicated everything he had to winning the coveted Mr. America crown. Now the question was, would he win?

As soon as the last man posed, the judges went under the stage for a conference on what they had just seen, which had been plenty. Once again we balloted. This time the voting turned to Howorth, who was selected the winner. Stonewall won his class and the Most Muscular award; Zane won his class—but Howorth won the overall title. He also took the Best Arms trophy; Stonewall got Best Back; Zane, Best Legs; newcomer Mike Katz, Best Chest; and Zabo, Best Abs—of course. And so another Mr. America event had passed and Don Howorth held the title.

The Tail of the Comet—1968 Mr. Universe

Joe Weider stopped his car in front of my hotel in New York. We had just spent another one of those night of nights watching the annual show of shows. It was now three in the morning and I was beat but inspired, and already looking forward to next year.

"When are you leaving to go back home?" said Joe.

"I thought tomorrow would be a good time, in the morning."

"No," said Joe.

"Huh?"

"I said no; I'm sending you to Miami." I thought for a minute he was joking.

"The Mr. Universe is being produced there next Saturday and I want you to go there to help cover the events."

"You're kidding?"

"Why should I kid?"

So I was going to Miami. I got out of the car and waved so long to Joe. Then, almost automatically I looked up at the walls of concrete and glass they call New York and wondered just what the fabled Miami would be like. I didn't have long to wonder, for in a few days I was looking up at the walls of concrete and glass they call Miami. The big difference was the place was loaded with many tons of sand, gallons of ocean water and beautiful girls in bikinis. The only thing missing was the sun. During most of my stay there, it was, unfortunately, overcast, and it rained.

Luckily, I didn't have time to waste worrying about the whereabouts of King Sol. The professional sports promoter Don Pope was recently appointed the IFBB director for Florida and he was out to show everyone why he was the success he was. With his associates Milton Berk and Walt Framer, who headed such memorable TV shows as "Strike it Rich," they arranged a publicity buildup that should be emulated by everyone who plans to put on a major event of this kind. The week before the contest was filled with press conferences, the shooting of new film, cocktail parties, live TV, rehearsals, briefings, interviews—you name it, we had it. This was a major event and it was being treated like one.

All during the week the contestants and officials arrived at the DuPont Plaza Hotel in downtown Miami where we were staying. It got so I would go to the lobby and wait around just to see the stars arrive. After Joe Weider, I'm the biggest bodybuilding fan of all.

By show time we had such men ready to compete as Kingsley Poiter from the Bahamas, Jay Gonzalez from the Philippines, Mario DaSilva from Uruguay, Vic Downs and Mike Galea from Canada, Takeshi Kimura and Nobuo Takemoto from Japan, Arnold Schwarzenegger from Austria, Roy Callender from England, Jose Donato Munoz from Spain, Frank Zane, Don Peters, Doug Betts and John Allen from the United States and Pierre Vanden Steen from Belgium. These were just some of those who were ready to compete for the Mr. Universe title.

It was no wonder, then, that we were all excited by the evening of the contest. On top of that, the weather cleared and the sky was sparkling diamonds on a blanket of black velvet. The palms swayed in the gentle ocean breeze and the mood was reflected in the happy spirits of those arriving at the auditorium. The locale of the contest was the fabulous Miami Beach Auditorium, which is the same place of the great Jackie Gleason show. Earlier in the afternoon there was a lengthy prejudging for both the Mr. Universe contest and the Miss Americana. After that, there was the final dress rehearsal and now it was time for history to be written.

Backstage all was mayhem. Contestants, officials, cameramen and newsmen were frantically crashing everywhere. It looked to me like there was almost too much disorder to ever be straightened out in time.

One of the more dramatic moments came when Sergio Oliva, Chuck Sipes and Dave Draper all met Arnold Schwarzenegger for the first time. Here in one spot were probably four of the greatest bodybuilders of all time. They sized Arnold up in a friendly manner and came out with the verdict that he was an official phenomenon.

Suddenly—wham! The show began.

The former Olympic champion and movie Tarzan, Buster Crabbe, announced the contestants who came out one by one to be interviewed. I'm sure many of the audience who were seeing their first physique contest were surprised how articulate a man with all those lumps could be. Each of the male contestants wore tee shirts so the fans only got a hint of what they would see. At last all the twenty-four Mr. Universe contestants had been interviewed and the Miss Americana contestants were standing around the vast stage. There was a giant backdrop with "Mr. Universe" painted on it and the flags of the countries represented flanked the panorama.

The IFBB President Ben Weider and Joe Weider welcomed the audience and described the activities of the Federation.

Interspersed through the show were sensational acrobatic acts.

The beauty contest began and it was obvious to me in spite of some stiff competition, Joe Nista's daughter, Sandy, the current Miss Western America, would win the Miss Americana title. She is one of the most beautiful young ladies

and the greatest advertisement I have ever seen on the values of training. Last year's Miss Americana, Christine Zane (Frank's wife), gave the crown to Sandy.

CARUSO

Florida: Chuck Sipes blows up a hot water bottle, bends spikes and twists iron bars for the audience; I do a posing exhibition and the following day we both pose for the cameras and magazine shoots. Guess who else is in town? It's the Governor.

Next the audience was treated to a Chuck Sipes strength exhibition. I have seen this many times, but I never get tired of watching. Chuck is a living package of dynamite. By the time the Mr. Universe contest was to begin, we had seen a show and a half.

Unfortunately there was no posing dais or posing light. The contestants had to walk on and pick the spot they felt gave them the best advantage with the light and audience view.

It quickly boiled down to two men: Zane and Schwarzenegger. Zane had come there to win. He never looked better. He had size, shape and cuts wrapped up in a golden bronze Florida tan. The audience went wild.

If they went wild for Zane, they went nutty for Schwarzenegger. I have seldom seen such a monstrous man. Standing six-foot, one, weighing 250 pounds with twenty-one-inch arms, fifty-five-inch chest, thirty-two-inch waist, twenty-seven-inch thighs and nineteen-inch calves, it was no wonder everyone was overpowered. Unfortunately, while Arnold had more than his share of size and shape, he lacked definition to properly delineate his musculature. On top of that he had no tan to display the big muscle.

Earlier it had been decided for dramatic effect only one winner would be proclaimed Mr. Universe, with the eight runners-up designated as ambassadors to the different planets in the solar system. I can't do that to you though—I mean you want to know how they placed. Right?

Before the final decision, however, Dave Draper gave a posing exhibition that proved why he is one of the greatest in the world. As if that wasn't enough, Sergio Oliva literally cracked the cement in the auditorium when he showed them how the world's best developed man should look. To me, he is the greatest I have ever seen and I've been around for a while.

CARUSO

This is Sergio Oliva, a young Cuban boy who showed potential in the '60s and '70s. If only he had worked his lats. And the lad will have to do something about that gut if he intends to compete seriously. Of course, those stringy triceps could use a little meat.

At last the winners of the Mr. Universe were announced. Frank Zane was proclaimed the winner; second (Ambassador to Mars)—Arnold Schwarzenegger; third (Ambassador to Mercury)—Johnny Maldonado; fourth (Ambassador to Jupiter)—Don Peters; fifth (Ambassador to Saturn)—Pierre Vanden Steen; sixth (Ambassador to Uranus)—Roy Callender; seventh (Ambassador to Pluto)—Vic Downs; eighth (Ambassador to Neptune)—Christopher Forde.

In the subdivisions: Best Arms—Arnold Schwarzenegger; Best Chest—Arnold Schwarzenegger; Best Back—Christopher Forde; Best Abdominals—Pierre Vanden Steen; Best Legs—Frank Zane and Most Muscular—Johnny Maldonado.

Unofficially I was appointed the Ambassador to California and I thought it was time to visit my province and my waiting family. On the plane I looked back on the memories of the night before. It was one of the best-staged events I had ever seen. It had been fired with excitement, imagination and some of the best physiques and strongmen in the world. In 1970 I understand the IFBB will be putting on the Mr. Universe contest in Japan. Wow! If only Joe will...Oh, well. That's a couple of years from now. In the meantime I can look at travel folders and dream.

•

Usually, after seeing the big show in New York, I find that pretty well covers the Eastern shows as far as gossip and your reporter are concerned. This year things were different since I was sent to the sands of Miami Beach for the Mr. Universe contest. Another thing that made things different this year was all the social activities. Usually I'm not too gregarious at a cocktail party since I don't drink anything stronger than Dr. Pepper. This time things were different. I was in my element so to speak. You know, muscle talk.

Tuna and water for the bodybuilders and fries and coke for the men in suits. From the left is Ben Weider, Pierre Van Den Steen, Joe Weider, Chuck Sipes, me, Arnold and John Lima.

Actually the parties were almost divided into two groups. Them with the muscle and them that stood in awe. I'd like to say I was in the muscle group, but there was too much muscle around for anyone not to be amazed. Even some of the contestants were fascinated by what they saw. Joe Weider was everywhere as was expected.

He's a dynamo of energy. I know I've mentioned this before, but Joe outdid himself. The disgusting part of the whole thing is the man is as fresh at the end of a day as when the sun rises. I'll bet that was Super Pro 101 in his champagne glass.

CARUSO

The pride of Latin America: Mr. Uruguay, Mario Da Silva, Johnny Maldonado of Puerto Rico and Jose Donato Munoz of Spain, share Miami's wealth of fresh air and sunshine before enduring the backstage closeness and the overhead lights of the evening's big show. Bring it on and let it rip

Probably the biggest thing at the Florida contest was Arnold Schwarzenegger (no kidding). I mean 250 pounds displacing the Florida sun was pretty hard to miss. Arnold seems to accept the stares of those who see him. He has to. I don't care how many times you've seen something like him—it's an experience. The crazy thing about the guy is that he looks as solid and hard as a student protestor's head. Not an ounce of fat.

In spite of this, Joe Weider confided in me he felt Arnold could use more definition and a drop of five pounds or more wouldn't hurt the cause. During prejudging, Joe, who refuses to judge any of his shows, turned out to be a prophet. Arnold looked big, well shaped and powerful, but a bit too smooth. As a result Frank Zane, who was in the best shape of his life, clearly won first, with Schwarzenegger placing second. On top of looking great anyway, Zane sported a coat of tan that made it look like he was made of bronze. Arnold looked like he had seen a ghost, he was so white.

All this contributed to a Zane win in the afternoon balloting. At night during the show, it was different. All the posing in the afternoon, the photos and the interviews had taken their toll at the expense of some fatty tissue on Arnold. He lost four or five pounds and as Joe had predicted looked one-hundred percent better. This time the balloting was split right down the middle with Zane winning on the strength of the prejudging. I spent the rest of the time in Miami looking for Joe's crystal ball.

•

Of all the people in the recent Florida contest, I'd have to say Johnny Maldonado made one of the greatest impressions. Just the week before in New York he had stunned the fans with his sensational physique. Sure we all know Johnny was one of the better physique men in the country, but no one dreamed he could transform a good physique into a great one. This is no exaggeration. He has muscle separation and definition added to even greater size.

He now ranks in my book as one of the greatest bodybuilders in the country. He looks like he went to a plastic surgeon; his muscles can't be for real. Joe says he has great muscle density. I'll say—as dense as a brick wall. The audience in Miami went wild when they let their eyes roll his way. Jaws hung and the applause was deafening. On top of all this he's like a boy scout, confident, quiet, friendly and helpful. With a few more inches in height he could be one of the greatest bodybuilders in history. If you think I'm piling it on a little heavy, just see the man yourself and then comment.

•

I'm seriously thinking of asking Joe Weider for collision insurance. Being backstage at a muscle show is dangerous work. You never know when you might be run into by some mountain of muscle. As an example, all 250 pounds of Arnold Schwarzenegger nearly flattened my dynamic body into the floor when it was announced Dave Draper was going to pose. From out of nowhere the Austrian express plummeted toward the stage. I, unfortunately, was in the way of the misguided missile. Luckily I slipped out of the way just in time. Draper is one of Arnold's heroes.

"Dave," he said as he watched the posing routine, "looks great even at his 215-pound movie bodyweight. He's one of the most popular stars in Germany."

I asked him if he was going to get a driver's license for the way he ran or at least register his body as a dangerous weapon. Funny thing about Arnold is that he is a man of inspiration.

On the day following the contest, Don Peters, Arnold and I were near the boat channel in front of the hotel. Suddenly Arnold bolted from us as if someone had just announced Dave Draper was going to pose again. Before we knew it, the white monster was acting like a porpoise amidt the ships in the water. Hope he never gets the inspiration to fly without a plane. Although if he was sky diving, those lats could carry him pretty far—maybe even up.

CARUSO

Don Peters and I pump up slightly before a photo shoot in Miami. It was the weekend of the '68 Mr. Universe when Arnold arrived in America to contribute to the gold of the Golden Era.

•

Blazing thoughts...Frank Zane, after winning the Universe title, was dragged all over town by newsmen and looking like he loved every minute of it...Austrian Arnold Schwarzenegger and Johnny Maldonado pulling towel while warming up backstage. It was like watching a bulldog fighting a polar bear...Frank Zane saying he was going to put on twenty pounds of muscle and give the big boys a run for their money...Sergio with his gold ring, gold wrist chain and gold necklace. Wanna make something of it?...Dave Draper sneaking looks at Arnold's arm when he thought no one was looking, shaking his head in wonder...I can't forget Joe wants this in pronto, so adios!

•

At the recent California State Powerlift championships things were more exciting than usual. This, in great part, is due to the fact that powerlifting is still fairly new as an organized sport and records are continually being created. I now make the lofty prediction the records of today, as great as they may be now, will be small compared to what they will be a few years from now. While feeling so wise, I think I'll go out on a limb and make a five-year forecast, so get the clippers and cut me out. I mean cut out the predictions, save, and see how close I'll be. That's what I call nerve, or is it just plain stupidity? But gimme a break, if I get twenty pounds either way I'm doing great. Ooops.

Back to the California championships—first I must say it was one of the best organized and run contests ever presented. This was so mainly through the efforts of Ramon Garcia, who's been a power booster for years. He also happens to be one of those who exercises the "get things done" muscles. As a result, things do get done better than ever. You couldn't have asked for more equipment or better facilities. And chalk? Why the powder was flying so much that I thought I was in a snow storm in a soft-drink commercial. But the final touch—the crowning glory—was the messenger service. That's right. People were there to aid the lifters by going out for food or making phone calls. I couldn't believe it. I didn't want to leave, but I had to face reality and now I'm back to making my own phone calls and walking through the yellow pages with my fingers.

•

I've found too many people think of the powerlifts as just a demonstration of crude power. This is opposed to the sophistication of the Olympic lifts. The theory is that timing and coordination play such an important part in the Olympic lifts that the slow, deliberate power moves are merely demonstrations of sheer force. I'll buy that. Who wouldn't, and be proud of the purchase? I do think the power boys are being sold a little short. Sure it takes strength, but it also takes great style and control. All moves must be done in the correct form and the lifts, being as slow as they are, are carefully observed and judged.

Peanuts pulls from the blocks for reps to break yet another sticking point. These guys really had a lot of fun and meeting at Peanuts' garage became a ritual for a powerful brotherhood. Some say the earth's surface beneath their feet was permanently dented by the repeated pounding of their lifts.

ZELLER

It's Hammer Thrower vs. Shot Putter in the Great Power Clean Contest

Some of the greatest athletic contests take place as impromptu training competitions when two or more outstanding men get together for a workout and decide to have a go at some event or another. I was fortunate enough to witness just such a day at Peanuts West's.

Photographer Art Zeller and I walked toward Peanuts' muscle factory to the accompaniment of a familiar sound indicating some very strong men were throwing barbells around. Clank... Wham...Crash...the sounds got louder as we approached.

"Sounds as though the boys are playing," Art remarked, as we entered.

Sure enough, the boy who was playing at the moment proved to be George Frenn, one of America's leading hammer throwers and the world record holder for the thirty-five-pound throw. His playground was the concrete driveway in front of Peanuts' garage gym.

"Dick," big George greeted me, "today I'm gonna try to power clean 350 pounds."

"I thought you were strictly a standard powerlift man, George," I replied. "Are you moving into Olympic-style weightlifting now?"

George just smiled and hauled a warm-up with 255 pounds to his chest.

For the uninitiated, the power clean is one of the best basic strength and power builders, used by competing weightlifters and by athletes in all sports, especially those who require great power. It looks simple enough. The exerciser stands close to a barbell, his feet on a line and extending under the bar so the bar brushes or almost brushes his shins. He bends his legs and leans forward to grasp the bar with an overhand grip, slightly wider than shoulder width. Then he crouches over the weight and pulls from a position with his legs bent, hips lower than his shoulders, and his back flat. With minimal movement of his feet and with no more than a quarter bend of his legs as he catches the weight at his chest, the exerciser hauls the weight up from the floor and whips his elbows forward under it to hold it across his upper chest.

Frenn quickly worked up past 300 pounds, but when he reached 335 it was obvious the load was making him work hard, slowing his powerful upward pull. Still, he made it and finally loaded the bar to 352 pounds. By this time George was sweating profusely from every pore. He paced up and down, psyching himself up to a real hate for that inanimate object, building his determination to lift it. Feeling ready, he approached the weight. He looked down at it, hard, daring it to defy him. He placed his hands carefully and I could see his grip become firm enough for his fingers to pale. George lifted his head and with a roaring grunt powered the weight chest high. But he couldn't hold it. Unfortunately, he was unable to whip his wrists under and secure the weight against his chest.

Down came the bar, but only to his thighs. Without a pause, Frenn tried to power it up again, but again he failed. Twice more he tried, after resting, and twice more he failed.

Then from a corner of the gym a deep voice rumbled, "Wanna see who can power clean the most, George?"

From such remarks great impromptu contests are born, but seldom do they involve athletes of such national prominence. Frenn looked over at the massive George Woods who had just spoken.

His face lit up. "Sure. Let's go."

Just like that we had a match going between two great heavyweight athletes. George Frenn holds the United States powerlift records for the 242-pound class in the squat at 732 pounds and the total for bench press, squat and deadlift at 1900 pounds, holds the world record for the thirty-five-pound weight throw (seventy-three feet, three-and-a-half inches), and had the second-best hammer throw by an American in 1968 at 226 feet, six inches with the sixteen-pound weight.

George Woods can't match Frenn in total weightlifting experience, but has great agility—he can do a standing back flip—and muscular size, usually weighing from 290 to 300 pounds. Woods was ranked second in the world as a shot putter on the basis of his sixty-eight-foot, quarter-inch put with the sixteen-pound ball at the Olympic trials in September.

The two track and field behemoths began to chalk their hands so their grips wouldn't slip when they tugged on the barbell. Art Zeller wasn't going to miss an opportunity like this, so he unlimbered his camera.

"Down at the beach I get sand in the lens," Art grumbled. "Here it's chalk."

Woods stepped up to the barbell for his first attempt with 295 pounds. It zipped up so easily he looked good for double the amount. Next it was Frenn's turn and he showed the hapless barbell no mercy.

The massive shot putter loaded the bar to 315 and made another nice success. Frenn shook his head and wiped the sweat from his brow. He chalked his hands, then decided to add five pounds, bringing the total weight to 320.

"You can do it, George. You can do it," he told himself, thinking aloud positively. Everyone quieted to watch him try.

Frenn gripped the bar tightly, threw his head back and pulled with a tremendous explosion of power. He tore the weight from the floor—but not quite to his chest. It dropped back to his thighs, where he held it in the completed deadlift position.

Still holding the weight, Frenn looked at Woods. "Can I try again?" he asked.

"Right," Woods answered. "Any way you like, as long as you get it up."

Without lowering the weight, Frenn tried to clean it from the dead-hang position across his thighs. No go. It was evident that his earlier efforts to clean 352 had drained off a lot of power.

It was Woods' turn again. He chalked his hands carefully, stepped up to the barbell, gripped it and pulled powerfully. Almost—but not quite. He was so close that a three-inch dip of his knees would have fixed the weight at his chest.

This was just the encouragement Frenn needed. This time his power would not be denied and he took a five-pound lead. Not interested in a tie, Woods loaded the barbell to 325. He pulled...and missed. The weight crashed down, almost through the cement of the driveway.

Frenn had won—this time.

Some of the most exciting athletic contests and greatest feats of strength are performed just this way, on the spur of the moment. Art and I had been lucky enough to be present for this one.

As we were leaving, Woods was telling Frenn, "I'd like to press 450 pounds on the incline. That's the best Dallas Long was able to do when he held the world shot put record. My best so far is 395."

"I've done 400 myself," Frenn stated, "and so has Joe DeMarco."

It sounded as though another contest might be in the offing, but hearing about all those heavy weights was making even my ears tired, so Art and I kept walking.

•

Years ago I used to go to Muscle Beach to train. From almost the earliest days, I remember seeing the exceptional Chuck Collras physique pushing the weights around. In fact, Peanuts West credits a great deal of his original drive in training to the efforts of Collras. The friendly rivalry has continued through the years until now Peanuts is a national powerlift champ and record holder.

What about Collras?

MOZEE

The sliced torso of Chuck Collras, a Muscle Beach child and Golden Era forefather.

Well, for a while I heard nothing about him and figured he had been lost in the California smog. That isn't too hard to do. This seems to happen to a lot of bodybuilders for some reason. I suspect it's because the pressures of business and family life consume too much time for the proper amount of training. Whatever the reason, too many promising champions seem to vanish.

So here we have Collras, a man in his mid-thirties with business and family responsibilities now making a comeback. The amazing thing about all this is that he isn't satisfied with just one aspect of weight training. Chuck is competing in both powerlifting and physique in an attempt to prove that a man needn't look like an elephant to be as strong as one. Right now he's able to do the same lifts he did ten years ago, but then he weighed 165 pounds while now he competes in the 148-pound class. He plans on winning a major physique title and power title on the same night.

That would be a first and quite possibly a last. I know a lot of guys who can't decide whether they want to enter physique or power competition...so they end up doing nothing.

•

The amazing Pat Casey did it again. That's right—he made me make a fool of myself.

I get this call from Peanuts.

The legendary Pat Casey prepares a pair of dumbbells for flight. If it wasn't rooted, bolted or set on foundations, Pat could lift it.

STERN

"Dick," he says, "Casey is now incline pressing 250-pound dumbbells."

I yawned. "I can do that," I said.

There was a silence from the other end.

"What was that?" said West at long last.

"I can press two fifty-pound dumbbells while standing," I replied confidently.

Peanuts broke into laughter. "Listen, I said Casey could incline a pair of 250-pound dumbbells."

I thought for a second. "No, I can't do that."

"I can't either," said Peanuts. "Come to the gym this Saturday and watch him incline 500 pounds."

To make a long story short, Pat pushed up a perfect 505-pound incline press. I leave you with a word of advice. When you hear of something Casey can do, don't say you can do it too.

•

With head bowed in shame, I must admit I helped lead someone down that rocky road of law breaking. Now don't tell the fuzz, 'cause they already got the culprit. You see it all started when I saw this muscular man running around the park near my home. He looked familiar, so I stopped my car and went over to say hello. It turned out to be Gene Mozee, the well-known writer and strength athlete. He looked in better shape than I had seen him in a long while. We talked for a few minutes and he said he'd meet me back at Vince's after he finished his run. That's where he made his mistake, he crossed in the middle of the street. That's right—he jaywalked, or should I say jayran! Don't worry, a policeman was right on the spot to catch him and the crime wave was stopped before it got going.

•

And a great record has at last been broken. It had been held by the Italian anatomy chart, Gironda. The record was for the half-mile run in the wash not far from Vince's muscleorium. Victorious Vince had negotiated the distance in 2:03 minutes. The record stood for a while until Galloping Gene Mozee clocked in at 1:57. Now, Vince wasn't there when Gene ran, and while he doesn't come from Missouri, he wasn't there to verify that obviously exact timing. So-o-o, arrangements are being made for a match race with the winner treated to a dinner at the loser's expense. That's the kind of steaks…er, I mean, stakes I like.

A Visit with Don Peters

CARUSO

Palm trees in Florida had just the right curve to accommodate the perfectly symmetrical body of Don Peters.

I said on the phone, "Joe Weider will be in town next week and he wanted to know if you'd like to pose for some of the pictures to be used in a new series of ads."

"I'd love to," said Don, "but I don't think I can."

"Why not?" I asked in my usual, none-of-my-business way.

"Well, Saturday I promised to take my wife and child to the zoo in San Diego."

"This is gonna be on Sunday."

'Then I can do it."

I arrived at Don's apartment in North Hollywood just after he did. It's a beauty of a place situated in the San Fernando Valley just a short way from Vince's Gym. In the setting sun you get a great view of the surrounding Hollywood hills with Hollywood's backyard spread around like a blanket of tinsel and lights. No wonder people from all over the world come to live here. The first thing that impressed me was the class of the place. It was obvious that the apartment was not just a place to live in, it was a home. Everything was done with care for detail and quality.

"Where did you get this fantastic coffee table?" I asked.

"I made it."

"Huh?"

Don laughed. "I mean it. I love working in wood. See that frame over there?"

I looked and would have sworn that it was an antique. "You made that too?" I said in disbelief.

"Right, and look at this desk over here."

"How did you do it?"

Don held up his hands. "With these."

Over against one wall were a whole set of trophies with enough gold to make King Midas jealous. In just the short time he had been in competition, he had garnered enough awards to be chosen the AAU Bodybuilder of the Year. Don picked up his AAU award and looked at it carefully. He put it down and then looked at me. "Now, that I'm in the big leagues, the IFBB, I have to work even harder."

At that moment little Steve (Don's four-year-old named after Steve Reeves) came running in and jumped on the old man. "Can I go for a ride?" he said.

"Steve loves to ride with me on my motorcycle," said Don with a smile. "Want to see it?"

"Sure."

We went downstairs and while I know nothing about motorcycles, I must say this one looked like a great machine.

"This is my pride and joy. It's a ball to ride. As long as you don't lose your head and start letting the machine tell you where it wants to go. When that happens you get in trouble." Don obviously carried the commonsense he used in the film world into his home life.

It was time for dinner so I sailed into the setting sun after bidding farewell to the friendly natives. I also wanted to get home in time to see Don on the Jack Benny Show. He works in the movies and on TV in addition to all his other activities. I can't figure out where he finds time to get everything in, but the fact is he does and is a success at everything he tries.

An Average Day—Going on a Photo Assignment with Russ Warner can be Quite an Ordeal

"Want to go to a cemetery?"

This was physique photographer Russ Warner's cheery greeting as we met one day recently. I thought it over for a second. While running amidt the graves is a ball when you have nothing better to do, I felt sure I could find something to do that was a little more lively.

"Uh, look Russ," I said finally, "you go ahead and have a good time. I think I'll stay home and play a crazy game of Scrabble."

"You don't understand," protested Russ. "I was going with Dave Draper."

"You mean?" I asked in horror.

"No, no, of course not," said Russ. "Dave's never looked better. I thought I'd go to one of the cemeteries for some physique photos with the statuary."

TYLER

Here we capture Russ Warner candidly taking a picture of himself at Bat rocks. Strong background, good composition, perfectly focused—Russ performed magic with his camera. How did he do it?

Russ, of course, was referring to one of Southern California's swank death gardens. They try to make these glorified graveyards so inviting you hope for an early death. They're filled with some striking art treasures, however, that would be complementary to unusual physique studies.

I said okay I'd go because of the unusual story value, and Russ went ahead with the arrangements. Unfortunately, the officials at the cemetery declined to let us use their facilities. I could see their point. After all, Dave posing against a thirty-three-foot statue of Michelangelo's David could detract from the sober atmosphere of the surroundings. With a little figuring, Russ came up with the idea of taking photos in a more conventional locale. I can't tell you the name of the place because it's unprintable. Let's just say it's a dramatic eruption of rocks known as Bat "fertilizer" Rocks and you fill in the details.

Whizzing along the freeway toward our destination we started talking about the recent results of the balloting for the top ten greatest bodybuilders of all time. I remarked jokingly I was not in the elite ten and I should demand a recount.

"I sure feel flattered," said Dave. "I mean, placing seventh right after Bill Pearl is pretty great."

"The fact that you've appeared in and won only three major contests in your life and still placed as the seventh greatest bodybuilder of all time is really to your credit," I said. "When people have seen you they've gone away impressed."

Dave frowned.

"What's wrong?" asked Russ.

"Oh, I don't know. It's just tough placing that high. It's almost like a responsibility."

"You're right, Dave," I interrupted, "a responsibility to be better all the time."

"Well, I try, believe me. I never want to let my fans down."

Soon we were off the freeway and heading towards Chatsworth where the rocks were located. I had never been to this particular spot before so their sudden emergence was a surprise. There they were, a giant mountain of boulders reaching for the sky. Unfortunately they had been defaced by nature lovers.

"These are the same rocks where those great photos of Larry Scott were taken, aren't they?" inquired Dave.

"Yeah," said Russ, "how can you tell?"

Dave looked at Russ, "By the writing, of course."

Now, the problem was to find the best way to reach the top. I suggested a parachute drop, but the idea was nixed in favor of our feet. Russ had forgotten where the path was, so we were stuck wandering around looking up and yearning. At last someone came up with the brilliant idea of waiting until we saw someone coming down and then start up in the same direction.

It worked and before long we were picking our way up the craggy surfaces. I almost felt sorry for Russ, who was loaded down with all his photo gear. Since Dave was carrying a bag with a change of clothes and some food, that left me with just my bodyweight to propel along with a feeling of guilt. I felt at least I should help Russ, but successfully fought off the urge until we reached our destination. After twenty minutes of climbing we were at last at the summit, and, exhausted, I plopped down on the first rock I stumbled over.

Russ, on the other hand, immediately set up his gear and soon he was operational. Dave stripped down to his posing trunks and Russ started taking pictures. Big Dave looked in better shape than I had ever seen him, even better than when he won the coveted Mr. America crown.

Looking at Dave, I kept remembering all the remarks I heard prior to the big contest of '65. Unfortunately, Dave was the fall guy for many jokes about vast expanses of blubber. This had always been unfair, to my way of thinking, but we are all allowed an opinion. Being a sensitive individual, Dave was always hurt by the remarks he heard. He is also a fighter and was even more determined to turn his detractors into admirers with every caustic remark he heard. With this determination, Draper molded his physique into one of the most sensational and respected in many years.

Gone now were any layers of excess tissue and standing before me was an amazing anatomical specimen who could literally become a model for muscular separation and definition. I predict Dave will soon be the most-cited example of what proper training methods can accomplish. I counted four rows of abdominal muscle flanked by great serratus and oblique definition. It was a great picture of what a muscular midsection should look like. There is little point in my going into the Draper arms and other bodyparts; the photos speak for themselves.

After an hour of steady work we took a break. Suddenly from around one of the boulders came two young men of school age. They ignored us and proceeded toward a lone boulder that loomed like a peak over the others. One of them had a stick with a tee shirt tied to it like a flag and it seemed to be their purpose to plant it at the top. It was quite an ordeal to make it up the sheer face of the rock, but they triumphantly planted their banner.

"That almost reminds me of the time we went out to Vasquez Rocks with Joe to take pictures of Scott and Nista," I said to Russ.

"You mean all the spectators?"

"Yeah."

"I remember the time I came to this place with Scott. It was a Sunday and you should have seen the crowd."

"Any trouble?" asked Dave.

"No," said Russ, "people were just curious to know who Larry was. They had never seen anything like him before."

"You can say that again," said Dave as be gulped down the last of his protein drink.

Frankly, up until now the posing had been good, but it had not been inspired. Russ worked like a dog trying to get the best shots he could. He ran up and down the rocks trying to photograph from different positions and had posed Dave for some great shots. Still, something wasn't clicking.

We were about to pack up when Russ said, "Let me take just one more roll of color."

TYLER

Russ was the greatest, but he didn't understand that a delicate bodybuilding star can't carry his gear around and be expected to pump up too. Feed me, I'm starving.

While he was reloading, Dave and I started talking about some of the bodybuilders of Muscle Beach. He stood up and started to demonstrate some of their favorite poses.

"Hey," said Russ, "that pose is great."

It was. That seemed to do it and Dave started warming to the task. He seemed to relax and move from pose to pose. Each one was a masterpiece of rugged muscularity and power. Russ got more great shots in fifteen minutes than he had for the previous hour.

Now it truly was time to go. We packed up the gear and started to leave. Believing the trip down would be easier than coming up, I nobly volunteered to carry some of Russ' equipment. The minute I got hold of it I was sorry. It was heavy, but it was too late to back out now. I had committed my troops. We went a few steps and came to a crisis.

"Which way is down?" We all looked at one another.

"Down this way," I said with finality. "I remember this rock that has 'Johnson loves Goldwater' painted on it was facing us this way as we came up."

Either I should be a little sharper on politics or carry a compass, 'cause we were lucky to get down that blasted pile of rock in one piece. Needless to say, I picked the wrong path and we all paid the price. Clinging to the sheer face of naked rock is something I like to watch some poor guy do on television while sitting comfortably in my easy chair at home. Now I was doing it, only there were no TV cameras around to record the event.

The whole thing had one advantage, however. At one point I was able to say to Russ, "Say, Russ, could you take hold of your equipment again while I try to make it down this dangerous rock?" I never took back the stuff until we got home and I helped him take it out of Dave's car.

After great sacrifice and a little blood we reached the car. As we were driving away I looked over my shoulder at those rocks with all the funny and sometimes dirty sayings scribbled on them and wondered if we had been allowed to go to that other place with writing on the rocks, would we have had an easier time of it. I shouldn't worry, however, because someday I'll spend an eternity there, at that other pile of rocks.

Excuse me? You actually want to take a picture of me pushing a rock around this forsaken, desolate valley? What'll my friends think? I told them I'm goin' west to hit it big. I ain't pushing no stinking rock. You push the rock.

TYLER

The ILLUSTRATED Muscle and Power Building Magazine Of The Champions
OCTOBER
Mr. America
WINNERS BUILD THEIR MUSCLES
ONLY 50¢
COMPLETE
ILLUSTRATED
COURSE
ON
championship
MUSCLE
BUILDING
TECHNIQUE!

WARNER

•

I called Gironda the other day and could hardly understand him.

"Dick, I goda colt dat wont stoppp."

Translated roughly, he had a cold. It had been going on for weeks. I even heard a rumor he was in the hospital. I knew the only way Vince would be found in a hospital would be for an autopsy, so I was frankly concerned.

"Na, I'll pull out aid. Nuttin like dis is gonna bed me downd." Honk! "Here's dews flash for ya. I dink World War Dree has begun."

"Why do you say that?" I asked.

Then he whispered, "Germ warfare, wud else could ged me dis sick?"

•

Got a call from Bob Green of our Muscle Beach Office.

"Dave is gonna be on the Johnny Carson Show tonight!"

Patiently I waited till the appointed time. Frankly, I'm sick of looking at the guy. Every time I turn around I see Draper. It was bad enough seeing his muscle on the covers of the Weider magazines. It was bad enough seeing him on local television. It was worse seeing him on national TV. It was agonizing seeing him in the movies, but this was the final straw. I was now being bugged in my own home to look at him and on a show as big as the Johnny Carson Show. Oh, the day I introduced him to my agent! If it wasn't for him, with his 230 pounds of muscle and two tons of talent, I would be on the Johnny Carson Show. As the time came closer, I found myself secretly hoping he would make some kind of mistake. No such luck—as all those who saw it will tell you, Dave was terrific.

When he was asked to display his bumps (natch) you should have heard the audience's reaction. He never looked better. I might say he was the most colossal sight I can remember. I thought maybe my set wasn't adjusted properly. Nothing could look that big without some kind of distortion.

On top of everything else he displayed what few bodybuilders are allowed to—brains. He showed, quite articulately, that all his waking hours were not spent concentrating on the formation of his biceps. We can all be proud our sport has such a representative.

STUDIO

Two East Coast boys standing on the beaches of Malibu, one has an empty box in his hand, the other a plastic shark's tooth hanging around his neck. Tony Curtis and I came all this way and the only real thing in the picture is the hillside in the background. The Muscle Beach set for "Don't Make Waves" during a shoot in the summer of '66.

Funny thing about all this is an attempt was made to get Dave on another late night show to plug his picture, but was refused because they weren't interested in a musclehead on their program. Rumor has it the producers caught Dave on their competition. They must have been embarrassed to see someone with obviously better developed brain muscles than theirs doing pushups with Carson on his back.

•

While on the subject of TV, I caught the Mr. Whole World physique contest on the tube the other night. It was actually a skit on the Steve Allen Show. The competition consisted of a mixture of comedians and the real articles. Several of our well-known local bodybuilders were present. Usually I get teed off when they make fun of us, but this was so funny I couldn't stop laughing long enough to work up a hate.

Physique champ John Corvello had a nice bit at the end. I hear a TV series is in the works for John. Hope it's true. Looks like muscles are getting to be a key, or more aptly the battering ram, to the doors of opportunity in the movie and TV industry. Think I'll take a workout and call my agent.

Like Rivers of Steel—Eddie Giuliani

"Eddie Giuliani will be coming with me," said Joe Weider as we talked on the long distance phone.

"Giuliani?" I asked.

"Yes. He's won a lot of titles here on the East Coast."

"Oh, I know who he is. He won the AAU New York City and state titles."

"He's also won the Mr. Brooklyn and the Mr. Long Island crowns."

"That's great, but what legitimate IFBB titles has he won?" I asked.

"He won the IFBB Mr. New York City, Mr. Tri-State and Mr. Northeastern States."

There was a pause.

"You don't sound too enthused," said Joe.

"I'm just thinking about our California audiences. It takes a lot to get them worked up and from what I remember of Giuliani he had a pleasing physique, but not a great one."

Joe started to laugh.

"What's so funny?" I asked.

"Well," Joe replied, "you're in for a pretty big surprise."

Joe Weider is one of the keenest judges of physiques I have ever known. By this time I should stop doubting when he tells me something about the physique of a bodybuilder, but all I could remember was the last time I had seen Giuliani at the Mr. America almost a year before. He had shape and size, but was as smooth as a skating pond. In California they would just turn him off like a commercial.

I kept these negative thoughts with me as I went to the Embassy Auditorium on the night of the Mr. Western America show. Giuliani was to compete for the title and I figured he'd be fighting it out for last place. Even when we were introduced backstage I had no inkling of what was to come. He was in street clothes, which told me only that he was obviously a bodybuilder, but what kind I was soon to find out.

To say the backstage area was a mad house is an understatement. It was chaos. I have never seen so many bodybuilders, their friends, beauty contestants and their admirers packed into one area. As a result I was running around like a mad man, which is nothing new except this time it was with a purpose. I had promised to manage the show backstage for Reg Lewis, who was producing it this year, but I could hardly find the contestants through the people.

Finally, most of the physique contestants were corralled into the dressing room upstairs and I was able to give them their numbers in order of appearance. Giuliani was next to the last contestant, which meant he would be on after some of the best physiques on the West Coast had made their appearances. This was a tough spot, because I figured he would suffer by comparison. Ed is a nice person, but I couldn't remember any place on the judge's ballot for the nice category.

No sooner had I passed out the numbers, I had to rush downstairs and check with Ron Haddad, who was handling the music in the control booth. The suspense was building as the last act before the physique contest finished with a flourish.

At last the big moment came; Reg cued in the music and the first of the contestants for the Mr. Western America title stepped upon the posing dais. I ran backstage to see that the men went on at the right time and in the right order. The music swelled along with the applause and we were on the way.

I was so busy I couldn't pay much attention to anything until I was shaken by violent cheering. Ed Giuliani was onstage, but I couldn't tell anything from my angle, so I raced out front to see what was going on.

Just as I hit the audience, Ed turned and gave a full back shot that nearly sent the crowd through the roof. For a moment I thought I was looking at the back of Floyd Page, who was a star of some years back. One of his greatest assets had been the deep muscularity of his traps and lats. Now before us all was the same mass of muscle that had made Page so famous. It looked like rivers of steel coursing down Giuliani's back. It was crevassed and creased with anatomical delineation that an anatomist wouldn't believe. The traps were high across the shoulders and formed a perfect "T" formation that ended in the mid-thoracic region. The deltoids and the lats framed this memorable array of sinew and power. The rest of the routine I saw was equally good and well received, but it was that back that captivated me. I could hardly wait to ask Ed the secrets of his back routine.

Clean lines and ripped, Eddie Giuliani stands before Marina del Rey, a long way from NYC. "Hey, have you heard the one about Zabo digging the foundation for Joe Gold's gym? Joe told him to dig "here" and an hour later realized he didn't tell him to stop. When he went to find Zabo, the top of his head was barely sticking out of a hole the size of a Buick."

True stories by New York Eddie.

ZELLER

The dressing room after the show is not the best place to conduct an interview, but I had to ask some questions.

"Ed!" I yelled above the noise. "Can I ask you a few questions?"

"Sure."

"First," I said, "I want to apologize."

"For what?"

"Well," I said with a shrug, "I didn't think you were as great as you are. In fact, I was disappointed when Joe said you were coming out."

"Well, we all make mistakes and that one was your problem."

We laughed.

"Seriously, what did you do to transform yourself the way you did in just the time between the last Mr. America contest and the show tonight?"

"If I made any progress at all it was because of two people. Joe Weider and Bela Lugosi."

Bela Lugosi????

"Er...maybe I didn't hear correctly but I thought I heard you say..."

"You did."

"You mean..."

"Yeah, the human blood bank."

I cleared my throat. "Okay, I'll bite. I mean I have to ask—why Bela Lugosi?"

By now there were too many people in the dressing room to hear myself think and I need all the help I can get. At last Ed was dressed and he invited me for a cup of coffee.

At the counter Ed went into greater detail. "Joe Weider advised me to split the split. By that I mean I split my routine in such a way as to allow the maximum amount of blood to remain in one area for the maximum amount of time. In order to do this I had to work one section at a time, with a long break in between. Before, I trained six days a week, but would cover more than one body section at one workout. This took the growth-building blood from a recently exercised area before it had a chance to do its greatest amount of good."

"So you exercise a body area thoroughly and just let the blood gather."

"Right, just like it was waiting for a vampire," he said.

I nodded.

"Bela Lugosi," we said in unison.

"Another interesting point," he said as he gulped his third cup of coffee, "is I relax my carbohydrate intake on the day of the show."

"Won't that smooth you out?" I asked.

"No, because the carbohydrates won't have a chance to show in that short a period, but gives me a good deal of energy for the work that goes into a good posing routine."

"Speaking of posing routines, I had a chance to see just a part of it, but your back was sensational. What exercises do you do for it?"

"I'm glad you liked my back," said Ed as he gulped his fifth cup of coffee. (He likes the stuff.)

"I consider it one of the most important areas of the body."

Ed follows a Weider principle of training called giant setting in building his back. That is, he does a series of different exercises for the same bodypart, one right after the other without rest. After he completes the series he rests for a moment to catch his breath and then does it again until five sets of the exercises have been completed. Each exercise is done strictly and with great concentration for six to eight reps. For his back Ed does a series of four different exercises.

In the cool night air as we walked to the parking lot, I asked Ed about his diet.

"Well, it includes plenty of Super Pro 101, but I have a theory on the best way to drink it, which I'll tell you about later. Right now I just want to hit the sack."

"So long, Bela," I said jokingly. But he had vanished into the misty darkness.

•

Now that the hard work is over, I can look back on the IFBB Mr. America, Mr. World, Mr. Olympia muscle show and reflect on the lighter side.

Here, friends, is gossip from the show of shows.

Hooray for Bud Parker! You seldom see anything about Bud in the columns except during the big show and he discourages any photos being published that might carry his visage, so this is my personal annual plug for him. No, he doesn't need the likes of me telling you what a great job he does—that's evident when you see his shows. But sometimes the gloss of the productions obscures the vision of those who can't see past the footlights to the one who turns them on. So for the record, Bud Parker produces the greatest muscle shows ever seen.

During the prejudging I had a tremendous shock. Walking from backstage while the Mr. America contestants were all lined up in front of the judges, I caught sight of this mutilated back. It seemed pitted with deep crevices and giant growths. It looked too fantastic to be just muscle. I had to see who it was, so I sprinted in front just in time to have the judges ask for a back pose. I still couldn't see who it was. The man had to be one of the most muscular specimens I have ever seen. Finally the contestants were told to turn and give a most muscular pose. Well, sir, the object of my wonder gave some most muscular shots that were testimonies to rugged power and carved muscle. Who was this new wonder man? Slowly it began to dawn on me that it was Johnny Maldonado. That is, it was Johnny's head, but not his physique unless he had been to a plastic surgeon. In a year's time he had undergone a transformation that was unbelievable.

One of the biggest thrills of the evening came when Zabo Koszewski was picked as the Most Muscular Man in America. This walking anatomy chart is a legend in his own time and yet he has never won a major title until this show. When he did win, he did it in the best of possible ways. Zabo beat out almost forty of America's greatest physiques. He beat men who were almost young enough to be his sons. He won in an open contest 3,000 miles away from his home territory. No over-forty bit for this one. He proved that he was all guts and I don't mean just his abdominals. We should all win the title of Most Muscular Man in America when we're forty-five years old. It's amazing just seeing it in print.

After the show is when it's the most fun. That's when you can relax and reflect back on the good times you've had. What at times would seem like utter chaos and confusion would eventually turn out just right. Sometimes it catches you a little off-guard, like the time someone decided the Mr. America competition was too tough so he dropped out just before his name was called during the actual show.

All this is forgotten when you leave the theater. Outside the door were the many fans waiting to get a glimpse of the stars. Sergio was mobbed, as was Frank Zane.

Me? I was just pushed aside. I can't understand it. I can get through a group of fans like a hot knife through butter.

Art Zeller and his camera were there and he couldn't believe the whole scene. "Look, look," he kept saying. "Will you look at that?"

The fans blocked the street. Joe Weider decided it was time for us to be on our way and signaled a forward move just like John Wayne does to the cavalry. The fans decided to join in, too. So, down the street we went with Sergio and Joe in the lead. The greatest sight in the world must have been Joe fanning himself with his Japanese fan as admirers tagged along asking questions. I got tired of eating dust in the rear, so I ran around to be in front. It's great to be a leader.

We all piled into Joe's car and took off for a steak house located in Greenwich Village. Now no matter what it may sound like at times, I'm not a square. But friends, I've never seen anything like the Village on a Saturday night. Some of the creatures walking on two legs seemed more like electrical shock patterns than humans. You get the idea you're visiting a therapy session at a nut house.

At last we reached the restaurant where we all proceeded to break our diets through the power of our forks. Frank Zane was there with Christine. Sergio was there with his legs—I mean, arms. Well, it's hard to tell the difference.

Soon we got around to talking about the hardness of Chuck Sipes' muscles.

"Feel that back," said Joe, "if you want to feel ridges of steel."

I did and Joe was right. Then we all had to feel Chuck's back and make a wish. Crazy, huh?

Anyway it's fun to be in the iron game. The bigger the star, the greater the man himself. Says something for character building and weights, doesn't it? Zeller's usual load of rotten puns was cut short because his mouth was full of food. It was a wonderful way to cap the night.

•

A lot of times I hear from the know-it-alls. You know—the ones who have never lifted a weight in their lives, yet they know all about it: you'll grow fat when you stop training; you get slowed down and muscle-bound; most bodybuilders are just so much puffed-up tissue with little real strength to back up their bulging biceps. We all know what bunk it is.

And, I'm glad to say, so do most people. Oh, the holdouts are still there. They can look at a man put the shot seventy feet and hear that same man tell how he uses weight training in his conditioning program, then turn right around and say that weights are no good. I've found most of the great critics are lard-butted fools who rest their brains every time they stand up.

What got me started on all this is this guy telling me recently that bodybuilders had muscles like pillows, and that his little boy could outlift Larry Scott. That got me wondering if any of you out there had any idea how Scott built his arms or delts. All too little is said about just how strong many bodybuilders are.

MOZEE

What an historical combination of behind-the-scenes bodies, minds and souls: the Trainer of Champions, the Guru and the Olympian—Joe Weider, Vince Gironda and Larry Scott.

I won't go into a list of Larry's feats, but I will tell you a little story to illustrate my point pretty well. Recently, Scott was taking his regular workout at Vince's. He was hitting arms in supersets. Since supersets take a great deal of energy and endurance, you don't push around great piles of iron. Larry just finished a set of curls and went over to the bench to do a set of supine triceps presses.

He finished the set and said that it felt a little heavy. Upon checking, it was discovered that Larry had just been triceps pressing 290 pounds. Think that over for a while. That's doing triceps work in supersets with close to 300. The weight Scott usually used in that exercise is "only" 250. How much you bet the guy who thinks bodybuilders have no strength can't read, so he may never know what I've just said?

•

Getting back to people who think bodybuilders are weak...I forgot to tell you about Chuck Sipes. You know how powerful he is. He bends bars, lifts cars and breaks chains. He told me recently he broke a chain he hadn't planned to. He broke the chain with his calves. Impossible? No! He loaded up his calf machine in the gym with so much weight the chain snapped as soon as he started rising up on his toes. The shoulder yoke snapped up when this happened and gashed his forehead. Lucky Chuck—a few inches lower and his mighty calves would have cost him an eye.

•

A new club has been started within Peanuts' Westside Barbell Club. It's called the 400 Club. No, dummy, it's not society's 400 club of the hoity-toity swells. This club is even more exclusive. In fact, only George Frenn and Joe DeMarco hold memberships in this exclusive group. I wanted to join and for a moment I thought they might be discriminating. I was organizing my pickets when I was informed it wasn't that I wasn't being allowed to join because I had red hair.

"Yeah," I said sternly, "why then?"

Frenn put his hand on my shoulder and said with great compassion, "Because, Dick, you're not good enough."

That did it—back to my picket plan.

"Okay," said George, "you can join."

"That's more like it," I said smugly.

"Only one thing," continued George, "you have to pass a little test."

With that, the bar on the incline bench was loaded with 400 pounds. Before another word was said I let 'em off the hook. That's okay, I don't want to join.

You've probably guessed, like I did, that to become a member you have to incline bench press 400 pounds or more. I haven't even had the nerve to dream like that. Leaping over tall buildings in a single bound, but not a 400-pound incline bench press. The only way I could press 400 pounds would be one pound at a time. I've seen Steve Merjanian do over 450 pounds, something to remember.

Now, I understand Pat Casey has incline pressed 505 pounds. I wonder if he's started a 500 club? Must be pretty lonely being the only member.

•

If you're following my monthly gossip for any length of time might remember my pitiful excursions into the realm of strength contests with Dave Draper. Dave hasn't yet begun to tap the reservoir of his great power. In fact, most of the things he does are done with such casual ease as to be frightening. You can't help but wonder what would happen if he ever exerted himself. An example is Dave's great gripping power on one of those infernal spring grippers. Every time you close them the wooden handles "click." Well, maybe not a click. I got the handles together so slowly all anyone heard was my heavy breathing. Dave made the thing click so fast and often it sounded like someone's false teeth chattering at the North Pole.

The other day I was in our West Coast Muscle Beach office and what do you think I hear? Yeah, the sound. I knew the Blond Behemoth was getting closer. I reasoned that my superior intellect would render me above the challenge of the clicking. I walked to the front office. While I hadn't seen him yet, I knew he was near, for the clicking followed me. Finally my great brain cracked.

"Stop it!" I sobbed.

"Huh?" asked Dave innocently as he rounded the corner. Click, click, went the noise.

I stared at the toy in his hand.

"Stop clicking, er, I mean squeezing that stupid thing," I said.

"This?" asked Dave, looking at the spring. "But I have to get out my reps."

I was almost afraid to ask. "How many reps?"

"I do several sets of forty reps."

I knew he wasn't kidding. For a moment I had to control myself to keep from slugging the guy. Luckily, I thought of what would happen if I did.

"Gimme that," I said instead. "Here, I'll close the thing once. Then stop it until I get outta here."

Confidently, I took hold of the gripper and squeezed, not until it was closed, but until I nearly passed out.

"Well, I did it once before," I pleaded.

"Yeah, over a year ago," said Dave.

Once more I bent to the task, only to be stopped short of my goal by a great pain in my chest. I finished the correspondence I had been working on, then went back once again to the torture rack. Finally, I closed the thing with a grinding "cl..." You couldn't hear the "ick." Once again I had triumphed over evil. Once again the forces of law and order prevailed as I rode into the setting sun ready to beat up the first old lady I could find.

My triumph was short-lived, for the following week Dave had conceived of an even more terrible fate for me. Let's start at the beginning. Dave Draper has one of the most fantastic upper bodies in the history of the sport of bodybuilding. In fact, his upper body is so colossal the rest of him pales by comparison. While his legs would look great on the normal bodybuilder, Dave is certainly not normal. In order to match his upper body musculature, Dave would have to have legs like that Austrian, Schwarzenegger. Weider bodybuilding principles being what they are, there is not a doubt in anyone's mind that Dave can and will succeed.

To help in the process, Joe Weider sent him the new Weider Seated Calf Bomber. You sit on the bench and place your knees under the bar and do toe raises. One of the great things about the apparatus is that it restricts the movement to the calves alone. None of this knee-jerking stuff, just calf power in the strictest sense.

Dave keeps the calf bomber in a corner of the warehouse and at almost every opportunity, he can be found working on it. He's got it so loaded with weight it almost looks like some kind of joke.

I wasn't laughing. When I first saw it, I immediately saw the dreadful challenge Draper had rigged. I told myself I wouldn't fall for it this time. But it was useless. I looked around carefully to make sure no one was watching. Then, ever so quietly, I crept over to the machine. I sat on the bench. Oops, it made a noise. I had to be quiet. I didn't want to take the chance of being discovered; I had to test the thing first. I had to make sure I could handle the weight it was loaded with. Now I put my toes on the block and my knees under the bar. I raised it just high enough to release the pegs that hooked the weight in high position. So far so good. Then came the big mistake. I let my heels lower with every intention of raising them again.

That was the last physical move I did on the thing; the rest was in my mind, only this time mind didn't win over matter.

What to do? Do I just sit there until I mummify? Do I notify my next of kin and hope they bring me food and water? Better still why not call for help? Hmm—never!

My knees were killing me now. Well, maybe I could just make some noise so someone would know I was there. I cleared my throat. No answer.

"Hey, anybody here," I asked weakly. No answer.

"Anybody here?" I asked louder. Still no answer.

"Okay, HELP!"

"Yes?" asked Dave as he appeared. "You need help?"

"Get this thing off my knees before the bones snap."

He lifted the bar with consummate ease.

"Thanks," I said gratefully. "I might have been there forever."

Dave looked a little puzzled. "Why didn't you just take off some of the plates until it was light enough for you to lift?"

I thought for a second. "And admit I couldn't lift the weight?"

•

In the last several years Gene Mozee has gotten pretty well established as one of the nation's leading physiques and was the holder of the California bench press record a few years ago. Every once in a while we like to prove to ourselves, if not to others, that we can still do the things we once did. More often than not, these forays to capturing past glories meet with disappointing results. Mozee's lucky—he still has youth on his side. A few months ago he entered a local physique show and looked great winning the Best Poser award. Now he's hitting the power trail again and does a touch-and-go bench press with 390 pounds at a 165-pound bodyweight.

Gene Mozee has been immersed in the world of iron and steel most of his life and is a walking encyclopedia of bodybuilding and weightlifting minutia. As a competitor he's won titles and set records, and he knows who won Mr. Southern Cal in 1962 and who sat in the third row, second seat from the aisle. He's written and reported for all the muscle magazines and his physique photography has been seen on covers around the world. Gene's a journalist of muscle 'n' might.

The Wheels that Knock

The bell on the front door of our Weider Muscle Beach office sounded. Dave Draper closed the file case and went to see who it was. He didn't make it to the front because he was stopped after he took the first step by a familiar "Hi!"

It was one of the boys who come in all the time to visit with Big Dave. One of the great things about Draper is he gives so much of himself to other people. He's never too busy to talk to his many fans.

"What's the matter, Tommy?" asked Dave.

"Nuthin," said Tommy with a shrug.

Dave went back to his work, but he could tell that something was wrong. Dave knew if he waited long enough he wouldn't need to ask again.

"Going to the Jr. Mr. America?"

"Yeah, I guess so."

Now Dave knew something was wrong. Tommy never missed a show. He lived for contests and could tell you the favorite routines of every physique champ since Eugen Sandow. Every diet ever digested by any great bodybuilder was carefully catalogued. He literally lived and slept bodybuilding. To him a Sandy Koufax or Johnny Unitas might just as well have been gas station attendants. His heroes were named Park, Reeves, Scott and Draper. Now here he was mumbling, "Yeah, I guess so," when asked if he was going to attend the Jr. Mr. America. Maybe the guy was sick.

"Okay, Tommy," said Dave, "tell me what's wrong."

Tommy turned almost defiantly. He had "hurt" written all over his face. Before he could stop the flood, Tommy was spilling his feelings like a bag full of marbles.

He started telling of a well-known bodybuilder who trained at the same gym. "He comes up to me in the middle of a workout and starts telling me what a nut I am."

"What do you mean?" asked Dave.

"He told me I was a fool to train the way I do."

"Maybe he was trying to point up some flaws in your routine," said Dave, trying to smooth things over.

"Naw, he was laughing all the time. Then, he wanted to know why I trained at all."

"What did you say?"

"I told him I wanted to get muscles like Scott and you and he told me that was impossible."

"Well," said Dave, "you should try to look as good as you possibly can. Maybe you'll end up looking better than both Scott and me put together."

For the first time Tommy cracked a smile. He got serious again.

"Yeah, but not according to this guy. He even went on to say physique contests were just a bunch of bunk, anyway."

Dave was surprised at that. "He said that?"

"Yeah, he said if he had to do it all over again he'd never touch a weight."

The man Tommy was talking about won numerous contests over a period of years. He had taken the lumps he had built and gotten several lucrative film jobs in Europe with them. You might say the expensive clothes he wore on his back had literally been placed there by barbells.

Dave started fumbling half-heartedly through the files again. "I can't figure out why he would say such a thing."

"He said he was just in the gym to cut down slowly on his training and said something about not being too big for his acting career."

"He was going to stop training altogether?"

"That's what he said."

"So he spent all that time knocking you and bodybuilding?"

Tommy nodded.

The sad thing about this story is it's not as rare as you might think. Unfortunately, there are all too many people in the world who use both people and things as stepping stones to achieve their own selfish ends. Once these things no longer serve their purpose they are discarded like a used toothbrush.

You'll always find the snipers outside the ranks who are ready to call bodybuilding all sorts of things. We are all self-centered egotists, mirror athletes, mental midgets, musclebound narcissists—the whole bit. That's okay when you examine the source, for the critics are usually puny, funny looking, tenuous people. The thing that hurts is when a member of your own family leaves, then turns around and denies having ever known you.

You who are reading this should remember well what bodybuilding has done and is doing for you now. Chances are you are one-hundred percent better off than you were before you started in the sport. Bodybuilding is an honorable and exciting sport of he-men. You should be proud to tell people you belong to the fraternity of strong men and bodybuilders. Hang the label of fanaticism! Who cares? Name one thing that was ever done of great magnitude that wasn't perpetrated by a fanatic.

This doesn't mean a raving lunatic. Fanaticism can take many forms. Edison was a fanatic in his belief he could create the electric light. Sure people thought he was nuts, but he didn't care. His critics have long since died and been forgotten, while he lives every time you turn on the light switch. Fulton was a fanatic, a fool who built the first practical steamboat while everyone was saying it couldn't be done. Joe Weider has felt the sting of the stupid, but has gone on to build the largest bodybuilding organization in history. His name will live on as long as man has pride in his physical well being and appearance.

You have achieved something few in the world ever do. Be proud of what you have achieved. Be proud of bodybuilding. Most of all, be grateful.

CASEY

Give this guy a haircut, tuck in his shirt, roll up his sleeves and teach him to smile and I think you've got it. Poster boy for the Oakland Fire Department and GQ ad for Fruit of the Loom t-shirts, your choice...Bill Pearl—bodybuilding star, strongman, gym owner, antique collector, lecturer, author, entrepreneur, he-man—he does it all...really well.

Zzzzz. Huh? Oh, I was just dreaming. You know—fantasies of things I'd like to see. The stage is set and I can see heavy bars and chains scattered around, plus an odd assortment of weights. There, amidt the dynamic setting, are two of the greatest physique men in bodybuilding history. They are about to engage in a strength struggle that will decide the best all-around strongman in the world. The contestants will challenge each other in the odd lifts as well as in the breaking of chains, the bending of bars and other various tests of strength. On the outcome will ride not only the title with all its prestige, but a thousand dollars in cash. If I squint a little I can just make out the faces. By golly, it looks like Bill Pearl, and, isn't that—why, yep—it's Chuck Sipes. Crazy, huh? Well, maybe not as crazy as you think. Steve Lockman hopes that dream might turn out to be the real thing someday. Even if it doesn't, it's a nice dream anyway.

The Inferno—a Joe Nista Photo Shoot

TYLER

You can lean on my car, but don't—I repeat, do not—slam the door. With his straw hat in place, shades carefully adjusted and tripod slung over his shoulder, Artie Zeller is ready for action. Joe Nista and his daughter, Sandy, are images of physical fineness and indeed make an interesting pair of subjects for the Zeller camera. Joe's five-six soaking wet and Sandy hits five feet, ten inches in those mini-heels. Hello.

Ah, yes, dear friends. It started out so nice. It was a good morning, which promised a good day. After all, wasn't I going to the beach with Artie to take pictures of Joe Nista and his beautiful contest-winning daughter? Sure, it was gonna be a day to remember. With these positive thoughts I hurried over to Art's apartment.

Art's wife, Josie, was wearing her biggest smile as she ushered me in. To my surprise Nista and Sandy had already arrived.

"Wow...you're late!" greeted Joe, looking at his watch.

"How much?" I asked. Joe did some quick figuring. "Two...no, three minutes."

Sandy looked at her old man with a smile. "Dad's anxious to get out in the sun."

"That's right," Joe agreed. "Every time I've gone for a posing session it seems to be overcast. Today it's different...it's fantastic. I must get out in the sun, now!"

I could see that he wasn't kidding. Just then Art entered from the other room with Zabo. He had been showing the Human Cut some of the results of his latest photo shoots. As usual they were great.

"Care for something to eat?" Artie asked.

"No, thanks...let's get started. Joe here wants to..." I stopped because I could see Art was paying no attention to what I was saying. He was looking out the window as if in a trance. It was the genius in him, taken over.

"The sun isn't in the right position yet," he decided.

"But..." protested Joe.

I looked over and shook my head. "It's no use. The nut has closed us out!"

After way too much fiddling around, Art suddenly arose and walked to the front door.

"This is it," I assured the completely frustrated Nista. Out to the car we went and off to the open road. Mile after mile we went until we were going through some shady canyons.

"Say," I said finally, "where are we going?"

Art darted a look over at me. "I don't know."

With that comforting bit of news I decided to sit back and relax. We were in the hands of a fate called Zeller.

We crossed a little bridge and suddenly Art exclaimed, "This is it!" It was like some religious experience. I half expected to hear choirs of angels and the voice of Charlton Heston.

"You mean," asked Nista, "we're really going to be allowed out of the car?"

"Just be careful closing the car door," was Zeller's reply.

What the bridge had spanned was what we were after—a piece of wilderness right out of a Disney wildlife film. The running water, the rocks and moss were all there. We scrambled down the embankment to reach the glorious scene. Unfortunately we weren't the only ones there—we were greeted by a welcoming committee of bugs.

After five minutes I was quite literally going buggy as our little winged friends danced about my ears. I couldn't stand it any longer. I ripped off my shirt and tied it around my head. Both Sandy and Joe were flailing their arms, trying to keep the invaders away. Art, of course, was in another world. All he could see was what he saw through the camera lens.

"Stand still!" he yelled.

What mattered was that he get the shots he was after. At last it was over and we sprinted for the relief of the car. I rolled up the windows, but to my horror found the blasted bugs liked their dinner so well they didn't want us to leave without being dessert. We opened all the windows again and sped along until the wind had cleared the car. Free at last, and now for home.

"Aren't we going in the wrong direction?" I puzzled.

"What do you mean?"

"Well, Santa Monica's back in the other direction."

"Who's going to Santa Monica?"

I didn't answer—what was the use?— and we travelled further inland. Every mile away from the ocean raised the temperature a few degrees. It was like going into a furnace.

"Good grief!" yelled Joe. "I'm about to roast!"

Suddenly we screeched to a halt. When the dust settled, Art said once again, "This is the place."

Stepping out of the car was my first big mistake—the second was staying out.

"Arghhhh. Ahllll, uugghh, eyeii!" I exclaimed to the mad photographer, but he paid no attention. "I can't breathe!!"

"Now, now...if we climb up this little hill we should get some great shots," the master said as he surveyed the oven.

Wisely, Joe carried along a thermos of iced tea and was guzzling it like it was going down a drain. We started walking up the hill. Halfway up I began to wonder if I had left my will where my wife could find it. Out of breath, the summit was crossed, giving us a beautiful panorama of the valley below.

"Okay, let's get started!" directed Art, who had the only cold thing there...his heart.

I looked at him trying to size up what kind of a thing he was. After all, he looked human. What a sight he was, sweat pouring down his face...straw hat soaked...and I could see little beady eyes darting around behind his sunglasses. I decided right then he had lost his mind. They say all geniuses are a little mad, so I figured Art must be a pretty great one.

"Take off your shoes," he commanded Joe. "I can't take a shot with your shoes on!"

Joe bent down and felt the ground with his hand. He shook his head. "Are you kiddin'?"

"Go ahead," Art insisted. "The sun is in just the right position. Hurry!"

Joe removed his shoes. Luckily Sandy was allowed to keep hers on. In the meantime Joe was hopping around like he had stepped on a nest of ants.

"Stand still! Hold it!" cried our genius.

"But my feet—they're swelling!" moaned Joe.

ZELLER

Handsome Joe Nista adds his might to the collection of California muscles.

Mercilessly Zeller drove us all. What I was doing there, I'll never know, since I could have been at home writing in the shade of the lemon tree. The heat was finally reaching Art, so we went back to the car. Joe quickly grabbed for the thermos of iced tea and poured Sandy a drink.

"How about some of that?" asked a parched Zeller.

Joe pretended he hadn't heard as he took a healthy swig. "Ahh-h! Want some, Dick?"

TYLER

High atop the silent and spacious hills of Topanga Canyon is a concrete platform measuring twenty feet by thirty feet constructed for emergency fire control. It acquired the name Muscle Rock some fifty years ago when it became an altar for sun-worshipping musclebuilders. Seasonal coastal fog drove muscleheads to seek the great ball of fire wherever it glowed Where there's sun there's heat, where there's heat there's thirst. Artie brought the film, but forgot the cool clear water. The Nistas hit a sweet pose as they vengefully refuse the relentless, slave-driving cameraman a sip from their jug. Artie offers them a measly buck a sip? No way!

"Thanks," I murmured as I poured myself a healthy cup.

"P-p-lease?" mumbled Art. "I've gotta have a drink."

"I didn't think you needed any," sneered Joe.

Art started fumbling for his wallet. "Money...I'll pay you money!"

Art took his drink and immediately reverted to his heartless self. Back in the car we headed for the beach area. On the coast highway it was like moving in a vessel of coagulated blood.

"At least we're headed home," I sighed.

"With the sun still out?" Art frowned. "Are you kiddin'?"

I nodded, "I forgot myself for a moment. We're never going home. We're having too much fun!"

Like the man says on the commercial, I now had such a headache I felt as if two bull goats were going at it in the front of my skull. After an hour of grinding poverty of motion, we reached the Pacific Palisades overlooking the beaches. A gentle ocean breeze caressed my weary brow. This was better, and the view was great. Again Art fought the sun for every one of its rays and won in what turned out to be a series of the most beautiful physique pictures I believe have ever been captured on film.

That night as I stood under the shower trying to wash away the dirt and heat of the day I began to plan our next assignment. Next time, I thought to myself, I'll take along a mosquito net and a couple of cases of ice-cold Super Pro 101. I'll do anything to work with a guy who knows what he's doing...even if he is crazy.

•

To most of the readers, Joe Weider is just a name. With some people this is just as well. However, with someone like Joe, you're missing a great experience. In the first place, while he's my boss, what is more important is that he's a friend, too. It's none of the "I'm the leader, do as I say" bit with Joe. He treats us like we've got some brains. He doesn't order, he discusses. If there's something he doesn't like in an article we'll sit down and hash it out. Sometimes this leads to arguments, but always to progress.

Another thing that always impresses me is deep convictions about bodybuilding, and there is no greater fan of our sport than Joe. (No, not even you!) Joe gives more of himself to his ideals and to others than most people I know. Sure, I'm getting some points with the boss here, but I really dig this man and what he's doing for bodybuilding. If you ever see him, do yourself a favor and say, "hello."

Dick, with his I-have-a-broken-foot trick, and I trudge across the sands of a Pacific beach toward Artie Z, Joe W and an impressive gathering of models. We have our work cut out for us.

ZELLER

I got started on the above because Joe was just here on the West Coast for a visit, one of his usual whirlwind trips. When the dust settled he was gone, leaving naught but memories.

One of his main reasons for the trip was to get together an ad campaign for some new products. This entails arranging the models and photographers, but most importantly, the concept. For this series it was to be boys and girls at the beach. The girls were to wear bikinis. I really wasn't needed there, but when I heard about the girls, I asked (begged) to come along and help.

There must have been ten cars in the caravan that set out for the ocean blue. What a caravan, with Joe in the lead car and the rest of us strung out along the highway.

I started singing hiking songs, but was soon asked to stop by Zeller. Unfortunately, I was forced to ride with him since I had a broken foot at the time(Peanuts and his crew had nothing to do with this), which made it impossible for me to drive myself. This entitled me to listen to an hour of his rotten puns. If you've never heard them, I can't expect to get any sympathy, but if you have, you know they can be rated alongside the humor of Calvin Coolidge. By the time we reached the beach I was too stunned to move. My ears were turning sickly green and I was in a state of shock. What makes it even worse is that he thinks his puns are funny. Believe me, anyone who likes his puns also thinks train wrecks are hilarious. The whole thing is depressing.

TYLER

There's no film in that camera, but who cares. Zeller is moving in to get a close-up, just one more close-up.

"Hey, Dick," said Dave Draper as he stuck his head through the door, "will you put some oil on my back?"

I got out of the car fully realizing that while I might be escaping the jokes, I was about to undertake a workout. Trust me, to put oil on a back as massive as Draper's is an all-day project. On top of that there was iodine in the oil to give a deeper color for the photos.

This means there can't be any streaks; the oil must be applied carefully. Well, it was certainly a ball standing there on one foot trying to put oil on a virtual wall of muscle. I've been seriously thinking of writing a book called "Backs I Have Oiled." It's great to be needed.

Joe couldn't have picked a spot of sand further away from where the cars were parked. On top of this it must have been the windiest day of the year. It was so windy the gale began to hum a tune through the wood of my crutches. I could see everyone getting ready for the shots and I wasn't even a third of the way there.

"Why did I come?" I sobbed to myself, as the balls of the crutches buried in the sand, making it even harder to make any headway. Just then I looked up and saw all those pretty little gals bouncing around the sand and I knew why. In no time at all I was there and by the end of the day some great shots were taken.

Poor Dick Tyler defends himself against a vicious attack on the beach. The perpetrators were later apprehended and revealed to be Crazy Seymour "Doc" Koenig and Don "the Beast" Peters. The Blond Bomber—me—one of three witnesses, risks his life to save Tyler's. Very heroic.

ZELLER

This turned into a productive shoot and several covers and dozens of ad shots were generated by the Zeller camera, Joe's finesse and the collective muscles and curves of the stunning talent...Joe is seen here meticulously smoothing oil on one of the talent de extraordinaire, a charismatic fellow with both modesty and charm.

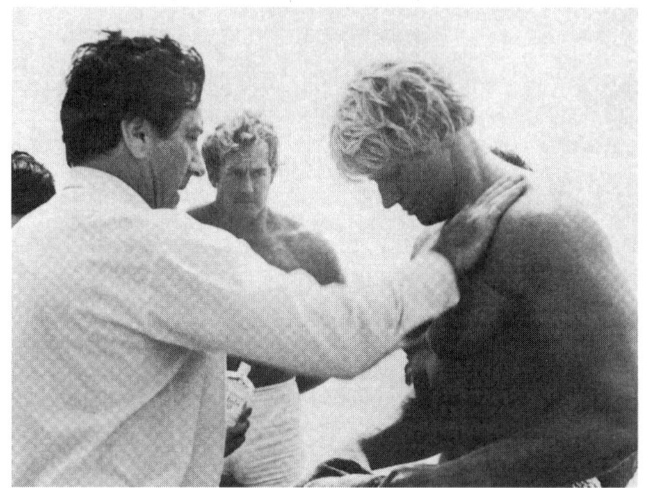

ZELLER

ZELLER

Auditioning for the Malibu Rockettes are, from left to right, Miss Polka Dot Bikini, Don Peters, Betty Weider, The Bomber, Sandy Nista and Dan Mackey. Impeccable choreography.

•

One of the oldest established gyms in the Southern California area just folded. It was the Pasadena Gym and I felt a pang of sorrow when I heard it passed from the scene. While I never trained at the gym, I visited it on numerous occasions over the years. Some great men trained there, leaving nothing but memories and a few dried drops of sweat.

•

Whenever something like a popular gym goes out of business, its former members have to be absorbed. You'd think they'd find someplace close to where they had trained, or at least close to where they lived. But no, a true believer won't be satisfied training anywhere but at the very best. The fella who'd walk a mile for a lousy cigarette has nothing on the man who wants a good place to train.

Now, Pasadena is on one side of town, while such places as Vince's and Gold's are miles away in the opposite direction. Yet, where do you think most of the big men from the old Pasadena Gym went? You guessed it. And I find it hard to walk out to my garage gym.

•

Joe Gold doubles as a movie extra every so often, as does Bert Elliott and many other musclemen around Hollywood. The other day these two worked on the show "I Spy." They played villains, natch. If you saw the show you couldn't miss 'em. Gold was wearing his California tan, while Elliott wore his mustache and shaved head. I understand they had a little trouble with Bert's dome. Seems they had to tone down the shine so it wouldn't overexpose the film.

•

"How can I build my low biceps?" asked Dave Draper.

Several of us who happened to be in Weider's Santa Monica office at the time slid looks in his direction, eyes narrowing defensively. We wondered if he wasn't putting us on, sure he shouldn't play games with us mortals. Out of polite habit we groped for thought, all our facial tics working, when one of us, suddenly remembering politeness was a lost art among advanced bodybuilders, said, "Why don't you try deep breathing, Dave?"

Dave's face remained a picture of Huckleberry Finn framed by a cloudless summer sky.

"No kidding," he said. "I mean it. I've tried everything and lookit." He held his arms out straight for a moment.

"Fantastic! Look at that," said Russ Warner.

"What did I tell you? Show them the forearm, Dave," Joe Weider demanded.

"Is it wrong for me to hate this guy?" asked Armand Tanny. Dave's arm straight out, an inch above the elbow, must have been a good eighteen.

"I've tried them all—concentration curls, incline curls, curls on the preacher stand, but the low biceps stay the same," he said.

We tried to feel sorry for him, our brows furrowing with regret over his tragedy, but instead decided to leave acting to the actors. We might have even felt sarcasm, but with the help of Dave's totally innocent look we decided the question was, oddly, a fair one.

"There's too much swing at the start of the concentration curls and incline curls, which cancels out the low biceps," said Joe Weider.

"I'd settle for the preacher stand, myself," said Russ.

Drawing on kinesiology, Armand said, "The fuller the stretch, the stronger the contraction. Curling while lying on the incline bench is the ideal position for total contraction of the biceps from the low to the peak."

"But the initial swing of the dumbbell cancels out the low biceps," said Weider.

ZELLER

Seated dumbbell incline curls at Joe Gold's gym in Venice one fine afternoon in the middle of life. Take me back where I belong.

"Do like the scientists in the space program—when in doubt, don't do anything," said Warner, smiling at this clever logic.

Dave, innocently observing all this chatter, suddenly responded as though he was the teacher teaching his pupils.

"Assume you're lying on an incline bench backed up to the wall, wouldn't you say curling with a low wall pulley in each hand would establish the perfect resistance?"

We hadn't thought of that. It was perfect. It was the perfect biceps exercise. We looked at one another for help, and when we saw none, we realized with a shock this giant young upstart had preempted a lot of our authority.

•

The other day I came across a duster of memories at Muscle Beach. Sometimes I go down there just hoping if I close my eyes and suddenly open them everything will be as it was so many years ago, when Muscle Beach was just that—Muscle Beach. This time I opened my eyes and there before me was a group of Muscle Beach citizens from long ago. They were all standing around talking. About what? You guessed it—the past. In the group were John Knight, Artie, Fred Kimball, Chuck Collras, Bob McKibbon and the former Mr. America, Dick Dubois.

"Chuck," said Dick, "you're looking bigger than ever and winning all the titles around."

"Some day you might fill Mr. America's shoes," said Zeller.

Collras sized up the big Dubois and said, "I'd rather fit in his jacket."

"Maybe you do already," said Dick with a smile. With that he took off his coat and put it on Collras. That was the last we saw of him. Rumor has it that somebody heard him calling for help from inside a tweed jungle. Hope we see him in time for the next contest.

•

While on the subject of Muscle Beach, I've got to tell you this. Wendell Corey, the actor, is also city councilman for Santa Monica. "So, big deal," you say. That shows how much you know. Councilman Corey happens to be a prime force in putting the muscle back into Santa Monica. It's his plan to bring back the weights and adagio platforms and make the beach once again one of the most famous spots on earth. For years the public has been deprived of the benefits of free weight training because of the whim of some politician. At long last the move is on to make amends for the actions of some dumbbell by putting the metal ones back on the sands where they belong. The old timers are still around, hoping and praying.

That Powerlifter's Paradise, Zuvers

"You wouldn't believe it," said one of them, "it's the most incredible thing I ever saw."

Hmm, that got my attention so I strained to hear more.

"The place has more weight than I've ever seen in my life," he continued, "and the apparatus defies description."

That did it.

"What are you talking about?" I asked.

"Zuver's gym."

"What's gym?"

"Zuver's. It's the most incredible gym I've ever seen."

He proceeded to tell me things that didn't seem real, so I dismissed the whole bit, thinking the guy was smoking something weird. I would have kept this line of reasoning if I hadn't begun to later hear similar stories. Each tale seemed to get wilder than the one before.

Finally I heard tell of a wall that had been handbuilt by Bob Zuver from boulders averaging a ton apiece. It sounded like one boulder too many for me. The next thing I knew I was calling Zuver and arranging a story.

Try as I might I couldn't convince Zeller the stories about Zuver's Gym were for real.

"Look," he said as we drove along the freeway to Costa Mesa where the gym was located. "I'll take the shots for you, but a gym is a gym is a gym is a gym. The only thing that really makes one different from another are the guys who train there."

I looked out the window at the passing palm trees that seemed to glory in the winter California sun.

"Guess we won't know till we get there."

Zuver's Gym is located in the little southern California city of Costa Mesa, a few miles south of Long Beach. As we pulled up, I noticed a small sign shaped like a dumbbell. On it was printed the name of the gym. That was the last small thing either Art or I were to see while we were there. We got out of the car and walked a few paces until we reached the sign. Only then did we realize the gym was set back off the street. Leading from the street to the front was a long promenade. On either side were potted plants and between those plants were Zuver Olympic barbell plates.

What plates they were! Molded into the facing of each was a golden muscle man spread-eagled so it appeared as if he were holding the rims apart. As we got closer to the front door, the plates went from fifty pounds to 200 pounds apiece! That's what I said—each plate weighed as much as 200 pounds.

There, finally, looming in front of us was the massive wall I had heard about. In front of that was a spectacular fountain. A drawbridge crossed what seemed like a moat. All this was surrounded by a massive chain that entwined over an archway that was surmounted by a loaded Olympic set. We hadn't even reached the door and I had enough for a story.

"Hi," said a voice. I looked to see a good-looking man with a pleasant smile. "I'm Bob Zuver." We shook hands.

"That wall..." I said shaking my head.

"That wall," said Zuver, "weighs sixty-five tons. Each boulder you see weighs an average of 2,000 pounds."

"That must have cost a fortune to build," I said.

Zuver smiled. "Not so much when you build it yourself."

"You really built that by yourself?" I asked in disbelief.

"That's right, my sons and I took the truck and went as far as 120 miles into the mountains to get the boulders. It took a lot of time, but the boys in the gym helped and we all had fun building it."

Now I was getting a little tense. Was this guy pulling my leg?

"Over here is the big doorbell," said Zuver as he pointed to a huge bell. Then he walked over to an enormous key. "And this..."

"Don't tell me," I interrupted. "The big key."

"Right. Which fits into the big keyhole."

"Which opens the big door," I said.

"Right again," said Zuver. "I guess you've noticed how I refer to everything as 'big.'"

"I've noticed."

"That's because I want everyone who trains here to think big and to act big. However, if he's too big to be nice, he's too big for the gym. Christ, and our faith in him, is big. Shouldn't our lives try to match the bigness of that faith?"

I looked at him intently. His eyes were set. He believed what he was saying. It gave me a nice feeling.

"Now here we have the big door handle," he continued, "which is a dumbbell that weighs 320 pounds. The big door alone weighs 4,000 pounds and took a year to build. It's perfectly balanced and even a child can open it."

With that he opened the big door. If the outside startled me, it was nothing compared to the explosion of sights that greeted Art and me as the huge door opened wide to reveal what must be the greatest layout of tonnage ever assembled for the training of the human being.

On racks angled against the wall were dumbbells that went in five-pound jumps from ten pounds to 300 pounds. I didn't want to meet the one who used 300-pound dumbbells in his workout. In the center were racks that contained curling bars that went in five-pound jumps from forty to 300 pounds.

"Bob," I asked, "who could ever curl a 300-pound bar?"

"Paul Anderson did it," he said without hesitation. I decided not to ask anymore dumb questions.

As I looked around I saw the Big Rope, which is the world's largest rope climb. I tried to figure out who would have hands big enough to hold on to it, much less climb it. Bob started showing us around.

"Now, here is the world's largest dipping rack," he said as we went over to a set of bars I was told measured twelve feet long.

"What are the wheels under the bars for?" asked Art.

"To hold the weights when you're through," said Bob. "Now here is the big hook we use to hold the weights around the lifter's waist." With that he showed us a hook attached to a belt. "The hook alone weighs seventy-five pounds."

Next we came to the big lat machine; the cable had a five-ton test. After seeing what I had so far, I wondered if that was strong enough. The weight-holding apparatus alone was a 100-pound anchor. At the far end of the gym was one of the greatest assortments of odd lift weights I have ever seen.

A power rack nearby had lights that flashed red when you stepped under the bar to let people know a strongman was ready to lift. A row of benches made just for bench pressing was next. And on a platform was the heaviest bench in the world weighing 652 pounds. It was complete with a seat for the spotter.

Zeller then asked for a drink, and laughingly remarked, "At the big fountain."

Zuver pointed toward the world's biggest fountain. That's right—it was a fire hose.

"That's the big scale there," said Bob, "and here we have the world's largest squat rack."

He led us to what looked like some medieval torture device. When you stand inside its confines, red lights blink.

"The bar alone weighs 200 pounds and the whole thing can be loaded to a ton."

"Isn't that pretty dangerous?" I asked. "I mean, who could spot you?"

Zuver didn't answer. Instead he pressed a button and down came

ZELLER

The state should have dipped into its pork barrel and funded Zuver's Gym as a museum to American Muscle and Might. It was a legendary place that captured the big heart and soul of iron and steel.

two hooks on some kind of hydraulic lift that grabbed the weight and lifted it clear of the man using it.

Bob could see the look on my face. "Look," he said with a smile, "I know this is all a little kooky, but why should we take training so seriously. Let's have fun while we work out."

This was all we needed to relax. I found Bob Zuver was one of the finest and most sincere men I have ever met. He is an ordained evangelist minister who quite literally practices what he preaches. He feels Christ is the answer and goes out to the youth with the word of God for the soul and barbells for the body.

Looking around all these weights I had to ask, "Bob, who can lift all this iron?"

"You mean do we have men strong enough to lift big?"

I nodded.

"Well, a gym member by the name of Wayne Coleman loaded so much weight on the lat machine that he couldn't lift it."

"See!" I said.

"So," continued Bob, "he just bent the bar around his neck."

I cleared my throat. "Okay."

Then I spotted a giant weight that was tagged The Blob. "What's that for and who can lift it?"

"It's for one-arm deadlifts, weighs over 500 pounds and I can lift it." With that he took hold and proved he was as good as his word.

At that moment a group of men smartly dressed in Zuver lifting outfits entered the gym for a training session. We were introduced to the team captain, Bill Witting, who introduced us to the rest of the crew, Rudy Lozano, Jim Waters, Willie Kindred and Chester Horvath. Not present were such power stars as the 165-pound California champ, Leonard Ingro, and the 181-pound national squat

Using my imagination and a little deduction I'd say Wayne Coleman (Billy Graham Superstar) is under that bar totaling about 500, and I'd say that bar is well on its way up and onto the racks. And I'd add it's early 1969 at Joe Gold's gym, between stops at Zuver's.

ZELLER

ZELLER

More monkey business at Zuver's.

record holder, Tom Overholtzer, who can pound out 575 pounds in that lift.

"That's quite a team," said Art.

Bob nodded. "I just hope one day very soon we'll hold the national team championship."

We walked outside again and I asked Bob about his future plans.

"The next thing we have planned is an outdoor training area under a cliff-like overhang called the Cave. Then there are the plateaus in which the men will be training on these cliffs and descend from them by fire poles."

At one time, I would have thought he was kidding, but after seeing what I just had, I didn't even blink.

We said goodbye and I was reluctant to leave. It had been a memorable experience. I had seen a gym that was unique in all the world, Zuver's Hall of Fame Gym, but what was more important, I had been privileged to meet a fine man who was dedicating his life to the youth of his country.

DOWNS

California's governor as a young man after six months of the good life in America. Here he performs freehand dips for the development of his triceps at Vince's gym in North Hollywood.

FIVE

1969

Schwarzenegger Heads West

Joe Weider called ahead. "I'm sending Arnold Schwarzenegger out to California."

"You mean the Oak?"

"You call him the Oak?"

"Do you have a better name?"

"Well, the Oak is coming your way, so you'd better call timber!'"

At seven the following evening, Art Zeller and I drove to the airport. The plane was a few minutes late, so I decided to wait in the car while Art looked for Arnold. After having to move eight times in a three-minute parking zone, I decided I'd see if I could help find our Austrian comrade. Inside the terminal I looked down the passenger tunnel and watched the passengers being greeted by friends and relatives.

Suddenly there he was, looming toward me like some colossus. To my surprise Schwarzenegger wasn't as tall as I had expected. I had heard stories about him towering over all he surveys. As he got closer, however, he began to tower. The crazy thing about looking at Schwarzenegger is that he's so w-i-d-e it makes him almost look short. Tucked under his arms were some trophies from a recent contest, and he had a smile as big as his shoulders. After our introduction, Art decided to go with Arnold to the baggage pickup while I moved the car for the ninth time.

The baggage comes down a chute and on to a revolving wheel and the passengers pick up their luggage as it comes to them. We all know this, but Arnold being new to the country thought you had to get your things on the first revolution. When his suitcase appeared he made a lunge for it so it wouldn't get away. In the process he accidentally brushed against some dummy in a Russian fur skin hat.

"Man, don't you push me. I don't like nobody to push me."

Arnold was stunned. "Vot?"

"You heard me, baby. Watch who you're pushing around unless you're looking for trouble."

People started to gather around. "Vot did I do?"

"Just don't think you can push me around, baby," said the jerk.

Zeller jumped between the two men. "Now, look," he said, "my friend meant you no harm."

"Yeah? Well, he'd better watch it."

Zeller shook his head with a smile. "Buddy," he said, "this man just brushed against you by accident."

He stepped back to give the troublemaker a good view of the "tree that walks like a man," who was no longer smiling.

"Now," continued Art, "if he wanted to brush against you on purpose, you'd be brushed for good."

The onlookers started to snicker at the obvious truth of the statement. For the first time the jerk seemed to take a good look at the man he was choosing off. He started to stutter.

"Wellll...I...yeah...Well..." And with that brilliant statement he left to find some little old lady to beat up.

As Arnold entered the car it depressed one side so much I thought for a moment the fenders on that side would drag on the ground.

"Can you sit on my side?" I asked Art who was sitting in the back.

He did, but it didn't help that much.

"What do you think of Southern California?" asked Art.

"Art, he just arrived. It's night. He's just gotten one gulp of smog and almost got into a fight and you ask how he likes Southern California."

"I like it fine," said the big Austrian with a laugh.

We stopped off at Joe Gold's gym so Arnold could see Zabo Koszewski. When we arrived Zabo showed him around and introduced him to Peanuts West, who was pushing some iron at the time.

Later, we went to a restaurant in Santa Monica. Arnold was so hungry he nearly ate the design off the plate. Zeller, no slouch in the eating department, decided he would have a salad because he had already had a full dinner earlier. He then proceeded to eat whatever he could find from other people's plates.

Zabo had to get back to the gym, so he took off in that direction, while Arnold, Art and I went to Art's apartment to see Art's wife, Josie. Josie comes from Germany and we thought Arnold might enjoy speaking his native tongue.

Time rushed by and before we knew it, it was time to meet Don Peters at his home. Don had been kind enough to offer his fabulous house to Arnold for a few days until he could find an apartment. This house is the one with the fantastic home gym, swimming pool, professional pool table, color TV, palm trees and genuine California sunshine.

After a few days in this perfect place, Arnold moved into an apartment that happens to be a block or so away from Vince's Gym, so you can guess where he's training now. Every morning at Vince's and every evening at Don Peters,' this massive Austrian Oak bombs his muscles.

I recently asked Vince how Arnold was doing and I thought he was going to mount a bandstand to tell me.

"He's a vast untapped reservoir of unused tissue."

"What do you mean by that?" I asked.

"For one thing he's never used a preacher bench before; he's never trained his legs or shoulders correctly and only recently has he started working his waist hard and started taking supplements of any kind. The other day I put him on a new deltoid exercise and you could see the insertion in the humerous literally burst out of the skin while he was doing it, only to disappear when the pump was gone."

Arnold shortly after arriving in California in '68 discovering an old American trick, the preacher curl. The secret to big arms at last.

Now Vince looked at me seriously.

"Dick, I guarantee in six months he'll put two inches on his arms and three inches on his shoulders. That's six months from now."

"But how will he cram on all that size?"

Vince walked away with a knowing smile. Don't worry though, I'll find out and let you in on any secrets. The Austrian Oak is in town and you'll get all the information from Vince's Italian Riviera.

•

It's now getting to be an annual event for me to visit Sig Klein's gym whenever I hit New York. Every time I go back, something seems to have changed. Faces, clothes and places all seem to be different. Only one thing remains unchanged, like an oasis of stability—Sig's gym.

Sig Klein, original strongman and physical culturist, lifting the iron in his New York City gym in the late-1960s. Sig exhibited an amazing physique and awesome power throughout an extended weight-lifting career. His muscles, like stones in a neat stack, withstand the wear of time.

For forty years this strength immortal has been holding court in the same location just off Broadway. The gym is on the third floor and can only be reached by walking up a narrow stairway. The trip is well worth the heavy breathing it might engender.

It's only a small place, but it's filled with enough atmosphere to spill over onto the street below. Sig told me some of his members have been with him for as long as he's had the gym, and he's trained as many as three generations of a single family.

While I was there I couldn't help but notice the reason for Sig's great and enduring success in a business that has more than its share of failures. It's the man's continuing interest in the welfare of those who train at his place. Time and time again during our conversation, Sig would leave to help one of his pupils. After all those years, he still cares.

While talking with Sig, a heavy step was heard on the stairway outside. I got up and looked out the door to see who it might be. The sight was blinding. Then, through my squinting eyes, I saw it was none other than the bald head of Bert Elliott. Fortunately, he had been able to time his vacation so he would be able to referee the arm wrestling championships the following night.

We had a jolly good time talking over strength—what else?—and made arrangements to get together later that night for dinner. It was a great German place zat vas filled mit steins along the vall and all dat. Sig and Bert got their steins of beer and said in German, "Kraft, Heil!" (Hail Strength!)

Me? I shrugged my shoulders and drank some water. Later, as Sig closed his gym, he softly said, "Goodnight, gym." After so many years it must seem like an old friend.

"Do you ever plan to retire?" I asked.

"No," said Sig, "not for quite some time."

I couldn't help but think that some day, as it must surely happen, Sig would have to say goodbye. When that day comes, it will mark the end of an historical era in the world of strength. Kraft, Heil!

•

MOZEE

I like that fat bar on the Smith Machine for pressing.. Here we see history in the making and major deltoids under construction. Neither the time nor the structure can be repeated or imitated. That's life, my friends. That's Don Howorth. Vince's Gym, 1965.

Poor Don Howorth. Several months ago he was in quite an auto accident. He and a friend were driving in the hills around Malibu, which overlooks the Pacific. Suddenly there was a sharp turn in the road, but not a sharp turn in the wheels. Don said the car must have flipped fifty feet in the air before it landed upside-down. Both the occupants were thrown clear, with Don walking away with nothing but a few scratches. His friend survived too, but Mr. America still gets the chills when he thinks of how close he came to competing for the Mr. Heaven title.

A short while after that his apartment above Vince's Gym caught on fire and all his trophies melted into a shapeless wad.

Now the latest: Bill McArdle dropped in for a visit. That in itself is okay, it's the way he visited. You see, Bill has this sports car and a very bad habit. He never puts on the safety brake, just leaves it in gear. That's not the best habit in the world under normal circumstances, but when you cling to the side of a hill like a man reaching for a lifeline it's nutty. So here's Howorth in an apartment just below McArdle's on the hillside. Bet you've already guessed what happened. Anyway, McArdle—or should I say his car—came for a visit, not through the door but through the wall. Fortunately no one was hurt. I was feeling sorry for Don as I started all this, but after reading it I think he's lucky to be alive.

•

I just got a package from Russ Warner. Russ, as you know, is one of the all-time greats in the world of physique photography. Since WWII he has taken pictures that can only be rated as classics. Hardly a physique immortal hasn't had his muscles engraved on film by a Warner camera. Russ finally decided to do what people have been urging him to do for years—bring out an album of some of his greatest photos.

So, I get this package and what do I see but a great color photo of Dave Draper looking like some colossus. What a way to begin. On the cover it says the Calendar of Champions. You wonder what can follow a color shot of the mighty Dave. So how's this for a lineup? Starting with January you get Mr. America/Mr. USA Dick DuBois. There's no writing on the photos; that's done on the calendar side with the name, titles won and dates. For February you get Don Peters, then Zabo Koszewski, Steve Reeves, Leo Robert, Vince Gironda, Larry Scott, Joe Nista, Reg Park, Freddy Ortiz, Clarence Ross, and for December, Draper again.

How's that for a lineup? As if that wasn't enough, a fantastic 8x10 glossy photo of Steve Reeves is included for framing, all this for only three bucks. The calendar is perfect for gym or den, if you have the chance to get one before they run out. I got so inspired when I saw it that I literally ran to the garage for a workout. Unfortunately I tripped on the way and got some lumps the hard way. I tried to measure them, but bruises just won't hold a pump.

•

Several months ago I had a talk with one of the managers of Vince's. Nice guy, fairly big, but certainly not ready for a feature story. During the conversation I suggested some day, when he was in shape, we could do a story on him. Frankly he impressed me so little in the physique category that I forgot about our conversation.

Last week I got a call from Artful Art Zeller telling me Joe wrote him about some photos he'd sent in from a recent contest. He wanted more on one of the men—Dan Mackey, by name. Art talked to Dan about my doing a story on him.

"Dan who?" was my reply.

Armed with this little bit of info I went to Vince's and asked for Dan Mackey. To my surprise I recognized Dan from our previous conversations. That is, I recognized the face. Any similarity between his body today and that of a few months ago is purely coincidental. If he continues to improve this way, I fearlessly predict he will be another Larry Scott.

Vince called me earlier today with the news Dan had just won the Jr. Mr. Pacific Coast title. He's the hottest prospect in Southern California. Yikes. I wish I could say I discovered him or at least have a polite "I told you so." Unfortunately I'm just a Tyler-come-lately, but I hope to make up for lost time.

ZELLER

Arnold the Oak and Dick the author, getting it down on tape for posterity. Looks more like two big kids playing muscle trivia.

Adventures with Arnold

"DICK," roared Arnold Schwarzenegger (he seldom just speaks), "I want to visit der udder gyms in Southern California. Can you take me?"

I thought for a moment.

"That's a pretty big order, Arnold. Why do you want to see all the gyms in the area? I mean a gym is a gym."

Arnold just looked at me as if I was nuts. He was right. All gyms are not the same. If they were all Vince's or Gold's, no gym would ever go out of business. The secret is great equipment, a good location and people who know what they're doing to run the place. Men with the proper training concepts attract progressive bodybuilders and everyone benefits.

"Yeah," I said after some thought. "Record the moment well. I was wrong."

"Vat?" roared the Oak.

"Nevermind. Anyway, my car wouldn't take us to the city limits much less all the gyms in Southern California. Unless..."

"Yes?"

"Well, I can't promise anything, but maybe I can get Zeller to drive us. He knows my car doesn't run well and you don't have one yet, so maybe, if the moon is right and the breezes from the ocean have caressed his car in just the right way, we may be able to get a lift."

"Vat?" roared Arnold.

"Nevermind."

Would you believe the following night I was just about to call Zeller when the phone rang and it was the world's greatest photographer on the other end.

"Is this Russ Warner?" I asked.

"No, this is the world's greatest physique photographer."

"It is Russ."

"Okay, this is the other greatest physique photographer. Is this the world's greatest writer, Armand Tanny?"

"Okay, Art, you win," I said. "What do you want?"

"Did you know Chuck Mahoney and Dave Saxe are opening a gym in North Hollywood?"

"You're kidding."

Chuck is an old buddy of mine from the beach days of a few years back. For years you've seen his muscles on the screen as an extra. More recently he's been working as an electrician for a local electrical firm. For some reason I just never figured he would want to go into the gym business.

"Why do you think I'm kidding?" asked Art. "He's been training for years and has worked out with the greatest bodybuilders in the world. He loves bodybuilding and..."

"Okay," I interrupted, "I admit I'm wrong for the first time."

"You mean for the second time in as many days."

"You've..."

"Yes," said Art, "I've been talking with Arnold. He'd like to visit some gyms and I was thinking since your car is a pile of garbage and Arnold doesn't have one yet and this is a new gym opening up, I could take you all there for a story."

The following Saturday was perfect weather for a drive. Art and Arnold were supposed to arrive at my house by ten. At eleven I decided to give Art a call; Josie informed me the two had gone out to breakfast. So that was it. Both of them decided to fill up before they got here. That filling up takes a long time, since both of them can salivate over an ice cube. I prepared for a long wait, but to my surprise they got here only an hour and a half late. After an exchange of pleasantries, we went on our way to the North Hollywood Health Club.

"Look!" Arnold shouted.

"Arnold," I said.

"Vat?"

"Wait till the car stops."

"Yes, wait," said Art, "I want to find a place to park."

"Vy not just park there?" asked Arnold, pointing to a vacant spot.

Art insisted we might be there longer than a nickel would buy, so we looked around until we found a free spot.

Inside the gym we were greeted by the smell of fresh paint. The walls were painted and new carpeting had just been put down. The only thing that was old were some of the weights. The powerlifting fans would be happy with that, because they were weights that had been used by Peanuts West and his garage-gym crew. This meant the place was loaded with heavy iron. It was to be a heavy training gym.

This didn't mean the weights weren't there for the beginners. The bars went down to a level Don Knotts would find easy. There was also a women's section adjacent to the men's with separate sauna baths and showers, meaning there wouldn't be any of the alternate-day bit. It would be open seven days a week for everyone.

"How do you like it?" asked Dave Saxe.

"Looks like you've got a winner."

Just then Arnold called my name from the dressing room. I thought he'd been hit or something. The run to the dressing room was worth it. Arnold was standing in his posing trunks in front of the mirror.

DOWNS

Arnold is a magnificent mass of muscle.

"Look at my lats," he said.

Friends, all I can say is that they matched his upper body. He is rounding into what may be the greatest bodybuilder in history. These aren't just words. You'll see for yourself in September at the Mr. Olympia contest. This showdown between Sergio and Arnold could be the greatest in bodybuilding history. I called Art in to see the phenomenon.

"And look at this," he said as he positioned himself near Arnold's flexed arm. "Stand where I am and tell me what you see."

What I saw was the most amazing biceps peak I had ever seen.

"Good grief," I said, "It's looking back at him."

Out on the floor of the gym, Arnold began to take a light workout. People began to come in to watch. Then she appeared. Framed in the glow of the afternoon sun, she stood in the doorway.

"What a body!" she exclaimed. She was wearing a mini skirt, boots and a navy jacket and was difficult to describe. Arnold ducked his head with embarrassment.

"Would you like your picture taken with him?" said Art.

He didn't need to ask twice. And so with his magic lens, Art captured another high spot in the career of Arnold Schwarzenegger.

After the workout Dave, Art and Arnold went for a bite to eat while Chuck Mahoney and I watched the NCAA basketball finals on the tube. By the time I got home it was evening. As I got out of the car Arnold said, "Now where do we go?"

"What do you mean?" said Art.

"I vould like to see the big gym next."

That could mean only one place—Zuver's Hall of Fame.

•

Death comes in many ways in the bodybuilding world. Not all the deaths come in human form. In weight training, the gyms take on a personality of their own. I have seen many gyms come and go and I've banked many hours in some of these sweat pits. You put too many hours of your time into a gym to let its demise pass without some thoughts.

PEARL

Behind the obscure door lay tons of iron, racks of steel and rows of rugged benches. In the midst of it all stood a mound of muscle and might. His name was Bill Pearl and he forged his way through the tangle of metal and flesh to the top. And at the top, so the story goes, there is only room for the destined few.

I'll never forget when the great Bert Goodrich Gym on Hollywood Boulevard closed. For weeks I felt lost. It was like losing a friend. I thought of all the good and the hard times we'd had together. Of the inches I'd worked to put on and the inches I'd worked to take off. Finally I resolved myself to the fact that my friend was dead and I must go on. Sob!

Now I must be the bearer of the sad news that another old gym has met with the ax, one I used to manage. This one is the Marcy Gym, owned by Dr. Walter Marcyan. It had been around for over twenty years when suddenly it died. Now only the California smog fills its empty halls.

Since all things die, it stands to reason some day there will be no more Vince's Gym, give or take another twenty years. And what about Sig Klein's Gym in New York, a monument in the same location for over forty years? Even Sig told me that one day, instead of saying goodnight to his gym, it would be a goodbye. He assured me with the next breath that he had no intention of retiring. Anyway I believe a plaque should be put up somewhere when a gym dies just like a tombstone for you or me. I called Forest Lawn Cemetery about it, but they thought I was nuts. Can you imagine that? Nahhh.

•

From the "it's about time" file comes this note of interest. The bodybuilding public has long recognized physique photography as an art form. The outsiders, however, usually just look at the physique and make some dumb remark prompted by jealousy. At least that's the way it used to be. In the last few years, with the advent of muscular screen heroes, people are beginning to admit what we knew all along: Men look better in a suit of muscle than the most expensive cover of clothes. At a recent art exhibit at the Los Angeles County Museum of Science and Industry, a photo of Dave Draper was put on exhibit and won a prize. Now it's to be sent around the world as part of the exhibit. So keep your eyes open; if the show comes to your town, one of our own is in it. For that we can all be proud.

•

Speaking of photos—great ones, that is—I can't help thinking about Art Zeller's recent masterpiece of Don Howorth. He's tentatively called it "The Dawn of Creation." It ranks as one of the greatest works of art in the field. No, I'm not going overboard and it has nothing to do with friendship. It's just that I've never seen a more dramatic approach to a subject. I'm hoping Art will enter the work in a contest. It's bound to be a winner or my name isn't, isn't...well, no lower than second, anyway.

ZELLER

It's a photo like this that stirs everyone to want a fine physique. Don Howorth, a picture worth a thousand words.

The Great Olympia Posedown

"I am ready for Sergio," yelled an excited Arnold Schwarzenegger as he came offstage. He had just finished giving a posing exhibition at the Mr. Western America contest. The audience had gone wild and was screaming for more.

I laughed. "Better go out there again and give them what they want."

Once again he strode onstage to the music of King of Kings and brought down the house.

Ever since Arnold came to this country, he worked toward one goal: meeting and beating Sergio Oliva. Arnold's life is almost consumed by the fire of bodybuilding. He trains like a madman and goes to every contest he can find no matter how small. He reads all he can on bodybuilding and practices his posing every day. He is the consummate bodybuilder, the distilled essence of desire channeled into the heaving of weights.

It was now just one week away from the day Arnold aimed for all this time. He knew he must beat the top man in order to prove himself the best. Arnold thought he was the best there was. This was not conceit, but confidence and honesty—nothing is worse than the man who is forever digging his toe in the sand and saying "Shucks, I ain't no good," when he really thinks he's Apollo.

The top bodybuilder is the man who holds the Mr. Olympia title and that man, of course, was Sergio Oliva, who many believe may be the greatest bodybuilder of all time. Arnold had done everything he could, and now, forged into steel by the sweat of his brow, he was girded for battle.

But what about Sergio all this time? What was he doing? Everyone knew he held a back-breaking job in a foundry. When did he find the time to train? How good could he look with such limited time to train? These questions could only be answered on the posing platform.

ZELLER

The tell-tale cinderblock walls say it's Joe Gold's gym
and the forearms, bis, tris, pecs, lats, abs, thighs and calves
tell me it's Sergio.
"How ya doin,' Serge?"
"Hanging in there, Drapes."

The following week, I was working at the check-in table at the stage door in New York when in strode the man himself. Sergio looked the picture of health and ready for the challenge Arnold was giving.

Having the NABBA Mr. Universe title, Arnold was eligible to enter the Mr. Olympia, but he wanted to compete for the IFBB

Mr. Universe as well. This gave Sergio a great opportunity to size up his opponent at the Universe prejudging. As the tall class came out on the stage it was clear the winner would be Schwarzenegger. By the look on Sergio's face, he knew he had a battle on his hands.

That evening I kept trying to get a glimpse of Sergio. No one had seen what he looked like. He was the great mystery man. Was he in shape, or just there for the visit? Arnold, in the meantime, was pumping like a fiend. When he wasn't doing that, he was striding back and forth like a caged animal. The tension was getting unbearable. The hours went by and at last Arnold was called to pose for the Universe title. He walked slowly to the platform and went through an abbreviated routine. He wanted to save his greatest effort for the Mr. Olympia contest. The crowd loved it. They could see why he was one of the most publicized bodybuilders in the world.

With the Mr. Universe complete, it was now time for the Mr. Olympia. The dressing rooms emptied and there were soon almost as many stuffed around the sides of the stage as there were sitting in the audience. No bodybuilder wanted to miss this one. I had the feeling this one moment might decide the greatest bodybuilder of all time.

Bud Parker stepped to the microphone and quieted the audience. It was time for the event people had come from all over the world to see.

"From Italy, the IFBB Mr. Europe, Franco Colombu."

Franco walked on the stage and gave his usual superlative routine. Just standing without flexing he could win many a Most Muscular. Franco proved to be one of the favorites of the evening.

I still hadn't gotten a look at Sergio.

"And now from Austria, Arnold Schwarzenegger!"

Once again Arnold went slowly toward the platform. This was it. This was the exact moment he trained and lived for. He posed as he had never posed in his life, for this was its most important moment. His mass and definition were unbelievable. The shadows from the posing light seemed to rip deep creases of black in his body while the massive mounds glistened with highlights. The crowd cheered him from pose to pose.

"And now," said Parker through all the noise, "Mr. Olympia, Sergio Oliva!"

But where was Sergio?

"Sergio, you're on!" yelled the stage manager.

"Where's Sergio?" we yelled.

With painful slowness, he walked toward the stage. He was still in his robe. Then he was lost behind a crowd of admirers. From where I was, I could only get a glimpse every so often between the others; I could barely see him remove his robe. Then I heard a gasp.

"Oh, my God!" exclaimed someone, and that just about summed it up.

On to the stage strode one of the most muscular human beings to ever walk the face of the earth. The audience let out a roar that almost peeled the paint off the walls. I cannot describe what I saw.

The words of an unknown bodybuilder said it all, "Oh, my God!"

After Sergio finished, the judges called the contestants back for another look together. Sergio wisely wanted Arnold to pose first, but Arnold would have none of that.

"Come," he said, "we pose side by side at the same time."

Sergio mounted the center platform and there began the greatest showdown in bodybuilding history. Two of the greatest bodybuilders of all time, matching each other pose for pose under the light. I will never again see anything like that.

Yet, still this was not enough for the judges, who by this time were even—four to four. And they insisted Bud Parker call them back again to determine the winner. The decision was a split one—a close, very close, decision for Sergio.

CARUSO

Sergio Oliva—take a minute to look at the picture. I'll start with truly remarkable. But that's not enough. I go to absolutely amazing. Not bad, but not quite. I give extraordinary a try, but it falls flat so I add super to extra and get super-extraordinary...how dumb. You see, mere words fail us in describing the Myth. He's also one of the coolest guys you'll ever meet. He's my brother.

Arnold looked stunned for a minute. Then he recovered his composure and showed the sportsmanship I knew he would. He threw his arms around Sergio in a warm congratulatory embrace. As a final gesture he raised Sergio's arm in victory. The greatest bodybuilding event in history had just concluded and its greatest champions side by side accepting the admiration of their fans. That moment can never be repeated.

After the contest Sergio told Joe Weider the miracle he had created in Arnold—in just nine months—proved within another year that Arnold would be out of this world.

"The greatest of all time!" Sergio said.

Coming from a true Caesar of bodybuilding, that's praise indeed!

•

In a feeble attempt to feel important I put out a list once a year of awards I think should go to outstanding people at a contest—the ones who don't always get the trophies.

Best Muscle Show Director in Bodybuilding History—Bud Parker

Best Physique (non-top-title winner)—Frank Zane...one of the greatest physiques I've ever seen

Most Muscular Man I've Seen—Zabo Koszewski

Greatest Improvement Since Last Year—Harold Poole

Best Mustache—Bert Elliott...no contest since Twichell shaved his off

Greatest Producer of Physique Contests—Joe Weider...sure, he's my boss, but just ask anyone else who was at the show

Most Promising Physique—Tie: Ken McCord and Don Peters

Most Tired Writer—Me...so long!

•

"Lose, baby, lose!" That's the phrase most often heard around the gyms lately. For years the big shtick of bodybuilders was bulk. Bulk at any price. It's like they felt security only if the lumps were bloated. Cuts only belonged to knives.

Now the trend is going the other way. Now the big thing is deep lines, not to be confused with wrinkles. Gironda—the leader of the cult—has been preaching cuts for years, only to be met by bloated bumps and looks of scorn.

When the boys listened, they won prizes. Unfortunately, some bodybuilders are like children who think of their trainer as they would a parent. After a certain age they know all the answers.

Maybe it takes the examples of the current champs to set the trend—if so, listen to this: Dave Draper has gone from 240 pounds to 210 pounds, Larry Scott from 210 pounds to 168 pounds, and Joe Nista has dropped a good twenty pounds, McArdle's down to something real weird. Pat Casey has indicated the same and has started losing weight like crazy. All of them look as if they've just been in a fight with a lion, they have so many cuts. What judge could vote against a guy like that? Personally I think they look better than ever. Now if only I could find that same lion.

•

You know, being a writer can be hazardous. After all, a guy could get lead poisoning from a broken pencil or get eraser's knuckle. Okay, laugh, but things can get pretty hazardous when you're working with a madman like Art Zeller. Artie has this idea the only reason I go out with him on a story is to watch him photograph.

I'll admit he's a great photographer and he knows how to work with his subject, but I can't go along with his wild scheme for backgrounds. He spends almost all his free time looking for locations for physique studies. His poor wife thinks she's going for a Sunday drive when instead it's a safari for backgrounds. Recently he found a great stretch of sand a few miles north of Muscle Beach. From its sweep of coastline jut out rugged-rock peninsulas every mile or so that act as breakwaters.

"The rocks," he yelled as we got down to the water's edge. I looked up expecting to see an avalanche.

"The rocks are out of this world," he said as he pointed to one of the peninsulas. Art burned such a track to the rocks I thought he might turn the sand to glass.

"B-but, Art," I stammered as I finally caught up with him. "The rocks are too slippery and the tide is in too far."

Oh, no, he had to have his shots.

"Are you kidding?" he said to me as if he couldn't believe the wisdom of his ideas. "The waves crashing on the rocks will create an aura, a majesty, a..."

I left to tell Dan Mackey what Zeller The Zealot planned. Dan looked at the rocks and the tide.

"But..." he looked back at the rocks and shrugged, "okay."

"Now," said Art as he came up to us, "I want Dan right out on the tip of the rocks."

Slowly we inched our way forward until only Mackey's toes let him know he was on land.

"Now," said Art as he started sighting down into his camera, "we'll just wait until Mother Nature gives us the right wave."

We didn't have to wait long. At that moment a big one crested over the top, getting Mackey and Art, plus clothes and camera all wet. Hee, hee, hee.

•

Now, what I'm gonna tell you is the gospel truth according to the deities of Muscle Beach. I'm back in school. A very special school with only one teacher and principal. Another unique thing about this school is that it's on wheels. I found out about it by accident.

This is the way it happened. I got into Artie's car to go on a photo story assignment. After I got in, I quite naturally closed the door. Doesn't everyone? There was a silence. No motor started. Nothing but the noise of my eyes blinking.

After a minute of this silence I innocently looked over at the driver to see what was wrong and why we weren't on our way. Zeller was just sitting there shaking his head.

"What's wrong?" I said.

The nut just kept shaking his head and muttering, "F, F, F."

"What do you mean 'F'?" I asked.

With eyes blazing he shouted, "You failed!"

"Well," I said, "in arithmetic once, but...wait a minute. What do you mean 'I failed'?"

"You closed the door like some kind of slob. It was way too hard." He started the engine and I could tell someone in the car was not all he should be upstairs, and it wasn't me, so that didn't leave the greatest selection.

"Er, look, great madman," I said finally, "I've never in my humble life seen someone get so excited about closing a door to a car."

"Well, everybody treats car doors like the tops of trash cans. As a result they end up looking like them, and wreck the hinges in the process. It doesn't take any trouble, in fact, less effort, to close a car door correctly."

Well, that told me and we didn't say much till we got to our destination.

As I got out of the car I closed the door without thinking.

"D-!"

"Good grief," I said in fear, "I did it again, by gosh." With that I opened the door again, but this time closed it as softly as I could.

"B+."

"You mean I don't get an A for that?" I said, suddenly realizing I cared.

"You can do better," said Zeller.

Well, I hate to admit it, but now I wait, brainwashed, for my grades. My wife says she can always tell when I've been on an assignment with Art because I come home and start slamming all the doors in the house. That'll show him.

•

CARUSO

Reg Lewis personifies Muscle Beach. Some bodies are meant for competition, some for demonstrating exercise and others work great on magazine covers when the photographer has arranged everything just right. I visualize Reg walking down the beach, emerging from rough, frothy surf or standing in the dramatic shadows of the late afternoon sun against a backdrop of swooping gulls, full sails and a pale blue horizon.

Got a phone call the other day from Mr. America, Reg Lewis.

"Dick," he said, "I'm going to be on TV in just a few minutes."

Needless to say, I tuned in. It was an interview show with Reg demonstrating the values of weight training to the audience. At one point the telephone lines were open for one of those question and answer sessions with the audience. Well, sir, the lines got so flooded with calls they had to stop them. Reg was in the studio long after his appearance answering all the telephone questions. If you have any doubt as to the interest generated by bodybuilding, you should have seen the reaction when the mighty Reg unveiled the lumps for the lens.

As a result of his appearance, this champ was picked for another show the following week. We should all be grateful bodybuilding has such an articulate spokesman. I can't figger out why dey don't ax me to talk on dem type o' shows!

•

Quick sets of muscle news: Joe Gold, the well-known Venice Beach gym owner, makes all of his professional gym equipment. He makes it sturdy enough to withstand the onslaughts of his mastodonic members, which means only dynamite could bust the stuff. He even makes his own Olympic barbell sets and they're better than anything on the market. Nope, he won't sell anything commercially so don't bug him about it. Just go in and look and admire...A special award should go to Chuck Collras for withstanding the ocean winds while on a photo assignment recently. With lats like his, he stands a good chance of flying away. Maybe he should wear an anchor on a windy day...While on the subject of awards, one should go to that rising physique star, Dan Mackey, for the length of his workouts. I hear he started working out last Saturday morning and missed church the following day. Wonder if he took a break for dinner.

•

There was a time when Hollywood was noted for many things. We had Hollywood and Vine, movie stars, and Bert Goodrich's gym.

Well, Hollywood and Vine is still there and we still have movie stars, but Goodrich's Gym has long since departed to the great big junk heap in the sky. A rather ignominious fate for so grand an enterprise.

The years have passed and Bert Goodrich went his way leaving a vacuum that can never be filled. Every now and then I see Bert and we invariably talk about the good old days. I always feel a little sad when we part, how wonderful it would be if we could just reach back for a while and reclaim some of those days for just a moment. People came from all over the world just to touch the weights that Reeves, Pedersen, Eiferman, Scott and all the others lifted. Now all that is left are the yellowing pages of old *Muscle Power* and *Your Physique* magazines to tell of the glories of the bygone eras.

Okay, so I get dramatic about it. You would, too, if you'd trained there. Then just the other day I came across an ad in the paper. You guessed it—Bert Goodrich has opened another gym! It's located in the San Fernando Valley in a community known as Granada Hills.

My next step was to call our very first Mr. America and check out what I had read.

"That's right, Dick. I've opened up another gym at last and you should see it," enthused Bert. "It's got everything, and I mean everything. When can you get over here and see my pride and joy?"

Needless to say, I was ready right that moment.

"You know," he continued, "it's amazing how many of my old members are coming over here. Why just the other day I got an autographed photo of Fess Parker recalling the fun we had at the Hollywood gym."

Now my advice to you, dear reader, is to grab hold of your bike or pogo stick and hop on over to see the great man himself, back where he should always be.

•

Dominic Juliano displays an early physique trophy from an East Coast win. For many years Dom put his muscles to work in clubs in Las Vegas and on TV variety shows demonstrating his awesome strength and exciting hand-balancing skills. With a female partner overhead and a Roman Chair below, it was showtime.

Dom Juliano is rolling in the money lately. He's traveling all over the world with his balancing act. The other night I had a chance to see it for the first time on ABC's "Hollywood Palace."

One of the stunts—and I hesitate calling anything a stunt when it's as good as this—combined a chair, his lovely partner and him, along with those barbell-built muscles. He takes his partner by the feet and lifts her overhead. With his feet hooked in the seat of the chair, he bends over the back of it as he lowers the girl to the floor.

The most amazing part comes next: With his partner's feet once more in his hands and his upper body draped over the back so his head is on the floor behind, he pulls her up with a straight-arm pullover motion. Then, he actually pulls his body back up—girl and all—until he is once again upright. It's a wonderful demonstration of power. Guess it comes naturally for a former training partner of the strength immortal, Marvin Eder.

•

Recently the top ten bodybuilders list for the year was published. Quickly I scanned the top boys to see where I came in. Incredible as this may sound, I wasn't even listed as a joke. Last year I believe I held down the ninety-second spot with Don Knotts. This year I was overlooked completely. But I bear no grudge. Ahh, that my lumps should be as big as my heart.

I know that you're all wondering about my list of the top ten. Hold it. Here goes:

1. John Grimek
2. Eric Pedersen
3. Steve Reeves
4. Larry Scott
5. Sergio Oliva
6. Bill Pearl
7. Dave Draper
8. Freddy Ortiz
9. Clarence Ross
10. Marvin Eder

Sorta dates me, doesn't it? Now that I've started, want more?

Best Arms—Freddy Ortiz

Best Chest—George Eiferman

Best Back—Floyd Page

Best Abs—Zabo Koszewski

Best Legs—John Grimek

Most Muscular—Larry Scott

Think of all the friends I just made...and lost.

•

The other day Don Peters went out with Artie on a picture-taking session that almost turned into a pretty wild event. As you know, Art always tries to find the best locations possible for the bodybuilder, ones that will complement rather than distract. What you see on the cover of any Weider publication is the culmination of many hours of work and artistic endeavor. So far-reaching is Zeller's artistic grasp that he seeks to implement the physical features of the locale as much as possible. This can turn out to be dangerous, as we shall see.

Excited? Well, Zeller was taking some photos of Peters in a rustic park area. Agile as his mind is, he spotted a large dog he felt would give an interesting approach to the picture—a strong man holding a strong animal. The dog appeared to be some type of German shepherd mix and had a great look. The owner liked the idea, too, handed the leash to Don and all was set.

Yeah? Not with Artie. Next he spotted a boxer. After all, if one dog looked good through the lens, two dogs would look twice as good, right? Now Don had a boxer on one side and the shepherd on the other. He felt like a sandwich. The dogs eyeballed each other carefully.

"Say," said Don as an afterthought, "do these dogs know each other?"

Zeller kept clicking off shots.

"Oh, no," was the bland answer, and at that moment both dogs began going at each other with a vengeance. Wilder than a UN Security Council meeting! Fortunately, Don escaped intact and some excellent photos were obtained.

Not every cover session is quite so wild—with animals, that is. The human variety is something else again. Over a period of time I've found the average person views what we do with mixed emotions. They'll see photos being taken with a bodybuilder and, more often than not, be just plain curious. Sometimes they'll inquire how he got all those muscles and other times they'll just watch in awe. Of course, there's always the wise guy with the flabby body who knows all the answers and has never-ending comments. When the environment is hostile, the photo results can naturally be poor.

Don Peters and two dogs in front of tree. Go back to page 64 and you'll see Don five years earlier standing on the shore of what was once Muscle Beach. His physique has improved considerably, along with his company some might say. His pose is the same.

ZELLER

One time Zeller found a little hidden valley. It was so hidden it seemed to shut out the rest of the world. In fact, the minute a foreign car entered the area you felt all the beady eyes in the world were on you. The feeling persisted as we got out of the car.

"Now there," said Art, "is the field I've been telling you about."

In front of us stretched the most beautiful field of green you have ever seen. In the middle was a solitary tree, all gnarled and old. On either side of the field were hills that seemed to cup it in a bowl of green. What a place for photos!

The bodybuilder for this photo excursion was Steve Davis. He's one of the fastest rising stars in the area and we wanted to be sure we got the best cover shots possible. Art picked up his equipment and we started across the field to the location he had in mind. After several minutes we got to the spot and started setting up. This would be perfect. Steve got ready for a few poses, when suddenly we heard this voice from atop one of the hills.

"Get out of the field!"

"What did he say?" I asked.

Zeller shrugged, "Something about getting out of the field," and resumed what he was doing.

Once again the lonely voice wafted to our waiting ears with poetic grace, "That's a planted field, you idiots! Get out of there!"

"I think he wants us to leave," said Steve.

As we were leaving I kept thinking how much more proper it would have been in this setting if the fellow had yelled, "Come back, Shane, come back!"

Not to worry. We haven't given up. We shall return.

•

Bits and pieces...Chuck Collras recently did six reps with 500 pounds in the deadlift! That's at a bodyweight of 150 pounds...Vince Gironda has been invited to participate in the Highland Games in Scotland. If he can find the time, he'll compete in the caber toss. I'd go, but they don't have an event for tossing the bull...Wound of the month came when Art Zeller complained to Chuck Collras that he slammed the door of his car too hard. He gave Collras a D grade. Chuck looked Art's car up and down for a minute. "If you've got a good car," he said, "you don't need to worry about closing its doors." Now that hurt...Larry Scott recently followed Dave Draper and Bill McArdle's example and visited the Los Angeles College of Chiropractic with me (it's where I'm studying chiropractic) to view the human dissection. As Larry put it after a few hours in the lab, "It was like some great adventure to see at last what we look like from the inside. Makes me appreciate anything I have that much more."

•

Have you ever had one of those days when you felt stronger than usual? Most of us have. You know, you feel you can tear apart a piece of wet tissue without working up a sweat. Well, I felt that way a few days ago. To make things better we had a pretty easy day of it here at the Weider West Coast office. It was time to go home and the summer sun was still shining.

"I feel unbeatable," I said to myself as I started to get into my car. That, good buddies, is as far as I should have gone. "I know," I continued, "I'll drop by Joe Gold's muscle market and see if I can buy a contest with Zabo."

You see, a week or so earlier Zabo had done a strength stunt I was unable to duplicate. This bugged me. Now that I was feeling mighty, it was time for revenge. Besides, maybe I could catch him when he was sick or something. So a few minutes later I walked into the gym. There was Zabo in the middle of the floor, instructing. He looked discouragingly healthy as usual.

Undaunted, I went up to him and said, "Zabe, babe, what's new?"

"Okay, Dick, try this one," he answered as we went over to the thigh curl bench. (He seems to know what I'm thinking all the time.) The bench was very high. Zabo stood beside it for a second. He leaped up and landed on top with both feet.

"Can you do that?" he asked. "A lot of guys are afraid they'll break a leg trying."

I looked at the bench and then at Zabo. Without saying another word I walked out of the gym. Driving home I was thinking I could at least kick my dog when I got to the house. After all, why waste all that power?

•

Michael Landon spent years building his muscles and was a regular at Vince's Gym when not before the lights, camera and action. His natural power and ability as a young man is demonstrated on this enclosure fence post somewhere in Hollywood. Ever try this?

The Batman TV series started a rash of comic book heroes invading the tube. This got me to thinking of how sick I am of seeing my idols being portrayed by fat old men or skinny young ones. Why not have a hero look like one? Can you see Superman played by

Dave Draper? How about Larry Scott as Batman? Who could be better than Chet Yorton as The Phantom? Leo Gorey and Huntz Hall as Batman and Robin? Okay, now that you're paying attention, how about Bill McArdle as the Flash or Freddy Ortiz as The Mighty Atom? I was going to try out for one of those roles, but decided not to when I discovered they were casting for Batman, not Fatman.

•

Got a preview glimpse of some photos of the powerhouse, Steve Merjanian, to be printed in *Muscle Builder* or *Mr. America* soon. I was floored when I saw them. How could one man have so much power, be so big and still look almost ready for a major physique title. Let me think, how can I describe him...hmmm... Have you ever seen a gorilla with shape?

Planet of the Muscleheads. Looks like Seymour Koenig, Zabo "The Chief" Koszewski, Jerry Trayler and Steve Merjanian having a bad hair day. Try Palmolive, guys.

STUDIO

•

I get pretty sick sometimes of hearing about what bums bodybuilders are. It seems like taking potshots at the muscleheads is going to replace baseball and football as a national pastime. The latest blast came from the *Wall Street Journal,* which should be more concerned with stocks and bonds instead of stacks of muscle. According to our latest critic, the average bodybuilder is a vain, psychologically disturbed boob who is constantly being taunted by them thar normal guys. Ordinarily, you forget such nonsense for being what it is—garbage. The writer obviously spent many long minutes getting his facts straight. When you approach something with bias, the natural inclination is to try to justify that bias by seeking situations that dignify the concept.

CARUSO

In 1966 the IFBB gave out the most attractive trophies I have ever seen: three precisely sculpted nickel-plated figurines symmetrically arranged atop one another and mounted on a dark walnut base. Sergio and I managed to dislodge a pair from the judges' mitts, while Most Muscular Chet Yorton and our Most Shapely companion gracefully shared our good fortune.

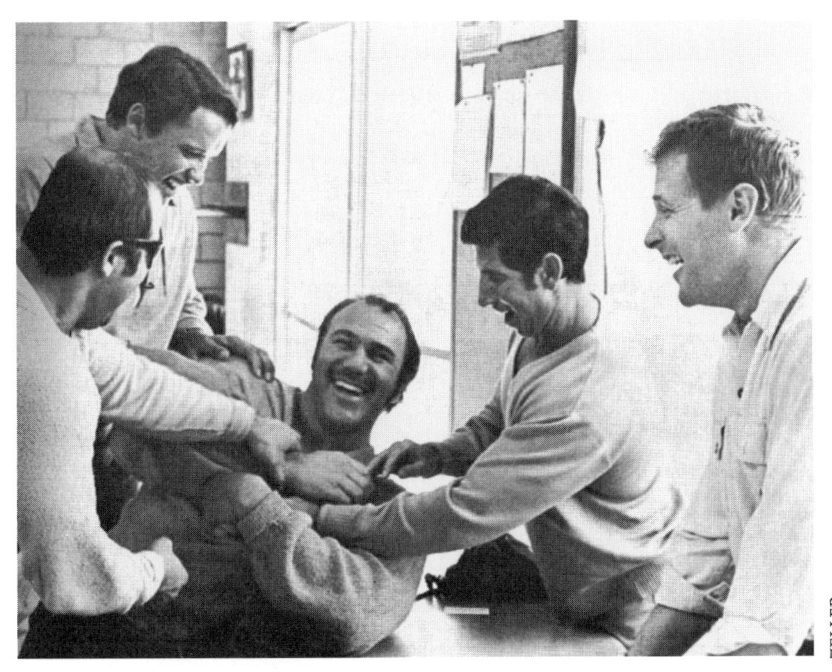

ZELLER

Wayne Coleman at this time—late '60s—was tossing men around the ring of the professional wrestling world as Superstar Billy Graham. Carrying 300 pounds of muscle mostly in his shoulders and arms made him good at crushing and thumping as well. It seems Arnold, Peanuts, Chuck Collras and Dick want to be sure all that mass is not eight or twelve sweatshirts from size medium to 4X piled one on top of the other.

The author of the article didn't like bodybuilding, so he put on the blinders and saw what he wanted to see. As a result, a warped and totally inaccurate picture of bodybuilding was presented. First, let's get something straight. Some bodybuilders are vain self-centered boobs who love to spend great chunks of their time admiring their reflection. These same people may never get a girl to be interested in them because they just don't have the time or desire to share themselves with anyone else. But please don't tell me that it's bodybuilding that makes them that way. It's just bodybuilding that makes you notice.

To blame bodybuilding for one dud makes as much sense as saying that every southerner is a member of the Ku Klux Klan just because a few were. Since it's my job to report the things that bodybuilders say and do and since I've been in the game for over twenty years, one feels I'm in a better position to report about bodybuilders in *Muscle Builder* than some reporter for the *Wall Street Journal* in spite of what the *Wall Street Journal* says.

Some of the best athletes I have ever met have been physique contestants and some of the best-educated professional men have held physique titles—doctors, lawyers and on down the line. Let me end this with a word of advice: Stick with the thing you like. Remember, a bodybuilder is the same as any other man ever born—he's just more muscular, healthier and stronger.

•

A few weeks ago Corsair Field at Santa Monica City College was transferred into a bit of Scotland. Amidt the wail of bagpipes and a hey nonni nonni, the United Scottish Societies held their thirty-sixth annual Highland Gathering and Games. Once you're on the field and in the midst of all the color and excitement, you tend to forget the everyday life of Santa Monica awaits just outside the gates. As part of the Games everything is contested from tossing the caber, to pillow fighting, to an old-fashioned tug of war. Now, in the latter event we had a special interest because a team had been recruited from Gold's Gym to do the honors for a local soccer club. As soon as the teams were announced, all eyes turned to the mighty mountains of muscle led by big 295-pound Steve Merjanian. With such men as 300-pound Hank Breaker and 250-pound Joe Kanaster holding things in place, they didn't have much chance of losing.

I suppose you might say rope pulling is one of the few sports you win by going backwards. After several struggles the men of Gold's Gym emerged victorious and immediately claimed to be the best in the world. No one seemed in a mood to argue the point as the excited fans stormed their horses.

Merjanian told me later he's forming a team called the Gold Ropers and they are challenging the world in this event. I got so excited that I volunteered my services.

"Sure," drawled the big 300-pound Texan Hank Breaker, "we could use a mascot."

•

Chalk talk...Merjanian plans to go from his present bodyweight of 295 to 330 pounds; they're building the power cage now. Steve's power was amply demonstrated recently when he pressed 300 pounds from behind his neck ten times, while in a braced, seated position. He's done 375 for singles...Tom Overholtzer did a squat in competition not long ago that was supposed to be 590 pounds. It turned out to be eleven pounds heavy, so he now owns a new squat record of 601. That's the kind of surprises a person can learn to live with...At the recent Los Angeles Powerlift championships, middleweight Bill Thurber made a nice 375-bench press, only to lose it by a foot. The foot moved while he was lifting, which disqualified the lift. That seems pretty stupid to me. How can a foot sliding on the ground aid the lift? Maybe they feel that the friction will impart some electricity to force it up.

A Challenge Accepted—Chuck Sipes, Mr. World

We were driving through the tunnel that leads to New York from New Jersey and the Weider home office. Joe Weider and I were talking about the Mr. World contest that was to be the following evening. As usual we both were getting worked up about the contestants.

"It's so great," said Joe, "to see bodybuilders coming from all over the world to enter physique contests. It's one of the greatest international brotherhoods in sports."

"I'll say. Of course, the greatest thing would be to have an event like this televised so that millions instead of thousands could see it."

Joe just smiled. I had the feeling he was working on that idea already.

"Look at that building there," said Joe suddenly. "A few months ago there were just a few flea-bitten stores and a bar there, now we have a monument in steel. What a place New York is."

"Speaking of monuments in steel," I said, "how's Chuck Sipes?"

Joe glanced at me. "Haven't you heard?"

"Heard what?"

"Chuck hurt his shoulder in training and won't be able to attempt his 600-pound bench press."

"You mean he won't be at the show?"

"Oh, no," Joe assured me, "he'll be there to perform his strength feats and to enter the Mr. World contest."

It took a moment for that to sink in.

"To what?"

"To perform his strength..."

"No," I interrupted, "I mean that thing about entering the Mr. World contest."

"What about it?"

"You've got to be kidding," I said.

"Why?"

"Well, what can he gain by entering that one when he's already entered the Mr. Olympia before?"

"What difference does that make?" asked Joe.

"Well, look at all he has to lose. What if he doesn't win? He'd never be the same in the eyes of the fans."

"I don't know about that," said Joe. "Regardless, Chuck has never won the Mr. World and he's willing to take the chance of losing a lot of prestige to put the title on the belt."

CARUSO

The Trainer of Champions and the Champion,
Joe Weider and Chuck Sipes

"He's quite a competitor," I said in the understatement of the year.

The following afternoon I got to the theater early so I could help check in the contestants. Bud Parker asked me if I could help assist backstage, which takes in a little of everything and a whole lot of time. Actually, I didn't have much to do; Al Townsend and his assistants did so well, they made me look pretty useless.

Useless or not I got a chance to see the contestants as they arrived, which is something else. I counted over thirty contestants from around the world, all who would vie for the Mr. World title. This was tough competition and I could only hope Chuck was in the best shape of his life.

As I was helping with the registration a familiar voice said, "Hello, Mr. Tyler."

I looked up to see my old buddy, Joe Nista.

"Joe, what are you doing here?"

"I'm entering the Mr. World."

Now there were two people for me to root for.

The sun slowly set on this warm day in Brooklyn. With the evening, the crowds that had been waiting around the Brooklyn Academy of Music grew into the frantic fans they always do. You could feel the excitement grow as the marquee lights were turned on and the front doors to the aisles were opened to the public.

Backstage was a mad house. Juggling acts were trying to move their equipment around without bumping into the belly dancer, who was getting stares from the bodybuilders, who were pumping up their muscles and oiling their lumps for the big moment under the posing light.

Unfortunately, I hadn't had the chance to see as much of the prejudging as I had wanted to because I was busy helping with the organization of the events and because of the arm wrestling event I was to manage. This resulted in an almost new show for me to see, and I think I was getting more excited about it than anyone with the exception of Joe Weider.

The National Anthem's powerful strains thundered the opening of the show of shows. No sooner had everyone settled back than they were greeted by the IFBB President Ben Weider. Ben was followed by a spectacular juggling act, a muscleman fashion show and a belly dancer. Now came the big moment. The lights dimmed and Bud Parker stepped to the microphone to begin the introduction of the Mr. World contest. I had to leave my post and run out front for this. The trip was worth it, as one of the best parades of muscle ever to grace the Mr. World contest marched before us.

Then it happened. Chuck Sipes was introduced and pandemonium broke out. It was fantastic. Before the thousands of screaming fans was one of the most powerful men in the world. A titan of explosive strength poured into one of the most dramatic physiques on earth. The crowd went nutty. Flash bulbs burst their eerie brightness like lightning on the surface of darkened clouds. Above all this, like some ancient god, stood the mighty Sipes bathed in the light and showered by the roaring accolades of his fans. It was quite an experience and, Chuck told me later, it was the greatest reception in his long career.

After it was all over you'll never guess who won. Sipes gambled and picked up almost all the chips. Not only did he win the title, but he was also chosen Most Muscular, and got Best Arms, Best Chest and Best Abdominals as well. Best Legs went to Nobuo Takemoto of Japan, with Roy Callender winning Best Back. The short class was won by Joe Nista, the medium by Sipes and the tall by Conrad LaFramboise.

Backstage Chuck told me he was retiring.

"But no bodybuilder has ever won the Big Four—Mr. America, Mr. World, Mr. Universe and Mr. Olympia—in bodybuilding history. All you have to do is win the Mr. Olympia and you've done it."

Chuck thought for a moment.

"You've just witnessed the shortest retirement in history!"

•

Plans for the Larry Scott Gym are really booming now. Talked with Larry the other day and he was pretty excited about all the ideas he's considering. The latest? The gym will be combined with the new Weider office. Also part of the gym will be a photo studio, convenient to grab photos of leading bodybuilders as they work on programs for Weider.

Sounds like a dream setup, and all under the direction of bodybuilding immortal Larry Scott.

MOZEE

Larry Scott doing wrist curls with, like, 165. Yeah, but can he scratch his nose? When Scott came on the bodybuilding scene with those arms, everyone from Boston to San Diego wanted a pair. This caused the bodybuilding population to double overnight and now look at it. There ain't no place to sit.

Can't go on about Scott's proposed gym without mentioning Vince Gironda's. What a change! Everything seems different. For years Vince's muscle pit was little more than that. This doesn't mean to say it wasn't clean, just that it was a place filled with the clutter of great equipment mixed with the clutter of great muscles. Well, the equipment is still there along with the muscles, but the clutter isn't. Under the stewardship of Gene Mozee, the gym has become a different place.

Sure the color is still there and always will be as long as the muscles remain; it's just the place has been spruced up with carpeting and a new coat of paint, with plans to put in an outdoor training area next to the regular gym. I hear memberships are booming. I frankly can't imagine where they'll put the new members unless they arrange a kind of series of nets or hammocks. In a few weeks I plan to visit the new Vince's and get some photos, if I can fit in the flash bulb.

From Muscles of Bronze to Stacks of Gold
The Chuck Pendleton Story

The girl had a body and a half and her bikini barely covered the half that didn't show. She and her skinny boyfriend were sitting on the beach when along came a big bronzed muscleman. Muscleman sees girl, kicks sand in skinny guy's face and walks away with faithless wench. Sound familiar? As familiar as the back of almost any comic book. Well, I thought this would be a whiz-bang funny way to start off a film I made back in 1960 called *Project Power* and it was an attempt to give weight training its own surf-style film. Unfortunately its weight was too heavy to float on any wave and it sank with a healthy chunk of my money.

Now that you've dried your tears I must tell you I had a reason for relating all of the above. You see, the muscleman who opened my film was to become one of the biggest stars in Europe within a year's time. Chuck Pendleton seemed perfect for the part of the muscleman. Not because he was some kind bully, but because he had the physique and air of self-confidence I felt was needed for the part. Without a doubt Chuck was one of the most popular bodybuilders at the beach.

Playing the part of a beach bully seemed almost paradoxical, for Chuck himself took up weight training because he was tired of being pushed around when he was a kid in Denver. Weights worked their magic and it wasn't long before the frightened kid turned into a burly athlete. By the time he was of high school age, he and his family moved to Southern California.

It was at Inglewood High School that Chuck began to carve his athletic reputation. By the time he graduated in 1942, he had lettered in football, swimming, gym and track. In college he received his degree and began to teach in the Los Angeles school system. He supplemented this income with occasional work as an extra in Hollywood films. It was about this time he met Joe Gold.

"This was an important moment in my life," says Chuck. "Joe and I hit it off right away. Not only did he show me the value of Weider training methods, but I've been hooked on them ever since."

The more he trained with modern methods, the faster he progressed until he had one of the finest physiques around. In spite of his development and his strength, Chuck never entered a physique or strength contest.

"The only strength displays I ever give," said Chuck one day, "are when I'm teaching."

"How's that?" I asked.

"Well, you see, I teach in some pretty tough school districts. Often, I teach shop and in order to establish who the boss is right from the start, I take an anvil that may weigh seventy-five to a hundred pounds and lift it overhead with one hand. I never have any trouble after that."

This is Chuck's simple and direct way of handling all of life's problems. He never side-steps an issue. He is honest with himself and it comes through to others.

Life could have gone on this way, but fate had other plans. One day a letter arrived at the gym. It requested anyone interested in being in Italian muscle films to send photos. On a wild shot, Chuck decided to see what would happen if he honored the request. He didn't have long to wait and before he could take another step, he was stepping off a plane in Italy and into a new life.

CHARLES

Slick as the wet sand by the pier's edge at Muscle Beach, Chuck Pendleton didn't carry any excess muscle to slow him down or require an explanation. A man, fast, free and cool.

That was in January of 1961. Since then Chuck has earned a small fortune, been in just about every corner of the world and become one of the most popular stars in the motion picture industry.

STUDIO

"Stick 'em up or I'll shoot." Raw Chuck Pendleton—filmdom's Gordon Mitchell,—playing a cigar-chewing commando in some nasty battlefield thick with jackals, scorpions and a merciless enemy. "I'll say it just one more time, bub. Hands up."

A few days ago I got a phone call. On the other end of the line I heard this deep voice say, "Hello, Dick, guess who this is."

I had to admit the voice sounded familiar, but the accent was all wrong.

"Chuck Pendleton?" I said in disbelief borne of eight years of not having heard his voice.

"Right! How about dropping by while I'm in town?"

I didn't need a second nudge. The following day I met him at Gold's Gym and made arrangements for an interview. A few days later Chuck and I were sitting in front of Joe Gold's home in Venice. It had rained the day before, washed the sky of all but a few brave clouds. Chuck was gathering in as much of the sun as he could before he had to go back to work.

"When do you leave?" I asked.

Chuck picked up a telegram and showed it to me. It was addressed to Gordon Mitchell from the famous Italian filmmaker, Fellini.

"What kind of part do you have in the film?" I asked.

Chuck lauged. "I play a psycho killer. I have to admit I've had a variety of roles and I think this has given me what success I may have achieved."

"You mean not being typed."

"Yes," Chuck replied, "being willing to work in all types of roles. I've considered each part I play a challenge and I think we learn from the challenges. I like to think I've learned a little more from each part I've played. The important thing is to let yourself learn from life without building up defensive walls first."

I nodded. "Now, about your name. Why did you change it from Pendleton?"

There was a momentary silence. "You may not believe this story, but I'll tell it anyway."

Now I was all ears for a change.

"It all started back in the middle '50s. Somebody suggested I see this clairvoyant."

"A fortune teller?" I asked.

"No. Not in the customary sense of the word. She was just gifted with the ability to see things in the future."

I shrugged.

"Whether you believe in such things or not, she told me about events in my life no one ever knew. During our talk she asked if I had ever been known as Gordon Mitchell. I told her I didn't know what she was talking about, but she assured me I would one day be known as Gordon Mitchell. I didn't think anymore about it until I got off the plane for the first time in Italy years later. The newsmen ran up calling me Gordon Mitchell. I'm told by the company publicity man that Gordon was easier for Italians to say. Believe me—the story is true. Ever since then I've been very happy being Gordon Mitchell."

He built his mind, body and soul and went to Italy to build his career and realize his dream as an actor and artist. Some folks called him Gordon Mitchell, the actor and filmmaker. Chuck Pendleton was blessed and gifted, and shared his wealth with those around him.

STUDIO

The phone rang and Chuck—I mean Gordon—went inside to answer it. A few minutes later he came back.

"That was my agent in Rome. I begin the Fellini film in a week. After that I do a film for Dino DeLaurentis with Rod Steiger."

By this time I was baking in that sun.

"Isn't it great to be able to take a sun bath in the middle of December?" said Gordon.

Since I was fully clothed and he was in trunks, it was all I could do to restrain what I wanted to say. Wiping the sweat from my brow I continued, "Gordon, what would you say was your greatest thrill in show business?"

"My first film." he answered simply. "On the very first day I realized I was getting the star treatment. Luckily that first film made over a million dollars in Italy alone, in the very first year."

"That's a great beginning." Gordon shook his head as if he still didn't believe what was happening.

"What a small world," he said almost to himself.

"What?"

"I was thinking of Jeanne Crain with whom I graduated from high school. Years later I was to star in a film with her. I knew Abby Lane when I was working in the Mae West show; years later I was starring with her. I met Jacque Bergerac, the Hollywood actor, in 1955. Later, I was to star with him in "The Fury of Achilles." It's a small world."

"Ever had a frightening moment in all the films you've made?" I asked.

"Not in any of the gladiator films. Funny as it may seem, my most frightening moment came in an Elizabeth Taylor film called "Reflections in a Golden Eye." The director, John Huston, told me what he wanted in the first scene I had. It was a very dramatic one with Miss Taylor. Suddenly she was on the set. Without so much as a hello, we began the scene with the cameras rolling. They printed the first take and ever since then my nerves have been made of steel."

"What are your future plans?" I asked.

"Well, a film I did with Terry Thomas called "Seven Times Seven" should be released soon and I'm writing some scripts with the actor George Nader."

"Along with the Fellini and DeLaurentis commitments, you sure keep busy."

Gordon shrugged his shoulders. "I can't complain. I've been just about everywhere and have a good deal of money and fame to show for it. I have a penthouse overlooking St. Peter's Square in Rome, complete with my own private gym. From my apartment I can see Steve Reeves' place. We often train together along with Brad Harris and Gordon Scott. It's a good life."

"What would you say is the reason for all this good fortune?"

Gordon put on some more suntan lotion.

"Love of what you're doing. Giving to something as much as you get from it. In weight training I give everything I've got. In films I do the same and that's paid off as you can see."

It was getting late.

"Chuck—Gordon—do you still train?" I asked.

"Is that sun hot?" he said.

I wiped the sweat from my brow.

"Before I go, do you have any words of advice to aspiring young bodybuilder/actors?"

"If anyone is interested, why don't they write me?"

"Are you serious?"

"Yes," said Gordon. "I'd like others to have the luck I have. Just have them write to you at the Weider Santa Monica office and you can forward my mail to me."

I got in my car and thought that if Gordon Mitchell never did anything else, he was a success as a human being.

•

DOWNS

Larry Scott is a mass of muscle wrapped around an iron stool knocking out wrist curls in Vince's gym one summer afternoon,

Prediction—I'm going out on a limb with this one, but I get the feeling in my bones Larry Scott will be coming out of retirement. From his low bodyweight of 168 pounds, Larry has begun to stack the muscle back on. Maybe it's the call of the crowd. It's pretty hard for a man to be idolized and then fade away. That only happens to old soldiers, not young bodybuilders.

I'll bet he goes into his den every so often and remembers the ovations he received and the glory he won as he gazes at the treasures and awards he received when he was the greatest bodybuilder in the world. As this is written, Larry is back to over 200 pounds. Can you see Scott in a rematch with Oliva for the Mr. Olympia? A contest with Poole, Sipes, Draper and Schwarzenegger also in it? It can happen, maybe this year. The chance for such glory is too much to pass up, not to mention the thousand dollars. Why for a thousand bucks, I'm almost tempted to enter—the stage door that is.

•

"The Adventures of Granny Zeller and his Electric Car" or "The Great Door War"—The scene is the alley in back of Joe Gold's gym. The characters: Art Zeller, also known as the little old man from Santa Monica who grades people on the way they close the door to his car—Ed Giuliani, champion bodybuilder, who owns a car whose doors have to be closed hard in order to hold—Dick Tyler, man about town, great intellect and all-around dummy who loves to witness other people's hang ups.

The battle lines were drawn by a Rembrandt. It was to be a classic struggle. I sat in the back seat of the car with my pen and paper in hand ready to record what I knew must happen. Art was behind the wheel as innocent as a lamb being led to the slaughter. Eddie got inside. His hand grasped the handle firmly for his all-out effort. His biceps twitched with anticipation. All of a sudden he flexed his biceps, his frontal deltoids and his pecs. The door slammed with the authority of several tons of TNT. My ear drum nearest the door quivered and threatened to break. The silence was awful. Cold beads of sweat ran down Zeller's wrinkled face. He just stared. For a moment I thought we had a case of cardiac arrest on our hands.

Slowly he turned his head toward Giuliani and opened his mouth as if he was about to speak. Before he could say a word, Giuliani lifted up his arm and gave a mighty flex.

"See that?" he asked.

Zeller nodded.

"Then drive."

Off into the fog we went. I kid Art a lot, but he's got a great sense of humor about all of his little idiosyncrasies and is one of the nicest men I've known. Genius must be served.

Peters' Pool Palace

How can I drink my 101 without a can opener?" complained Ed Giuliani. "Why doesn't Joe put on those fliptops?"

With that he went into the kitchen of Don Peters' combination gym and home. Actually it's sort of a sixty, forty split with the majority being the gym. Joe Weider was swimming in the pool, while his lovely wife, Betty, was sunning herself. Art Zeller and Gene Mozee were comparing cameras and Vince Gironda's son and mine were looking for trouble and finding it. In other words it was a nice day, clothed in a veil of California sunshine.

After a while I decided Giuliani had a good idea and a Super Pro 101 would hit the spot. As soon as I got inside, my ears were greeted by the ominous click of pool balls. Ahh, the evil of that game. I could almost see Robert Preston in "The Music Man" giving a sermon.

I wandered into the living room to see who was playing on the fantastic table that has turned the living room into a pool hall. Sergio Oliva was eyeballing a shot into the corner pocket while Don was casually chalking his cue.

"Who's winning?" I asked.

"We're just taking a few practice shots. The game will begin in just a few minutes."

"My friend, you are going to lose," said Sergio as he sank his shot.

I got the feeling this was going to be quite a game. I went to the back door and yelled for Zeller to bring his camera so this historic match could be enshrined forever on film. The word spread and soon the room was filled with spectators.

ZELLER

Now here's a rare combination of characters. Chicago Sergio, New York Eddie, Montreal Joe and California Vince playing pool at Texas Don's digs in the San Fernando Valley. The stakes are high.

"Anyone got a can opener?" asked Giuliani.

Then all was quiet.

"Be my guest, Sergio," said Don with a confident air.

"Man, you mean you want me to break?" said Sergio.

Don nodded. Sergio leaned forward and zeroed in on the cue ball. Everyone just looked at the Oliva arms. They're so big you feel like you're looking at a four-legged freak. No arm I have ever seen looks bigger. His shot was a beaut. It looked like the pool-king Peters had met his match. Now it was Don's turn. He sized up the table carefully.

"Somebody must have a can opener," said Giuliani.

Don's concentration was broken. "Will somebody get the guy a can opener?"

Once again he leaned forward for his masterful shot. Suddenly it was off, the white cue ball headed toward the red and white ball. It got closer and closer. Finally it was right upon the red and white ball. Then it went past the red and white ball and straight into the cushion.

"Ha!" exclaimed Sergio. "My turn!"

But the mighty Sergio had spoken too soon. The cue ball had not yet finished its journey. Across the green felt battlefield lay a blue and white ball. The cue ball from Don's shot went unerringly into it and sunk it into the side pocket.

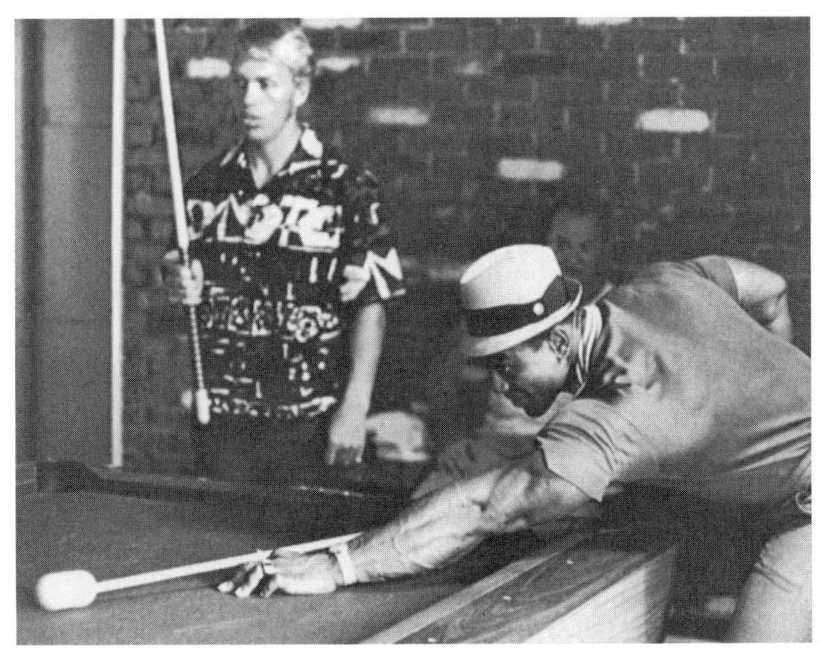

ZELLER

Gene Mozee acts as judge while Sergio hits a three-quarter back shot with the triceps fully extended for maximum effect. The pool table serves as a cool setting, the pool cues clever props.

"Garbage shot!" said Sergio as he held his nose.

I nudged Mozee. "What's a garbage shot?"

"A fluke shot. You know, one that gets the job done by accident."

"Listen, man," said Sergio, "are you gonna play like that?"

Don looked innocent. "That's house rules."

There's no point in going into the whole game shot by shot. Let me just say Don Peters could have been chosen the Man of the Year by the sanitation department. I suppose Don won, but poor Sergio was looking for a clothes pin because he said his hand was getting tired of nose holding, which is a pretty lousy way to treat a guest.

In the weeks that followed, the reputation of Peters' Pool Palace began to grow as fast as the muscles of a Weider champion. Then it happened. The Austrian Oak arrived. Since he likes pool, Schwarzenegger draped all of his 250 pounds around the table and it's been there almost since he arrived. Every evening Arnold trains at Peters' home gym and every evening before the workout they play pool. So far Peters is in the lead. After each game Arnold will say, "Now, let's have a hard workout."

While Don undoubtedly wins the majority of his games, I long suspected the record didn't prove as much as it would seem. I had a chance to prove my point a few days ago when Zeller and I went over to Peters' gym to cover an arm story on Schwarzenegger and were left stranded. What happened was that the signals got crossed and Arnold went for a skin-diving class instead of meeting us.

So, what to do? Yup—pool.

"In New York we played a pretty mean game of pool," said Art as all the pride of the famous East Side Barbell Club welled up in his manly pecs. Don sized Art up for a second.

"That statement sounds like a challenge to me," he said as he took a couple of cues from the rack.

Art took some powder and rubbed it on his hands.

"In New York," he said to me out of the corner of his mouth, "whenever we make a good shot we rap our cues on the floor as a sign of applause."

With that I took cue in hand and got ready to applaud.

Art broke and the battle was on. Actually there were enough garbage shots on both sides to make Sergio hold his nose all the way back to Chicago. There was, however, enough good play to make the whole game respectable. Slowly Peters began to pull ahead as he often does. Why? Why did he always seem to pull away?

"Sorry, Art," said Don, "you can't shoot from that position."

A moment later, "Sorry, Art, but if you don't hit the eight-ball with this shot you'll lose the game."

"Sorry, Art, but your left foot was not in place."

"Sorry, Art..."

Yeah, that was it all right. All games played at the Peters' Pool Palace were played by Peters' rules. These rules changed more than a baby's diapers. Four games were played and Art lost four times.

All this doesn't mean that Artie has given up. Quite the contrary. He seeks revenge, but the rules will be all worked out before the game begins.

One more thing—Giuliani found the can opener for his Super Pro 101. How do I know? Simple. He's getting bigger and more muscular every day.

•

Hesitate to start this column. I don't want to be accused of running a gag into the grounds, but what I'm about to tell you is the truth. I'm a great admirer of Joe Weider, but I'm afraid I must be honest and tell you he has feet of clay. Yes, you read correctly, Joe Weider isn't as perfect as he might appear. Oh, I know he's the trainer of champions, the most knowledgeable person on the science of weight training in the world, the publisher of the greatest physique magazines in the world, the manufacturer of the best and greatest variety of food supplements in the world and the manufacturer of the best weights and most advanced and unique bodybuilding equipment on the market, but I still must say he let me down on his recent visit out here to Muscle Beach during Christmas.

With little regard for the feelings of others he almost sent Zeller to a mental ward. That's right, poor Art is still recovering from the traumatic effects of Joe's visit. It all started when Joe first got into Art's car. I think you can guess the rest. Joe is a vigorous man to say the least. When he closes a car door he closes it for keeps. You know by now how Art is about his car—like a little old lady from Pasadena. Closing the car door is a ritual. It must be closed softly and each person is graded on his performance.

Well, Joe closed it so hard Art started yelling, "It's an air raid! Run for your lives."

"No, no Art," I said trying to calm him.

"A sonic boom?" he said in wonder.

"No."

"An atomic bomb test?"

"No, no. Joe just closed the door of your car."

Tears started to well in his eyes. "You mean Joe Weider, my friend for so many years, would do this to me? I don't believe it."

Joe was watching all this and not saying a thing. Finally, with the utmost calm he said, "Let's get started, Art."

Art started the car.

"I think he loosened the bolts," he mumbled as we headed into the traffic.

When we got to our destination Joe got out of the car and slammed the door so hard that it almost cracked the paint—on the walls of my living room twenty miles away.

"He didn't mean that, Art," I said to the stupefied person behind the wheel. "Joe drives a big car and is used to slamming the door."

Art didn't answer. He got out and ran to catch up with Joe. Later we got back to the car that had by now become a battlefield.

"Joe," said Art pleadingly, "please don't slam the door."

TYLER

Another day at the beach: sun, sand, surf, bodies, oil, pump, cameras, tripods, lenses, film, spectators, disorder, bottled water and outdoor john; hanging out, directions, commands, lights, camera and pose and smile and flex, good, again and again.

"Okay, okay." Joe got in and, I suppose, tried to close it easier.

"F, F, F," said Art in despair.

"Art, you're like some little old lady about this car," said Joe in disgust.

Art just shook his head. "F, F."

"What is he talking about?" asked Joe as he turned to me.

"Well," I said clearing my throat, "you see, Art has this grading system and you just failed."

Joe started to laugh. "And I got an F, eh?"

I nodded. We arrived back at the office. Joe got out first and wound up like he was going to really slam it good.

"Go ahead!" yelled Art suddenly.

"Huh?"

"Go ahead, I don't care anymore! Slam it! Go ahead, slam it!"

Joe whispered to me, "Art's gone nuts."

I nodded and we walked inside, leaving Zeller alone with his car doors. So, if you see some guy around Santa Monica repeatedly slamming his car doors, it's probably just Artie not caring anymore.

•

It heavily dewed out here recently. That's Southern California's term for rain. The rain came on just the day Joe Weider was to take a whole crew out for a photo assignment. We waited around the office for a couple of hours hoping it would pass, but no luck. While killing time I made a discovery in the form of a thirteen-year-old kid. He thinks Dave Draper is the greatest (natch!) and hangs around the office almost all day when Dave is there. The kid trains like a fiend and has started to make real progress.

"Dick," said Dave, "I want you to see something."

We went into the back room and Dave had the kid take off his shirt and throw a few poses. It was such a great display I had Joe Weider come back for a look. Before long around twenty people were watching the show. This youngster has abdominals you wouldn't believe. His back—particularly his traps—are anatomically right out of Gray's Anatomy. You can see every line. He has the potential of being a great future star. My only thought is having so much so early in life might make him take his gifts for granted. If he doesn't and sticks with it he could be a truly great star of the future.

•

Arnold Schwarzenegger got into a car accident the other day. At first I was worried he might have gotten crushed or something. Well, he got some gashes all right, but he never missed a workout. No kidding. All those coats of muscle can save your life in more ways than one. If a tank bumped into Arnold I'd look for the dents in the metal, not the bone.

And the beat goes on. Arnold knocks out a set of inclines as Joe Weider looks on. We're near 1970 from the looks of the mural on the wall of the now-famous, frequently photographed and highly visible cinderblock gym on Pacific Avenue in Venice, the refuge of the Golden Era muscle builders.

ZELLER

•

The big-muscle boys and their clothes...California fashions call for comfort and sport attire, but Jack LaLanne is the neatest dresser of them all. Looks like a fashion-plate in his made-to-order suits...Steve Reeves wears sandals and the loudest sox...George Eiferman delights in noisy shirts...Clarence Ross hates neckties... Mac Batchelor's usually in sport slacks and filling out a dark coat...Bert Goodrich mostly wears well-chosen suits...Malcolm Brenner sports a sport-jacket and any old kind of trousers...but most of the other boys are just so-so! Anyway, I thought you might like to know.

Gold Strikes it Rich

ZELLER

That's the man, Joe Gold, and that's his dog, Thunder. The quaint neighborhood is a cul-de-sac about a mile from the gym where Joe set up housekeeping at one of his Venice properties. Big Steve Merjanian lives to the left, Zabe lives to the right and Joe has his shop for designing superior gym equipment in the back. Stay tight, keep it simple, enjoy, appreciate.

The volleyball arched over the net. Joe Gold dug his feet into the sand and with a quick move leaped high in the air. At the same time his hand slammed against the ball with tremendous force. Back over the net it went with such speed no one could reach it. Joe had scored the point that won the game.

He walked off the court and went over to the adagio platform to watch some of the performers. Some of the greatest balancers in the world trained on these platforms every weekend. They loved the warmth of the Southern California sun with its soft ocean breezes and the companionship of the other great athletes who came from around the world to train there.

After a few minutes Joe moved over to the weight pen where for over a quarter of a century some of the greatest bodybuilders in the world trained. The crowd around the pen was ten deep as the tourists snapped pictures of the bodybuilding stars. This was Muscle Beach on a weekend. This was the Muscle Beach that had carved its memories into all who trained there, and brought people from all over the world to see it. Just a few acres of sand—but what acres!

Gold worked his way through the spectators until he was able to step over the fence and into the training area. One of the bodybuilders came over to Joe with a worried look. "Have you heard?"

"Heard what?"

"They're gonna get rid of Muscle Beach!"

"Hold on a minute," said Joe as he tried to calm the bodybuilder, "What do you mean 'they're gonna get rid of Muscle Beach'?"

Now, the man slowed down and emphasized each word with deliberate slowness.

"They say they're gonna close down Muscle Beach because they don't like the element."

"Come on!" said Joe. "What are you talking about?"

By now the other men who were training gathered around, each one assuring Joe the rumor was out that the weights and the platforms that put the muscle in the beach would soon be hauled away.

"I don't get it," said Joe. "Why would anyone want to do that?"

"They say if they take away the training equipment the bums like us will leave."

Joe shook his head in disbelief. "I don't believe it. This is one of the most famous spots in the country, if not the world. They couldn't do that. It would be like taking Rockefeller Center away from New York City."

The men looked at each other. They were hearing the reassurance they wanted to hear.

"Don't worry," Joe continued, "they'll never get rid of Muscle Beach—they can't."

Later Joe walked down by the ocean as the sun hung low in the sky. Almost everyone had gone home. The ocean curled into the glassy surface of the wet sand and the seagulls danced and chattered on the evening breeze.

"They can't take this away from bodybuilding," he said softly to himself. The words, however, seemed hollow. Deep inside he felt there might be a chance his worst fears would be realized. As all of you who remember your muscle history know, the misguided elements of the Santa Monica City Council destroyed this landmark. It was not achieved without a fight, however. Petitions were circulated and meetings were held with the net result of nothing.

Suddenly—overnight—everything was gone. The weight men and balancers came down to stare at the vacant hole that was left by "progress." They kept thinking it couldn't last, that it was all some kind of a bad dream. That dream turned into a nightmare that has lasted to this very day. Even now, after almost nine years, many of the old trainers still come down and sit in the warm sand on a summer weekend and tell of times past.

Life must go on. The Muscle Beach Gym was formed and tons of weight collected. It has since moved from place to place all over

Santa Monica. Venice Beach, a few miles down the coast, expanded its outdoor facilities to accommodate the expected rush of homeless trainees. The rush never came. Things were never the same. Muscle Beach was Muscle Beach—it couldn't be replaced.

ZELLER

The gym at night looking southwest from the rear door. Across Pacific Avenue is a block of old Venice houses, then the crazy mixed-up Speedway, then the sand and the wide Pacific. I wonder. Is the guy in the center not a guy at all, but the trainer of champs, Joe Weider? Hmmm. In flipflops?

Joe Gold did like so many others. He got together with his friends—Chuck Pendleton, Chuck Mahoney, Zabo Koszewski—and built a little training complex in the apartment house where they all lived. (Shortly after that Pendleton left for Italy where he was to become one of Europe's biggest stars.)

All this time restless thoughts stirred in the Gold noggin. Too many of his old buddies were looking for a place that would offer them the best in the way of equipment and iron—a place that was roomy and bright like the outdoors, yet had the convenience of apparatus that could best be served inside. Slowly plans began to develop. When Pendleton came back to California, Joe got together with him and they decided to become partners in a venture that was to become known as Gold's Gym in Venice Beach.

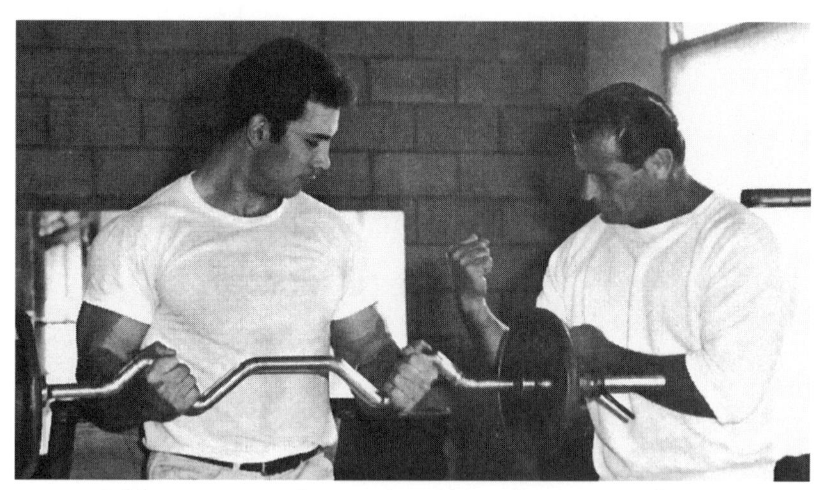

ZELLER

Joe Gold gives Ron Dipolito worthy advice at his Mecca in the summer of '68. In the summer of 2003, Ron and I talked about our friendship, which began at the Dungeon in '63 and survived 40 years of feast and famine. While reminiscing we stood in Joe's World Gym in Marina Del Rey where today Ron is a personal trainer. I believe we've gone full circle...or something.

That was several years ago and since that time Gold has struck it rich. Not just in the monetary sense of the word, but in the service he has given to the sport he loves. From the very beginning, he was determined to have a gym to reach everyone who trained. He wanted to get the businessmen, the bodybuilder and the strength athlete. All he was wanted was the man who believed in his health and was willing to do something about it. To cover this wide spectrum he needed lots of weight. He needed dumbbells that would fit in the hands of the weak and would test the arms of the mighty. With patience and a burning goal, he tooled and pieced together one of the greatest selections of weights ever assembled.

There is no one so weak he can't lift the lightest weight and no one so strong he doesn't struggle with the heavy stuff. From ten-pound dumbbells to those weighing hundreds of pounds, the place is a feast for the serious trainee. As if this wasn't enough, this man, Gold, made—by himself—the sturdiest benches and apparatus to be found in a professional gym anywhere in the world. A gorilla couldn't break any of it, and believe me, the men who train there can really give that statement a test.

At one time the Olympic sets were being bent by some of the mastedons who train in the gym. Joe decided he would have to get a better set of Olympic bars. If you haven't guessed already—Joe Gold made the bars to order and they probably are the best on the market.

All this equipment is set in a large sunny building near the beach. While it's filled with equipment of every description, it never seems cluttered.

You get the feeling you're right back at the old Muscle Beach, which is just what Joe wanted. Bodybuilders and strongmen from all over now train at this fabulous gym. Even if once again the weights were brought back to Muscle Beach, which Joe is hoping for, this would have little effect on his gym. It was born of the desire to give something to bodybuilding that had been taken away. It was forged by a dedicated man who worked miracles with his hands and his will. It will remain a monument to that man, because it's too good for anyone to ever give away.

ZELLER

Muscleheads line up like thirsty cattle at the watering trough to do their curls. Arnold looks on as Ken Waller, the Bomber and Frank Zane blast it.

•

The last few weeks have been the days of the floods here in sunny Southern California. I thought for a while our neighbors left their bathtubs running. Almost overnight we had a pool in the back yard. It covered the entire area and for a while I was thinking of planting rice. In spite of the California dew, people still get around. One of the movers was Dave Draper. The doorbell rang and I bundled up to get to the door.

"Who's there?" I asked.

"Dave," said the voice in the storm. "I've come to hear the music."

I opened the door. "Is your car radio on the fritz?" I asked.

"No, no," said Dave as he shook the rain from his coat on my floor. "I came to hear the music."

I knew immediately what he meant. I took out the records and we listened to several pieces.

"Ron Haddad, the Music Master of Muscle Beach, has the best selection of music in the world to pose by," I said.

"That's right," said Dave. "I'll take the one you're playing now."

It happened to be the musical score from the film "The Ten Commandments." Its powerful and sweeping score seems to fit perfectly into the majesty of a great posing routine. In fact, this music is the most requested posing music I know. It seems like such a short while ago that bodybuilding champions were posing to "I'm In The Mood for Love," played by a sour sax and an out-of-tune piano. Draper and the "Ten Commandments" should really impress the audiences. If they aren't impressed, they should get a new record player because what they see in the way of muscle can hardly be improved.

•

The other day I was sitting in front of my TV set looking at the Tonight Show when Johnny Carson says one of their ushers is the current Mr. USA, Chris Dickerson. Immediately I thought it would be one of those putdowns—like "Who wants to look like that?" and "Do the gals really dig all that muscle?" or "What do you plan to do with your life besides swing from trees and eat bananas?"

Anyway, there I sat braced for the worst. Suddenly Dickerson bounds onto the stage and an interview begins. To my surprise Dickerson almost takes over. He's articulate, dignified and interesting. It was an impressive performance by any standards. Then it was time for the acid test. Carson asks if he'll give a display of the muscle that won him the title. Chris stripped down to posing trunks and ran through a few poses.

To say I was surprised is putting it mildly. I was amazed. I'd met Dickerson a few times when he was out here on the West Coast, but he didn't impress me as having great potential. That shows how much I know. His upper body is rapidly catching up with his legs, and when that day comes he could be unbeatable. He looked as hard as granite and the audience seemed genuinely impressed, as was Carson. This type of thing can really give bodybuilding a shot in the arm. The image of the duck and his barbell is being replaced by the image of the professional man who enjoys training because he enjoys being healthy and strong thanks to men like Dickerson.

More of New York. Chris Dickerson was attracted to the Pearl camp of trainees in the '60s and '70s, as I recall, and maturity in behavior was one of their noteworthy qualities. Big arms, thick calves, strong backs, monster shoulders and symmetry were also among the nifty qualities they displayed. We beach guys were like rascals, man.

•

ZELLER

The power that is represented in these six guys is incredible: Peanuts West, George Frenn, Jim Hamilton, Hal Connelly, Franco Columbu and Arnold Schwarzenegger. They are a who's who of the iron game: heroes, champions, record setters, gold medalists. And get this, they're all reading the same comic book. Who's that on the back cover?

After thoughts...Just got the latest copies of the magazines in the mail today. Gee, I love seeing my things in print! When it's here in the typewriter it just looks like words, but when Joe finishes splashing it with artwork and pictures, it's something to behold—he could make the telephone directory exciting. A lot of credit should be given to the artists and layout men Joe supervises, who have helped create the Weider image of excitement and news.

Popping Questions at Arnold Schwarzenegger

I looked at the clock in our Muscle Beach office.

"I gotta get going," I said to Draper.

"But, you just got here," he replied.

"Yeah, but I've gotta interview the tree that walks like a man."

"You mean Schwarzenegger?"

"Yep."

"What a great guy," Dave enthused as he followed me to the parking lot. "No hangups."

"What do you mean no hangups?"

"Just that," he continued, "he doesn't let things bug him. He enjoys life and won't let unimportant things get to him."

"And anything that bugs him is unimportant?" I decided.

"I guess so," Dave replied. "On top of this, or maybe because of it, he's one of the most likable men I've ever known."

ZELLER

Draper, Schwarzenegger and Zane playing at work and working at play.

I waved goodbye, and after a ten-minute ride on the freeway to the San Fernando Valley, I was in front of Don Peters' house which should be renamed The Bodybuilder's Paradise. I thought I would be late, but I found Arnold hadn't arrived.

"Where is the great Arnold Schwarzenegger?" I asked Don.

He looked at his watch and said, "I talked to him and he said he'd be here soon—he's just stopping off for a bite to eat."

We looked at each other and suddenly realized the significance of that remark.

"That means he won't get here till tomorrow."

"Or until they run out of food in the restaurant," seconded Don. "Anyway, Gene Mozee is with him," he continued, "so he might be able to push Arnold to the door before too long."

Just then we heard a knock on the screen door and there, blotting out the view, was the big man himself. With him was Gene.

Dick: Hey, you guys are late.

Gene: Have you ever seen this guy eat?

We all laughed at that one. We went to the back hall so Don could show some new equipment he had just installed. It was a press and squat machine with an adjustable incline bench. To get it in the room, the washing machine had to be removed. Already Don has converted two rooms of his house into a gym and now it's beginning to creep into the kitchen. Soon the family might be sleeping on rafts in the pool, but Don will have the greatest gym in the world. One reason why he continually adds equipment is because men like Sergio and Arnold train there and they practically eat weights for breakfast. We went back into the living room and turned on my recorder.

Peters: You look better than ever, Arnold. Don't you think so, Dick?

D: Yeah, but I saw a recent shot of Sergio's arm that must be the biggest thing I've seen. Hey, incidentally, let's see an arm shot. I've never seen your arm flexed, in person.

Arnold: You've never seen a picture of it?

D: Sure, I've seen pictures of it, but never the real thing.

P: Why don't you go in back and pump up?

A: No, no, that's all right.

And at this point the Oak rolled up his sleeve and flexed. Once in a while, after seeing so many great arms, you think you've seen 'em all until something like Schwarzenegger makes the scene. Where will it all end? It's almost getting nutty. His arm was bigger than both of mine together, plus a leg. I got the feeling the weight of his arms alone was what had built his enormous shoulders!

D: Have you always favored specialization on your arms?

A: Yes.

P: I want you to know the size of his arms doesn't improve his pool game at all. 'Cause I still beat him nightly. Right, Arnold? Right? Every night before we train we play a couple of games of pool and I always win.

A: Yes, but I make you pay for that in sweat when we work out.

D: Why did you start training?

A: I wanted to be big.

D: You think you've succeeded? (That brought a laugh.) How long ago was that?

A: About six years ago.

G: Good grief, Tyler, you've been training for over twenty years. Why haven't you got results like that?

D: I've been on a layoff. (More laughter) Arnold, how much did you weigh when you started?

A: 150 pounds.

D: At the same height?

A: Yes, six-foot, one inch.

P: Tell him you got inspired by me.

D: Yeah, what was your inspiration when you first started?

A: Reg Park.

D: Are you going back to enter the Mr. Olympia this year?

A: Yes. But before that I'll enter the Mr. International in Mexico.

D: Arnold, what kind of exercises did you do to develop those arms. I mean, when you first started?

A good looking young fellow demonstrating a seated one-arm dumbbell curl. Look at those arms—the potential is there, but does he have the heart?

He has the heart of a lion and the strength, courage and respect as well.

Regal Reg Rules.

A: I did Zottman curls where I used dumbbells and rotated the dumbbells with each rep. Also cheating curls. Those were the only two exercises I did for my biceps.

D: And what did you do for your triceps?

A: I did narrow-grip bench presses and pushdowns on the lat bar. Up until two years ago these were the only exercises I ever did for my arms. With them I sent my arms from thirteen to nineteen inches.

P: Almost all the exercises Arnold does are good basic movements. They act as a foundation for his program.

D: Yeah, but you believe in doing variations now, don't you? For instance, what does your arm program consist of now?

A: Roughly, the cheating curl, the Zottman curl, and now I've added the preacher-bench curl. I had never done a preacher-bench curl until Vince Gironda put me on it at the gym. I'm getting great results with it. It works my lower biceps a great deal.

D: I talked to Vince the other day and he claims you'll have twenty-five-inch arms in six months. What do you do for your shoulders?

A: I do the press behind neck, seated side lateral raises, incline bench flys while I'm face down, and finally lateral raises with the pulley machine, one arm at a time.

D: And this is the first time you'd ever done these exercises?

A: Yes, I only used to do things like the press behind the neck. I've never done such direct moves before.

D: What do you do for your legs?

At this point we had to move again so Mozee could make a difficult pool shot. He succeeded, and with that, Peters felt it was time to bring out his special collapsible cue stick he keeps in a leather bag.

A: What do I do for my legs? First I do hack squats, then front squats, and then some leg curls.

D: What do you do for your calves?

A: Well, I do those things where you bend over and someone sits on your waist.

D: Donkey calf raises?

A: Yes. That's it.

G: He does them with two guys on him, making it over 400 pounds.

D: What do you do for your abdominals?

A: Nothing.

D: I've been doing that, too, but it doesn't seem to work out the same way.

A: I'm kidding. I do five sets every day in the situps.

D: How many times a day do you train?

A: Six days a week, twice a day. In the morning at Vince's and at night here at Don's house. Each workout lasts about two hours. I do exercises Joe Weider recommended, and in the split routine. In this way I keep the blood in the exercised areas longer. Do you want me to give you my complete routine now?

D: No, let's wait a few months until after you've experimented with the exercises Joe Weider gave you, those he feels will get you into the Mr. Olympia contest. What's your diet?

A: I eat everything.

P: Regularly.

G: He also takes Super Pro 101 four times a day, plus Insta-Power twice a day and a glass of Instant Nature Breakfast every morning. He must be breaking Joe financially!

D: Do you have any hobbies? Aside from trying to beat Peters in a pool game?

A: I used to collect stamps.

P: I gotta tell you something, Gene. Arnold's a pretty great swimmer. We were down in Florida for the Mr. Universe, staying in this nice big hotel called the Plaza, and they have a channel for yachts and other boats in front of the hotel. We were standing there when all of a sudden Arnold's gone. The next thing I knew he's swimming like a porpoise in the water!

D: People must have thought it was some kind of a great white whale.

P: Yeah, he was right in there in the middle of all the yachts and everything. What a sight. He couldn't swim enough. He had just finished with the prejudging and he comes up to me and says, "Can we go swimming now?"

A: Where I live now there are three swimming pools. The same man owns these three apartment houses all in a row, so anyone can use any pool he wants. This is good. I like all types of physical exercise. Back in Germany a group of us would get in the car in the morning, take weights and drive out to the lake and do squats until sunset. Some days we'd do only bench presses.

D: That's wild! There's something really great to that because you stimulate a muscle area like you might never get in any other way. Some like a shock to jolt the muscle into new growth. How do you like it out here in California compared to Florida?

A: I like it better here. It was too hot in Florida. Here it's hot during the day, but always cool at night. I can't breathe deeply enough when it gets too hot.

D: What kind of workouts do you take? Are they serious, or can you kid around? Some people almost shoot you if you interrupt them.

A: I train nice and slowly.

G: He concentrates while he does the exercise, but when he's through with a bodypart he'll relax and talk with anyone. He doesn't have any hangups at all. If someone comes over and asks him a question he'll actually go over and demonstrate the exercise. All the guys at the gym think he's the greatest!

D: Arnold, what are some of your best lifts?

A: I've done a 460-pound bench press, a 500-pound squat and a 710-pound deadlift.

D: Since you've been in this country, what would you say is the most interesting exercise you've encountered?

A: The press machine. Every exercise on the press machine.

P: The Don Peters Press Machine?

A: Yes. The Don Peters Press Machine.

P: Have you got that on tape?

CARUSO

When he first stepped on the posing platform, Arnold, barely twenty, displayed muscle size, shape and density not yet conceivable. It took scores of photos from different angles by numerous photographers and plenty of scrutiny by wide-eyed bodybuilding professionals and enthusiasts to conclude that what they see is what there is.

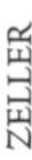

Front squats. I go, you go, he goes or is it he goes, you go, I go or you go, he goes, I went?

The Bomber, The Oak and The Stallion

SIX

1970

Golden Impressions

It all began so quietly. The men started to assemble in the cool of the evening. The sun set over the horizon of the Pacific and the soft blue of the evening was beginning to accept the blackness of night. An ocean breeze drifted across the sands of the beach and wound through the crooked little streets of the city. The lights in the homes and apartments flicked on as the windows of the hippies' pads glowed with crazy hues of blue or red bulbs and the sounds of hard rock music fought those of Lawrence Welk. It was night in the city of Venice. Still they came. First there was Zane. He quietly nodded to Zabo, who was sitting behind the desk, and went upstairs to the dressing room. Soon Franco and the current Mr. Belgium, Serge Jacobs, arrived.

Draper was next, followed by Eddie Giuliani and Mike Katz. After a few minutes, Don Peters came in and within seconds, Arnold arrived. Gold's Gym was now busting with championship lumps. Already at work was Ken Waller, who is one of the most massive bodybuilders of all time. The cannon was loaded and was ready to explode.

All this concentration of bodybuilders was for the sole purpose of getting ready for the big contests in New York. With the exception of Waller, all the others were IFBB bodybuilders and were stomping like mad bulls for the tension of the big event.

Already Zane and Jacobs were working abs. This would last for as long as an hour and a half without rest. Arnold and Draper went over to the squat rack in the corner. They started loading the bar, which was already bent from the tons of weight it had been forced to carry over the years. Katz took some dumbbells from the rack and started blasting away at his delts. Columbu was on the calf machine lifting a stack of weights that was almost taller than he, while Don Peters was warming up with some light presses.

What made the whole scene a little scary was the almost unearthly quiet that seemed to descend. Everyone was concentrating on what they were doing. This was serious business and there would be no useless rapping this night.

I looked over at Arnold, who was heavily clothed in a sweatsuit. The stains of sweat began to show under the arms and around the chest. Dave slapped more plates on the bar. Now it was his turn. Again and again he went down to the full squat position, only to fight to stand. Arnold leaned forward with each rep and counted them out.

When it seemed Dave would burst if he made one more effort, the Oak would lean even closer to the Bomber and say, "You can do it, Dave. You can do it."

Then as if in some kind of hypnotic state the mighty Draper thighs would ram out another rep.

"Do another one, Dave," said Arnold softly, another rep done.

Then it was Arnold's turn and he worked until his thighs looked like they would split his pants. There was no resting between the supersets, then both Dave and Arnold started doing sissy squat moves on the hack machine. All that could be heard was the clank of Olympic plates and an occasional yell of encouragement.

"Dick," said Arnold finally, "I think my thighs are going to come off my leg. They feel so heavy with blood. Tonight we are doing torture routine number two."

"Torture routine?" I asked.

"Ya. On Monday it's torture routine number one. That's the heavy day. On Wednesday it's torture routine number two, when we combine the heavy with the supersets, and on Friday we do nothing but supersets for the legs. On Tuesday, Thursday and Saturday, it's the same thing for the upper body."

"Why do you call them torture routines?"

ZELLER

The blood was flowing, the heat was on and the pain was welcome. We wallowed in our workouts like hogs, snorting occasionally and rooting around improvised pumping and shaping movements for added burn and final touches.

Arnold looked at me with baleful eyes under his brow, now dripping with sweat. "What else would you call a routine that makes your whole body scream for relief, that makes you want to vomit or pass out from exhaustion?"

I nodded. "Torture."

When you're done, you're done. Tomorrow's another day. Nevertheless, it is very good—splendid, in fact—when you crown the fiery, intense moments with gratitude, mutual recognition and encouragement. God's speed, brother.

"It's your turn," said Dave as he got off the leg curl machine.

By this time Mike Katz was doing presses behind the neck. He was seated on a back-supported bench and ramming out reps that forced him to grind his teeth until I thought I saw the enamel crack.

Zane and Jacobs were still doing situps. I got seasick just watching them.

"Do another set," I heard the familiar voice of Arnold roar from across the gym.

For a moment I thought he was urging Dave on. Instead it was aimed at Don Peters on the preacher bench. Don was standing in a pool of sweat. I could see his muscles twitch involuntarily.

"You want to kill me or something?" he asked.

"If that's what it takes for you to win the Mr. America this year, yes." He couldn't have made it much plainer than that.

"Okay, but I have to take a rest first."

"No," said Arnold as he turned back to the calf machine for another set, "you wait too long."

Don shook his head in disbelief and went back to another set of curls.

By this time the whole place was chugging away like a steam engine. I've never seen anything like it. There were more shouts of "Go, go, go!"

I got up on the stairs that lead to the dressing rooms. From the balcony I could see the entire gym. Everyone was now dripping with sweat. Great pools of it seemed to surround each apparatus. The smell was getting pretty musty. The yelling was increasing with the clanking of the plates. Nostrils were flared, eyes were wide and staring, teeth were grinding, blood vessels looked like they would burst and steam was almost seeping from the floor. For a moment it reminded me of Dante's inferno. No money on earth could make men toil in a hell like this, but they were doing it all for just the glory of a few minutes on a posing dais.

After the workout Peters and I walked toward his car.

"You come here every night?" I asked.

"Yes," said Don, "but it's worth every long mile. I found myself getting in a rut. I had it pretty soft. I had a whole house to train in with a pool outside and soft music on the stereo. It was pretty great if I was training to win the Mr. Pismo Beach title, but not for the Mr. America. In order to have the kind of muscle that wins the big titles, you have to suffer. It's not suffering laying by a pool and listening to the stereo playing Doris Day or Johnny Mathis. No one ever won a title with those two as training partners."

As I was driving home I began to think back on my bodybuilding past. I began to wonder if I could have ever won a physique title. Maybe, I thought, if I had really tried. I turned on the car radio. It was Doris Day.

No, I guess it's best I stuck to writing.

ZELLER

Katz and Arnold receive reassurance and advice from Dick Tyler. "Let's see, a ham and Swiss cheese on whole wheat for Mike, lots of mayo and Arnold, all you want is a box of animal crackers and a quart of milk...I get that right?"

•

I've gotta write this while I'm thinking about it. I've got bad news. My eyes are failing me. I used to be proud of the fact that I had twenty-twenty vision. I also used to think once I had seen Sergio Oliva there was nothing left to see. He was the period at the end of the sentence. Nothing was as muscular or ever would be as muscular as Sergio. Even when I met Schwarzenegger, I stuck to my belief that no one was as muscular as the mighty Oliva. Today, I saw something that made me either doubt my sanity or my eyes. It all started off with a phone call from Art. He was so excited he could hardly get out the words.

"Arnold is back in town."

"You mean he just got back from Hawaii?"

"Yes, yes."

"Hold on," I interrupted, "take it easy. I like Arnold, too, but not that much."

"You don't understand. You should see the way he looks."

My mind conjured up Arnold in a wild kind of native outfit. "Funny, huh?"

"Whatdayamean, funny! You haven't seen anything like this, Tyler."

"You mean he looks good?"

"He's out of this world."

"Well, not as great as Sergio."

"Now you're talking about the old Arnold," said Zeller.

"You mean there's a new edition?" I asked.

"I don't know what it was, but something in Hawaii changed him. Maybe it was the tan he got or the food or something, but he has lines and cuts he's never had before. He..."

"Okay, okay," I interrupted, "when do I see the new Arnold Schwarzenegger?"

A few days later I was at Gold's Gym getting a story, when in strides the Oak. The first thing I noticed was the tan.

"Arnold, Zeller tells me you look better than ever."

He just smiled.

"Well, take off the shirt and let's see," I insisted.

"Warm up first," said Art.

"Vot? Who needs to warm up?" said Arnold with injured pride. With that he pulled a Superman, only without a phone booth. Since that time, I've really doubted my faculties. I won't describe what I saw. I'm not that good a writer. He has clearly broken the muscle barrier and the vibrations will be felt around the world. For once in my life I'm left without a thing to say.

•

For the last month or so we've had so much rain out here some people started praying for a drought. People here have a crazy desire to build homes on the sides of hills...Something about a view. Every year during the rainy season—yes, we have one in Southern California in spite of what the travel folders say—more houses slide down the hills than were built on them. (That's pretty hard to do.) It got so bad I hear some houses are now coming equipped with outboard motors. Just about everyone was affected by the downpour.

One of the hardest hit was that national shrine, Vince's Gym. The gym, you see, is right up against a hill. Every time it rains, water comes rushing down the hill into the gym's backyard. For years it stood as a defiant beacon in a windswept sea during the rains of the past. This year brought a little too much rain and not enough defiance. One day the mud and water came rushing into the gym. Soon crews were cleaning up and once again it stands as the temple of power it has always been. I'll bet no one even missed a rep during the mudslide. Or to quote the immortal words of Vince Gironda, "Right."

•

September and New York seems awfully far away and yet as you read this, the Mr. Olympia contest is just about to be written into the record. Even now Olympia fever is beginning to make my massive biceps twitch with anticipation. Joe Weider didn't help any when he called to tell me of the latest happenings.

First of all, I started to tell Joe how incredible Arnold looked lately, but before I could finish Joe was telling me the IFBB director from Belgium, Juilian Blommaert, had a sensational discovery that would make Arnold look like a child. I cleared my throat.

"Wwwhat did you say, Joe?" I said. "Maybe we have a bad connection. I thought I heard you say that some creature would make big Arnold look like a kid."

"You heard correctly," said Joe with a laugh. "According to Blommaert this guy is six-foot, three inches, weighs 260 pounds and is built like a mountain with all the jagged ridges to go with a man who could be the greatest bodybuilder in the world."

The whole conversation left me doubting my sanity. I remember when it was said no one would ever be as great as John Grimek (and in some ways I believe this is still so). In more recent times it was Reg Park, then Bill Pearl, then Harold Poole, then Larry Scott, Dave Draper, Chuck Sipes, Sergio Oliva, Arnold Schwarzenegger and now a new one. Each of the aforementioned men has at one time been considered the greatest in the world. At present, this year's Mr. Olympia contest might very well decide who truly is the greatest in the world.

Now I hear about this new guy who'll also be at the contest and I don't know what to think. Just when I reconcile my thinking to the fact that I know all the answers, along comes the startling info about a bodybuilder better than all the rest. I'd better stop trying to set limits on physical standards. After all, if God had wanted men to fly he'd have given him wings, wouldn't he?

•

The other day the former Mr. Western America, Dan Mackey, dropped by the office. I knew it was him the moment I pulled into the parking lot. Not just by the muscles he wears, but by the roses. No, he doesn't hold one between his teeth or wear one in his hair—he wears them on his eyes. Let me explain before you think I've had mental atrophy. You see, Dan wears sunglasses that are rose colored. At first I thought it was pretty dumb—that is before I put them on myself. You know a view of the world through rose-colored glasses ain't bad. I almost hated to give them back and look at a three-color globe again. Soon Dave Draper came out of the office. In a few minutes Art Zeller drove up with Arnold Schwarzenegger. It was getting crowded and everybody's looking rosey.

Finally Bill McArdle arrived and I thought we might hold a convention. I'm now in the market for rose-colored glasses, but the people in the stores think I'm selling a philosophy instead of trying to buy a product.

Peters, Mackey and Draper, AKA Don, Dan and Dave, hoist a surfboard full of pretty girls, Sandy, Betty and Dot. The ocean beyond looks like a vast lake on a peaceful day. So much for the stunt we planned to perform, the six-high human totem pole on the board catching a giant wave from a mighty south swell. You'd have to see it...

ZELLER

•

If you go up to Vince and innocently ask, "What's cooking?" you might get an answer like "crushed mushrooms marinated in guava sauce," or "stewed eggplant au gratin." He'll be referring to the restaurant to be opened above his gym. That's right. Vince is going into the restaurant business. Actually, the Italian anatomy chart will just be leasing the place to a group of health food gourmets and devotees. From what I understand, John Barrymore, Jr. (son of the famous actor and a fine actor one in his own right) will be doing the cooking with Roger Montgomery and Don Howorth helping out.

I went upstairs the other day just to check things out and had quite a surprise. What the place lacks in size, it more than makes up in quality of decor. I was particularly impressed by the massive furniture which I understand was all done by Dave Draper.

"Pick up one of the chairs," said Vince with a sly grin. I took one hand and started to move it into the table. Nothing budged. I took two hands and tried. The only thing that happened was my knuckles turned white trying. I looked under the chair to see if it was bolted down.

"Dave sure makes heavy furniture, doesn't he?"

"Well," I said, "if the meals are that heavy you've got a problem."

I was assured only the finest and tastiest health foods would be served. From the description of the menu I started to salivate. They are obviously taking their time to come up with a quality product that should be well worth your stomach to discover. Oh, yes, it'll be called the Earth Foods Inn and is located above Vince's muscle pit.

•

While on the subject of the venerable Vince, I think I'll relate another little bit of information. You may not know it, but Vince

WARNER

Very tan and symmetrical, Vince Gironda had clear and specific ideas on how to build a physique. They had to do with pinpoint focus, total concentration, maximum muscle intensity and you didn't dare squat. Chins and dips and hack squats and sissy squats earned a trainee As. Protein from meat and eggs won honors. Carbs were frowned upon, which meant the possible loss of a tuft of hair. Vince liked discipline...that's good.

has a gym and a half. This half-gym consists of apparatus like chinning and dipping bars that are on a platform outdoors beside the gym. It started out as a major project for those who wanted to train with the rays of the California sun bouncing on them while they heaved the iron. Enthusiasm waned and what is left are some bars and a platform hanging onto the main building. While looking over the equipment I asked Vince who used it.

"I do," he said with a grin.

"What do you do?" I asked.

"I take a workout that lasts twenty minutes."

"And you can get results from that?"

"The way I do—yes."

Naturally I had to ask the way he takes a workout.

"First," said Vince, "I chin for ten reps, then do ten pushups followed by ten dips. It's, of course, all done without a pause between sets. This is then repeated until I've done the whole thing ten times over. So far, I've been able to do it all in twenty minutes and I'm aiming to cut that time down."

Just looking at the amazing Gironda physique makes you wonder how he does it. Then he gives you a routine he's working on and you realize it takes wisdom on the shoulders of experience to do the trick. Whatever the answer is, the results speak louder than these printed words.

•

Local physique sensation Art Peacock was sitting at the opposite end of the table at Java Time, the local Santa Monica hangout for many of your musclemen. It's a nice little restaurant that really packs the food on the plate. We had just come from a show, so there we were: Art and Josie, Frank and Christine, Peacock and yours truly.

"You know, Dick," said Peacock in his clipped British accent, "I don't want to criticize your writing, but don't you think you've told the story of Zeller and his car door too many times?"

ZELLER

One day "they" got together and selected rocks of varying sizes from the nearby rugged coastline. Shaped and polished, the stones were carefully placed on top of one another until a fine form appeared. They covered it with exquisitely thin skin and stood back. They marveled and called it Art. Art Peacock.

I nodded. "Yeah, I suppose so. But every word of it is the truth. Of course, Zeller has other little quirks that are worth writing about."

Zeller wiped his mouth and took a big swallow of water. "Like what?" he said challengingly.

"Well, for one thing, people have to touch your photos in just the right place."

"Right," agreed Zeller, "so it won't hurt in reproduction."

Everyone agreed that made sense. It began to look like I was picking on poor Arturo. After a few minutes Zeller said, "Frank!"

Zane looked up.

"Behind you."

Frank looked around. His back was to the wall, so there wasn't much to see.

"The picture on the wall is at an angle," said Artie.

Zane glanced at the picture behind him and nodded, "Yeah," and went back to eating.

"Well," said Zeller.

"Well, what?" Zane took another mouthful of food.

"Don't leave it like that."

"Like what?" asked Zane.

"Straighten the picture out!" said Zeller with growing impatience. Frank looked at me and then at Art. He saw he was serious; turning around he straightened out the picture so that it was fairly level. This wasn't good enough for Zeller, who kept fighting until the picture was perfect. I looked over at Peacock.

"Well," he said with a shrug. "Guess you've got another story."

•

A few weeks ago Zeller got a long distance call from Arnold Schwarzenegger, now known professionally as Arnold Strong.

"Listen, Art," roared the big man, "I'm here in New York starring in the movie "Hercules in New York."

"I know," replied Artie.

"Why don't you come back and watch me work?"

"That would be fun," Zeller assured him, "but I can't afford to take the time off from work."

"I'll pay half your fare," said Arnold.

Zeller was startled to say the least.

"Why?"

"Because," said Arnold, "I want you to take photos of what's going on. No one takes pictures like you, Artie."

Well, that was too much for any man's ego, so the following week Art was on his way to the big city. He had many adventures while there, but one of the most amazing he related to me was about a chariot ride. The ride didn't take place just in Central Park as you might expect. It took place right down Broadway. Can you just picture big Arnold dressed as Hercules and riding a chariot on Broadway right behind a cab? I wonder if he had to stop for the red lights. Bet someone mistook him for a hansom cab.

Zeller said the Oak drove by a girls' school and created a panic with the ladies packed in at every available window as they screamed their adoration. Tough life, ain't it? And all you need is good looks and one of the greatest physiques the world has ever seen.

ZELLER

Before Arnold came to America he was a poor farm boy living in Austria. In a rarely published photo we see Schwarzenegger as a lad tilling the fields outside his hometown of Graz seen in the background. Oops. Wrong caption. I'll go with the original as printed in a muscle magazine some thirty-five years ago: Arnold Strong is Hercules in New York.

•

Quite often at this point, I toss in some of the gossip written in times past by that great master of the muscle world, Earle E. Liederman. He was associated with Weider Publications for close to fifteen years and in my neophyte stages of bodybuilding I found him a great source of inspiration, as did so many thousands of others. Liederman's career spanned many years as a strongman, athlete, stage performer and writer. In the latter he achieved great prominence in the field of literature outside of physical culture. I have never met such a memorable person as the Earle of Hollywood.

Now he is gone. He was in an auto accident, the injuries in turn caused pneumonia while he was fighting to recover. The complications of emphysema made the battle for life too long and hard for a man of his years to win.

The last years of his life were spent in a small room by himself. He was writing until the very end. He never retired from life, even though he was well into his eighties. I pray the spirit of this great man knows peace and that we all take the example of his life as a guidepost for our own. Farewell, my friend.

•

Good news for bodybuilding fans on the West Coast—Joe Weider is coming our way. No, I don't mean into your home, but pretty close. He's decided to move his headquarters to the land of palms, sun and sand. Actually, this isn't a sudden move. He's been contemplating it for quite some time. You might say he's been edging towards the door for the last three or four years. The holdup has been in Joe finding the right area to build. For a while it was going to be right at the ocean. Then it was going to be in the hills overlooking the ocean, but now it looks as if he'll construct his new offices in the land of Robin Hood. That's right, Robin Hood.

The office will be built on several acres of the old Warner Brothers ranch in the San Fernando Valley, where Errol Flynn once cavorted before the cameras with his merry men. It won't be like any office you've ever seen. Probably the most interesting thing will be the Hall of Fame dedicated to the immortals of bodybuilding. Life-size portraits are being painted of the greatest. Recently, Arnold showed me a photo of the one being painted of him. I looked at it wistfully.

"I wonder if they'll do a portrait of me?" I asked.

"What?" howled the Oak, "A life-sized portrait of a typewriter?"

BELLAS

One of the very best men in the world, Dick Tyler. He wrote the words that compile this book, the words that entertained and inspired us thirty-five years ago in the middle of the greatest era bodybuilding has ever known. That time has become fondly termed the Golden Era of bodybuilding, those years when the sport had matured enough to become something grand, but not so mature that it was old or imitating itself or in love with itself or all used up or tiresome. Few people have a talent—a sensitivity—to see life as it is and embrace it and have fun with it and offer it to the reader with love and understanding. He's an all-American healer, straight from the heart.

•

Just got the latest issue of *Muscle Builder.* Wow! Is that Rick Wayne great?! Every edition seems to get better. Rick does the editing now and it's a true labor of love. Shows doesn't it? Also in the same issue is the ballot for the greatest bodybuilder. It showed photos of some of the great champions of the past and present. I was shocked to see I wasn't represented. You can laugh, but one year I was voted in something like ninety-sixth place by twelve of my admirers. Let's see there was Mom and Dad, my wife and kids, etc. Well, here's your chance again. Remember to spell my name correctly—it's G-R-I-M-E-K, or, is it S-C-O-T-T? No, it's D-R-A-P-E-R, or maybe Z-A-N-E. Anyway you get what I mean.

•

Got a letter recently from my old buddy, Chuck Pendleton, who's still starring in movies in Europe.

In his latest letter he told me about someone we all know and admire—Steve Reeves. Are you ready for this? Chuck told me Reeves will soon be running a giant health club in Yellowstone Park. Now don't stampede up there. Give the guy a chance to catch his breath.

Thinking out loud—I wonder if this has anything to do with the multi-million-dollar resort project the famous newscaster, Chet Huntley, is investing in. Steve has always been an excellent businessman and I've got the feeling this great Mr. America/Mr. Universe and former movie Hercules will be where the coins are gold. Anyway, a tip of the Tyler tin cup to the big man.

•

The month between September and October will go down in bodybuilding history as one of the wildest we've ever had. In that period two Mr. Universe titles, a Mr. World and the Mr. Olympia title were decided. I'm writing this just a week and a half before the Mr. Olympia contest and already the roots of bodybuilding have been shaken.

ZELLER

Behind the scene: Me, Arnold, Frank in the center, our buddy from Holland, Serge Jacobs, and Artie Zeller framed in a mirror hanging on the wall. I'm just glad to be there. Summer of '70, preparing for shows in September from New York to London, Columbus to Munich.

In early September Franco Columbu beat the great Chuck Sipes for the IFBB Mr. Universe crown in Yugoslavia. Two weeks later the NABBA Mr. Universe contest was held in London. The line-up was the best the contest has ever enjoyed. Competing were Chris Dickerson, Franco Columbu, Frank Richards and Frank Zane in the amateur portion and in the professional ranks were Reg Park, Boyer Coe, Dave Draper and Arnold Schwarzenegger. Wow! Zane, Richards and Dickerson each won their height classes, with Zane winning the overall amateur Mr. Universe and Franco Columbu taking the Most Muscular title. Schwarzenegger beat Park, with Draper taking third and Coe fourth.

•

You know, in the magazines we try to bring as much of the excitement of bodybuilding to you as words and pictures will allow. Even though I pull out the cork on my barrel of adjectives at times (okay, most of the time) and the magazines are filled with the most exciting and inspirational photos of physique greats ever published, it still doesn't take the place of the real thing.

You've got to be there to make your own value judgments. You've got to be there for this swelling excitement of the audience. No words or pictures have been able to capture the excitement of thousands of screaming fans and the inspiration that comes from viewing a truly great champion.

I remember for years I never thought John Grimek was so great. Then I saw him compete for the 1949 Mr. USA title and since that time I've thought of him as the greatest all-around bodybuilder who ever lived. The photos and words could never begin to capture the greatness of Grimek. You had to see him to believe him.

This is true of so many of today's bodybuilders. I remember seeing photos of Rick Wayne. He looked great. He was massive and cut up, but he wasn't in the immortal class as far as I was concerned. A few nights before the 1965 Mr. Universe contest in New York, Rick arrived with Earl Maynard to compete in the big event. After dinner Joe Weider, Maynard, Wayne and I went up to the photo studio for some pre-contest shots. Joe was bubbling with excitement.

HANIGAN

No book about bodybuilding that has 160-some pictures among its pages and speaks in any way of its history is allowed to be printed without a photo and mention of John Grimek. Grace and power were his before the sun rose high.

KAYE

Rick Wayne was a rare combination of muscular beauty, might and a strong mind. He was cool, insightful and confident. Ambition stirred in his blood, but he channeled it into the rivers of determination and righteous accomplishment. Rick added highlights and color to the canvas of the Golden Era with his writings, observations, opinions and competitive participation. I'll bet he's as ripped as ever today, 2004.

"Rick, take off your shirt for Dick so he can see that arm!" Rick did and this was the first chance I had to see him in the flesh.

"Wow!" was the only thing I could think of saying. Not too brilliant a remark, but it seemed to sum up what I saw. Wayne has to be one of the great muscular phenomena of our time. The reason for all this build-up is simple. Reg Lewis has made arrangements for Ricky to appear on the West Coast for the first time—he'll give an exhibition at the Mr. Western America contest. On the same event we've programmed exhibitions by Schwarzenegger, Columbu and Zane. If that isn't enough, we're also having the Miss Western America contest and some surprises. This promises to be the most exciting Western America we've ever had. Nothing I can tell you about it can match what your own eyes will see, so don't miss it.

•

I think you should know more about Draper. I don't mean how he blasts his biceps or devastates his deltoids or terrorizes his thighs. I mean you should know more about the man under the muscles. I know you dig hearing about the glamour and the fun, but many fail to realize the champion has the same problems and sensibilities as anyone else. The fact of the matter is Dave was often unhappy. Sure he has everything going for him: looks, muscles, a beautiful wife and child, a great home overlooking the blue Pacific, a movie career and an ideal job.

How could anyone be unhappy with a setup like that? Most people would give their eye teeth for such a deal. Not Dave. It wasn't that he was playing the prima donna. Quite the contrary. Few men I have ever met have been more self-effacing or filled with as great a sense of humility. Dave's biggest problem seemed to be summed up in one word—pressure. He couldn't take the great wad of it that came with success.

For years he trained for the sheer joy of it. Eventually he found he was training to be at an almost constant physical peak. He never knew when he would be called upon to give a posing exhibition or have photos taken. He couldn't afford to relax and be anyone but Dave Draper, champion bodybuilder. Finally he decided to chuck it. He loves training too much to let it turn to hate.

Fortunately, Dave loves to work with his hands. He began concentrating on woodwork and presently is one of the finest carvers of trees I have ever seen. Each piece of furniture he makes is a masterpiece that will be a monument to the person long after he has left this mortal scene.

He's happy now. He's doing what he likes. He trains the way he likes and the only weights he carries about his shoulders is in the form of a barbell. As a result he's never looked healthier and more muscular.

ZELLER

Arnold would come up to me in the middle of our off-season training and ask things like, "What should I do with my future, Dave, I'm so mixed up?" or "Do you think it is okay if I talk to girls, Dave; I'm very shy?" or "How can I make money so I can rent a room and buy sneakers for my feet?" I would say, "Arnold, you stick with me, kid, follow my moves, do what I do. Got it? Watch close, kid, 'cuz I'm fast." I like helping him out, you know what I mean. He's like a big puppy.

•

I know I told you this before, but I've got a purpose for telling it again. A few months ago the human lens—Zeller—brought his latest photos of Zane over to view. When he's proud of his work (which is always) he'll go further than a king-sized cigarette to show you what he's so proud of. I must admit these were the best photos of Zane or, for that matter, any bodybuilder I had seen. It seems like I'm saying this all the time.

ZELLER

Amazing what a tan, good lighting and twenty years of intensive training will do for a guy. Frank Zane is perfect. I personally like ugly a lot, but perfect is also very interesting. You can put Frank in a big jar, shake it vigorously and toss him on the sand and in whatever position he pops out, it's perfect. Weirdest thing.

The only other set of pictures that have ever been comparable in my eyes was the set that Zeller took of Don Howorth at Howorth Rocks. The photos of Zane have the brilliance of a diamond with an almost three-dimensional effect. To make the picture literally complete, Zane looks sensational. On the strength of the photos alone he could rank as one of the greatest bodybuilders of all time.

CARUSO

One of those photos the day after competition in New York City. Nerves are still raw and energy is confused with adrenaline. Jimmy Caruso was behind the camera and Joe was behind Jimmy. Arnold, Ricky, Franco, Draper, Chuck Collras and Frank Zane were before the camera.

What a mob.

•

Sometimes we have some of our most sound reasoning when we think twice about something rather than when we make a snap judgment in the heat of frustration and disappointment. Arnold has always had a pretty cool head in this department. The closest I've ever seen his face come to a look of tragedy was when it was announced that he had been beaten by Sergio Oliva for his first Olympia. Up until that time the word defeat had never entered his mind. I used to wonder what he would do if by an outside chance he was beaten. No sooner did the look of disappointment come, it left. He was the first to embrace Sergio and raise his arm as a symbol of victory. Still, I wondered what the long-range effect would be on his training. The answer is nothing. He accepted the loss, as close as it was, with a shrug and a smile.

"Just wait until next year. I plan to be 250 pounds and cut to ribbons." You could see he meant it. He seemed to reflect for a minute. "You know," he said, "Sergio is truly amazing."

We all agreed.

"No, I mean unbelievable," Arnold protested. "All during the show I kept watching him. I watched him in his robe and when he was stripped down for training. I thought, 'This man is nothing.' He looked out of shape and fat. I was quite pleased and felt sure that I had an easy win."

"Did you ever think differently?" I asked.

"Oh, yes," the Austrian Oak replied with a broad grin. "It was the most fantastic thing I have ever seen. There I was standing right behind him as his name was called to come on the stage. He just stood there talking to someone. They called his name again. He did some more pumping exercises. I thought the audience might leave. He finally took off his robe and something seemed to happen. He changed before my very eyes. Right before my eyes he pulled in his waist and spread his lats. I mean this, it was like two completely different people. The fat man became one of the most muscular men I have ever seen. I couldn't believe the transformation I witnessed in the space of a couple of seconds. That last contest he was a great winner."

"And this year?" I asked.

"Oh, that's different," said Arnold, "I beat anything in the world then." He meant every word of it, and this is precisely what he went on to do.

Friendship forged by muscle and power. Arnold leans a mighty forearm on the colossal shoulder of Sergio Oliva. Their expressions of contentment say another fierce workout has just been completed. How good does it get?

•

It seems young people of today have this thing about change. That's great as long as they don't ignore the past, which had been the prologue of the life they lead today. In strength and bodybuilding I'm always surprised that so many weight trainers have such a lack of knowledge about the history of their sport. I know of one well-known physique champion who couldn't give you the name of a bodybuilding or strength great who existed a single day before he started his own training. This is pretty sad, especially when we have so much history to be proud of.

It's for this reason that I was doubly happy when I heard Frank Zane was going to give a series of exhibitions in the California schools. Frank made a tremendous impression with the performance he gave at the school where he teaches. This eventually led to his being contacted by the California Association for Health and Physical Education to develop a muscle-and-health act to be given in schools around the state. At this point Frank is in the middle of the preparations, which he hopes will lead to a great expansion of his activities. He hopes he'll be traveling and spreading the word about weight training a la George Eiferman. The nice thing about Frank's act is it will be based on the classical strength presentation of the Sandow days.

"You've got to capture the imagination of kids if you want to hold their attention," said Frank recently. "Once you have their attention, it's up to you to get the message across."

Frank, with the aid of the romance of yesterday, will relate to the kids of today. If the message is heeded, we could see the inspiration of the champion of tomorrow.

•

The Biceps of the Sardinian Samson
Franco Columbu

Francesco Columbu sat alone in the room that was lit by the glow of a television set. He was looking at one of his favorite programs, the wrestling matches.

"And now," said the interviewer, "let's talk with the sensational strongman who just won the match—Hercules."

The screen was then filled with the massive bulk of the wrestler.

"Hercules," continued the interviewer, "you've been going all through Europe and you haven't lost a single match. What would you say is the secret of your power?"

The big wrestler smiled. "My strength. I am one of the strongest men in the world."

"That's a pretty big statement," said the interviewer.

"Well, I'm a pretty big man."

"How can you prove such a statement?"

Hercules thought about that for a moment.

"Well," he said, "arm wrestling is a pretty good test of a man's power and I've never been beaten, so I'll just offer to take on any man alive in an arm wrestling match in the center of the ring."

That was a challenge to everyone listening and Francesco Columbu was listening.

Several weeks passed and the interest in the arm wrestling grew with each wrestling show. Hercules was as good as his word. With ease he would dump the best arm benders in the territory. The word was getting around that this was no phony wrestling promotion; this was the real thing. Hercules was indeed a genuine strongman in every sense, a weight-trained powerhouse who wasn't shy about demonstrating his power. By this time some of Columbu's friends were beginning to prod him into accepting the challenge.

"But, he's so big," Francesco would modestly protest. "What

chance would I, a 175-pounder, have against a man who weighs nearly a hundred pounds more than I do?"

"And who was a genuine strongman to boot," said one of the men standing nearby. That did it. Francesco had quite a reputation as a strength athlete as well as a great bodybuilder. Just to infer that he was not a genuine strongman was not to his liking. No, he would accept the challenge of Hercules. He would sit in the middle of the ring, and on television, before his countrymen, accept the challenge of the great Hercules to do battle in arm wrestling.

The following week the word had gotten around and the arena was filled with enthusiastic strength and wrestling fans. While Francesco was genuinely admired for his enormous power, few of his greatest fans felt he stood much of a chance against the massive wrestler.

At last the moment arrived. The announcer took the microphone as the mighty Hercules stepped through the ropes.

"And now ladies and gentlemen," he said, "the mighty Hercules issues his customary challenge to one and all to engage him in the manly sport of arm wrestling."

With that a table was brought into the center of the ring and chairs placed on either side.

"Come," repeated the announcer, "there must be some men out there who want to show their lady friends how strong they are."

Then, with considerable prodding, one giant of a man fumbled his way into the ring. The audience gasped at his size. Surely here was a man to really test the vaunted power of Hercules. The contestants shook hands and sat at the table. They clasped hands and prepared for the referee's signal. Hardly had the command to start been given before Hercules had his opponent's knuckles embracing the table—he won with ease.

"Nobody can beat Hercules," someone yelled. Then, almost unseen, Francesco stood up and made his way down the aisle.

SANTANGELO

Who more appropriately stands among the remaining granite columns of the great Roman Empire than Franco Columbu? The mighty man himself resembles a statue of stone sculpted by a thick-hand master 3,000 years ago.

"Come now," said the announcer, "there must be other men out there who would like to test their strength."

The attendants prepared to remove the table and chairs.

By this time Francesco was in the ring. No one, however, paid any attention to him. He must be one of those cleaning up the ring.

Francesco tugged on the announcer's sleeve.

"I wish to accept the challenge."

The announced looked startled. "Are you joking?"

Francesco assured him he wasn't. With a smile on his face, the announcer once again stepped to the microphone.

"May I have your attention, please? We have one more challenger."

The attendants put the table and chairs back.

"From the island of Sardinia, we have a challenge of Francesco Columbu."

Francesco stepped forward. A wave of laughter swelled throughout the vast arena. It must be some kind of gag. How could one so little have the nerve to challenge one so big? The laughter only made Francesco all the more determined to make a good showing. Hercules patted him on the head in a mock gesture of condescension.

"All right, my friend, we'll play some games," he said as they sat and readied to do battle.

They engaged hands and waited for the signal.

"Go!" cried the referee. With incredible speed and power Francesco rammed Hercules' fist deep into the wood. The audience could hardly believe what they had seen. They began to cheer and applaud. Hercules immediately stood and grabbed the microphone.

"Wait," he cried, "I wasn't ready. He was gripping the table and prepared before I had a chance. I'll show you how I can beat him."

Francesco agreed to a rematch and once again they sat across from each other. This time the mighty Hercules wasn't smiling. He had tasted the power of the Sardinian Samson and he didn't like it.

As they prepared for another match, Francesco took his free left hand and held it high above his head in obvious scorn for the remark Hercules had made about gripping the table. The crowd was delighted. They had found a new hero. A David to challenge Goliath.

"Ready?" said the referee. "Go!"

This time Hercules went down to defeat even faster than the

first. Pandemonium broke loose and Francesco Columbu was immortalized in the hearts of strength fans.

ZELLER

Mike Katz and Franco bench pressing at Joe Gold's sanctuary.

This story was told to me by Arnold before Franco arrived in this country. That story, along with the photos I had seen, made me quite anxious to meet this amazing athlete. It was not until a couple of weeks after our first meeting that I had a chance to see him in posing briefs. It was at Gold's Gym right after a workout and he decided to practice his posing routine. What an incredible sight. Then he flexed those arms and I was astounded by what I saw. They almost didn't look real—as if someone had carved a sculpture of a baseball on his arm. I had to find out how he got such shape and power.

When I asked Franco what Weider training principles he uses in his arm workouts his swift reply was "almost all of them."

He added, "Wherever I go, to every country, show or exhibition, whatever gym I visit, I find all the champs using the Weider training principles. They use the split system, the double split, supersets, forced reps, flushing—you name it, the champs are using them."

"For my arm workout I use the cheating principle. This enables me to handle the heaviest poundages possible, so I can keep my arms bulked up with massive size. In the other four exercises I use the peak contraction and continuous tension principles. I perform these exercises strict style, slowly, tensing all the way up and down as this helps to build shape and definition into my arms. I always combine the two principles because it enables me to keep and build my bulk as well as keep my arms shapely."

"I also apply the forced reps principle in every exercise, forcing out with all I've got the last two reps. I do each set as if it were my last. If I do not get a powerful force-out in the last two reps, I feel I have cheated myself."

"And I believe in total concentration, by feeling the action of the movement all the way from beginning to end. I concentrate so deeply on the movement that I can actually sense the full movement of the muscles as they contract and relax."

"In all exercises, whether cheating or using strict style, I fight the weight all the way down. I never let it drop. I work my biceps twice weekly; just before a contest I may work them three times a week."

"I vary the way I do my arm exercises—sometimes in superset fashion, incorporating a biceps and triceps exercise. But when I am really out to blast my biceps, I do all six exercises one after the other with a slight pause between each set."

"I want to advise all the readers if they want large arms, they must build up their weight, because without bulk large size is almost impossible to get. I have found if I add ten pounds or so of weight, my arms will grow a full inch, solid and muscular."

"If I have the time," Franco told me, "I will enter the arm wrestling championships back in New York."

When I told him there would be two weight classes, he laughed. "I beat them all," he said, "And, Dick, will you mention in the article that although I haven't met Joe Weider and will not see him for a week or two, I am grateful to him for having paid my way to the USA and also my expenses while here so that I may train with Arnold, Dave and the Weider gang. He must be a very generous man, as well as a brilliant man to have done so much for the sport. I am looking forward to meeting him and working out with him. Arnold keeps raving about Joe and the workouts he takes, even in his late forties."

When Franco C. is not in Rome doing as the Romans do, he hangs around with Eddie G. They make a good pair, serious about life and the wonders it has to offer. Here Franco dangles by his toes and does some sort of brilliant inverted row as Eddie encourages him. Right, guys.

ZELLER

CARUSO

One of my all-time favorite physique photos, the champion is discovered candidly at work backstage readying his body, mind and soul for the judges and the fans. His preparations are successful, everything's in order; he's up, he's on, he's pumped and the audience is packed. "Arnold, stand by...you're next, go." And the house came down.

SEVEN

1971

Mr. Pacific Coast Report

It started as an off-hand remark by Frank Zane and grew into what promises to be one of the most exciting series of contests presented on the West Coast.

Frank Zane was facing the blackboard and explaining a math problem to his students at Mark Twain Junior High. He could hear murmuring behind his back and finally turned to see what was causing all the commotion.

"All right," he said as he put down the chalk and wiped his hands, "What's going on?" There was a short silence. "Well?"

One of the boys timidly raised his hand for recognition. "Mr. Zane," he began amidt some snickering, "are you a muscleman?" Now there was embarrassed laughter all around.

"Do I look like one?" asked Frank.

At that point no one seemed to agree just what a muscleman looked like.

"Haven't you been in muscle magazines?" asked one of the kids, "There's a guy in one of them looks exactly like you."

"It is him," said another boy. "It said Frank Zane under the picture."

"Did you ever win the Mr. America title?" asked another. Everyone was talking at this point.

"Okay," said Frank holding up his hand. "Let's have some quiet. Yes, I'm what you call a muscleman and I was Mr. America."

As you might imagine, nothing in the way of math got done for the rest of the day. Up until that day Frank had always been liked by the kids, but now he was a hero. What surprised him most, however, was how little the kids knew about physical culture.

The more he thought about it, the more he felt a physique and strength demonstration in the school auditorium would be just the thing to educate his pupils and all the others to the benefits of weight training.

With this in mind, arrangements were made and a show was put on one afternoon after school was let out. It was a tremendous success and this started the Zane brain thinking about putting on a full-scale IFBB contest at the school. It was at this point Frank contacted Ben Weider. Arrangements were made for the sanction and for financial support of the event and I was notified the proper arrangements had been made and to aid in whatever way I could. The next step was to find someone as a co-sponsor of the event.

Frank wanted someone to work with whom he felt was not only enthusiastic and energetic, but also commanded the respect of the bodybuilders. The one who filled the bill to overflowing was Arnold. Now two great men of muscle were in the harness together and there would be no stopping them.

Saturday night at the Mark Twain Junior High School Auditorium in Venice, California, Frank Zane and Arnold Schwarzenegger presented the Mr. and Miss Pacific Coast contest for 1971. It had been raining earlier in the week, but now it cleared and the evening skies were sparkling with the good news. It seemed like an omen of things to come.

The show began a little after eight with all the contestants onstage for the playing of the National Anthem. Frank and Arnold were fortunate in securing the services of Ron Haddad and his Magic

Music, so the Star-Spangled Banner matched the stars in the sky. After this impressive beginning, it was time for the contests to begin. Zane acted as the emcee for the first part of the program and introduced the contestants for the Miss Pacific Coast crown. What a great job this is—just imagine calling that work.

Next on the bill was "Mr. Charisma" Franco Columbu. I say this because I know of only a handful of people who are born with an ability to charm. All Franco has to do is walk on the stage and the audience is pulling for him. Maybe it's his smile or the way he combs his hair, but whatever it is, if it could be sold I know a lot of people who should buy it. (I'd be standing in line, right behind a certain photographer named Zeller.)

ZELLER

Looks like 495 to me. Franco must be doing reps. I've never met anyone as strong as Franco, who can lift enormous weight in an exhibition of bench press and deadlift strength, blow up a hot water bottle, tear a license plate in half and then slap on some oil and give a knockout posing routine all in one night. And he smiles and jerks around though the whole catastrophe.

Franco started by doing some deadlifts. The heaviness of the bar was visually projected to the onlookers when the spotters couldn't even lift one end of it to add more weights. The next thing he did was bend a large metal bar held in the vice of his teeth. This left the audience gasping. So he could be gasping too, Franco ended this portion of his act by blowing up a hot water bottle with the power of his lungs. The shock waves from one of these things exploding is almost enough to blow you out.

An appropriate follow-up on the bill was an endurance contest for some of the teenage athletes in the audience. This event had everyone cheering like they were at a football game.

The object was to see who could clean and press a weight the most repetitions. The first boy did eight reps. The second pressed the bar ten times, with the third contestant upping that to fifteen reps. The final entry, who was bigger and older than the others, decided that he would win the contest fairly by pushing the weight out as often as he could. Since he was the last contestant he knew all he needed was sixteen reps to win. Instead he put his muscles in gear for a fine thirty-seven reps. It's nice to see the youngsters competing in strength events. Makes you think the future of weight training is in good, powerful hands.

For a change of pace, Franco came out again to give his posing routine. I'd say a good half of the audience had never seen a physique contest before, so you can imagine the impact his muscles had. As soon as he finished, Zane turned the microphone over to me. Since I babble like I write, I had the feeling some of the people might edge toward the door. With a good show like this was proving to be, however, I didn't have to worry.

Now it was time for the Mr. Pacific Coast contest. Since this was the first time for this IFBB title, we only had four contestants. The quality, however, made up for the lack of quantity. Another nice thing about this contest was just about half the judges were with the AAU. This is the way it always should have been and this is the way it will be from now on. The music and the lighting combined to give the crowd more than their money's worth and those judges got a tough exercise in figuring out who would win what.

After the contest, Frank Zane came out again. This time it was to give a posing exhibition. The previous day Frank, Arnold and Franco had been in Palm Springs to soak up all the rays from the sun. They wanted to look their best for the show they were producing. I can tell you now, the sun wasn't wasted on any of them as the audience went wild watching Zane glide from pose to pose to the strains of the music.

The next act defies description. Before I introduced him, he was shoving bananas, candy bars, books, funny hats and marachas at me. He was prancing around backstage like an organically grown carrot with a hot foot. (Whatever that's like.)

"Now, when you introduce me, say something about my new book, "Barefeet and Good Thinks to Eat." I assured him I would. Five minutes later it would be something else he would want me to add. In self defense I finally got him onstage with, "And now, here's Gypsy Boots!"

For the next ten minutes it was Gypsy's show. It's hard to review his act since he hasn't really got one. It just...happens...until he's pulled off the stage. Got to give the guy credit. He's almost sixty years old and he has the energy, strength and endurance of a kid of sixteen. Maybe it's in the carrots he eats. Whatever it is, it works and while we laugh at his antics, he should be given credit for forcefully demonstrating good health.

At last it was time for what most of the people had been waiting for—the Oak was going to pose. Arnold had trimmed down from 240 pounds to 220 pounds for his first exhibition since winning the Grand Slam of bodybuilding. He had just defeated almost every great bodybuilding champion by winning every major title within a few short months. He didn't disappoint anyone and assured us he would compete for many years to come.

"I don't want anyone to ever have to wonder if I could have beaten the tops in their day." He said with a smile. "I'm going to be around so long there won't be any doubt."

After Arnold's triumphant exhibition, there was nothing left but to give out the awards.

ZELLER

Eddie Giuliani has rock hard muscle and it's piled up in a most appealing way. That's good. But Eddie has something nobody else has. Filed away in his exhaustive mind and available at a moment's notice is his immeasurable collection of bodybuilding stories. They have been directly gathered from coast to coast over forty-five years by uncanny observation and meticulous storage. Some have been passed on by word of mouth from reliable sources and most of them are true...though a little elaboration never really hurts. He is a bodybuilding historian in his own right, and I think of his colorful sagas as cartoons vividly depicting the craziness of the world of bodybuilding and its classic characters.

Ed Giuliani won the Mr. Pacific Coast crown, plus the Best Chest and Best Legs awards. Chuck Fautz came in second and earned the Best Back, Best Abdominals and the Most Muscular awards. Third place was won by Russell Eiler, who also grabbed the Best Arms award. This guy is a relative newcomer and should be a top winner in the near future. Randy Harris came in fourth.

The awards were topped off with the presentation of the IFBB's highest honor for service to bodybuilding, the Certificate of Merit, which went to Arnold. As the president of the IFBB for the United States, I did the honors and I could tell he was visibly moved. It seemed to mean more than all the titles he's won so far because it was given not for what he's done for himself, but for what he's done for bodybuilding.

After the show I stepped into the cool California night. It had been a good contest, the beginning of many from the muscular IFBB-approved hands of Schwarzenegger and Zane.

•

One of the nice things about bodybuilders is they seldom become bored or blasé about their sport. Some, like myself, collect old magazines and films on strength and bodybuilding. Ed Giuliani is one of those people. The other night he showed a film that had been taken at recent contests. Big Arnold happened to be there and he was pretty excited by what he saw.

"Can you believe some of these men?" he asked me recently. "Giuliani showed films of a contest that Chuck Sipes was in and I've never seen anything like it."

"Good?" I asked, knowing what the answer would be.

"He was terrific!" enthused the Oak. "He had everything. His arms were especially massive. I couldn't believe it. His arm went all over the place. It was fantastic. One of the shots was of Bill Pearl, but his didn't begin to compare with the arm of Sipes."

STERN

Bill Pearl is found by heavy light pouring down from the sky above. The shadows are thick, the contrasts are ice-cold and the blackness is fearsome, yet alluring. The sound of steel is heard in the dark silence, and the heart is pierced. Inspiration.

"Now that's really saying something!" I said in surprise. "Pearl must have one of the most massive and well-proportioned arms of all time. How could Sipes be that good?"

"Believe me, Dick, it is so."

"Don't get me wrong. I think Chuck has two of the greatest arms in the world, but to indicate that it wipes out the arm of Pearl is pretty hard to swallow."

“Then take a large gulp,” said Arnold, “because Sipes is that good.”

I haven’t seen the films yet, but my appetite is sure whetted. Makes me wonder if Chuck will be entering the Mr. Olympia this year. And wouldn’t it be something else if Bill Pearl entered?! He’s one of bodybuilding’s immortals—it would be nice to see him in action again. And not just in an exhibition.

•

I don’t like to brag (not much), but do you realize the great service I’ve done for bodybuilding? I’ve assigned nicknames to many of the famous bodybuilders. I’ve told you this before, but some seem to forget the fact. The other day I was really hurt when Dave Draper was in my new chiropractic office and said he didn’t know I had made up the “Blond Bomber” title for him. He thought someone else had. It all came about when Joe Weider wanted me to think up a title for Dave’s letters column. I came up with “On Target with the Blond Bomber.” I freely adapted it from the Brown Bomber handle attached to the great fighter Joe Louis.

After that it was all fun and games as I came up with the Sardinian Samson for Franco Columbu, the Austrian Oak for Arnold Schwarzenegger, Sandman for Zabo Koszewski, and the Black Knight for Sergio Oliva. And I mustn’t forget ole Stretch Marks whose blubbery body is scarred from exploding fat and whose mouth is the most muscular thing about him. Some unkind people might suggest I modeled Stretch after me, but I come back with the witty retort, “Oh yeah?”

•

Reg Lewis is entering the Mr. Olympia contest this year; I just got the word from him over the telephone. Actually this doesn’t come as any big surprise. Reg has been teasing himself with the idea for a couple of years now. The final straw came at a recent party. They were showing old films of great bodybuilders. He couldn't take all the derisive remarks he heard about some of the men who were developed along the more classical lines. Reg believes strongly in the Steve Reeves approach to physical perfection. This means he is a silhouette bodybuilder. He believes too many contests are being judged along the wrong lines, too many men are being judged solely on mass rather than where that mass is put. You might say Reg's entry into this year's Mr. Olympia is a protest action.

When he called, he told me he wanted me to print his decision in the magazines. This way it would force him to enter, instead of procrastinating about it as he has in the past. Okay, Reg. There it is. Now you have to enter. If you've never had the opportunity to see this Mr. America in action, you're in for a spectacular treat.

•

I went to the AAU Mr. California contest the other evening. I went mainly because I wanted to see Boyer Coe. I'd seen many of his pictures in the past, but never the muscles in person. The whole evening turned out to be something of a social event. I was even looking forward to the intermission so that I could get up and visit all my friends. I came with Reg Lewis, but almost didn't leave with him because we became separated several times.

The guest list included George Frenn, Peanuts West, Armand Tanny, Zabo, Bill Pearl, Joe Nista, Arnold, Franco Columbu, Artie, Chuck Fautz, Ron Haddad, Don Peters and so many more I can't think of all the names right now.

One thing was lacking from the whole evening: music. Just the deadly sound of the contestant's feet slapping the ground and the droning of the announcer's voice like he was reading the latest stock market quotations. The Master of Ceremonies for the girl's contest was different. He went to the trouble to tell the audience how rude they were and that he'd been watching the country go to hell for the last fifty years, which was kinda thoughtful of him when you think about it.

•

Bits of chalk…Sure wish Eddie would stop laughing at every thing Zeller says. It only causes the mouth to tell more rotten puns and jokes. I also wish Zabo would stop mellowing. Listening to him used to be half the fun of going to a contest…Some of the clothes worn at the AAU Mr. California show were almost more exciting than the contestants…Jim Morris, who won the senior title, has promised to let me do a story on him. He's got a great set of muscles and a great personality…Peanuts plans to retire from powerlifting competition this year. Wants to end it all with a win in the upcoming power meet with Great Britain. Whatever he does he'll go down in history as one of the founders and pioneers of the sport. Think I'll end this column on that high note.

•

So I was telling you of all the nicknames I've made up for the different bodybuilding champs. The Austrian Oak, the Blond Bomber, the Black Knight and others are mine, do you hear, mine.

So anyway, I've been thinking for a long time that Rick Wayne must have some kind of emblematic objective. After all, he's one of the most well-known bodybuilders in the world and he deserves more than just his name. He deserves an accolade. Recently Rick gave a posing exhibition at the Mr. Western America show that was pretty unbelievable. His body looked like a battlefield with all its mountains, ridges and fortresses. You could almost see the battle being waged by his abdominals on his serratus and his biceps looked like they were about to attack his deltoids. Every time he moved to another pose it was accompanied by visual explosions of muscle.

With the music supplied by Ron Haddad, he came across like a mighty fortress of muscle and power.

That was it! Rick Wayne was The Fortress of bodybuilding. I'm now taking this opportunity to enshrine Rick in the Tyler Hall of Name. I'm putting him between Zabo "The Abdominal Sandman" Koszewski and Wayne "SuperStar" Coleman. I can't think of a name for myself. I let others do that; so far none of them are printable.

•

The other evening I had Rick Wayne, Joe and Betty Weider and the Zellers over for dinner. Joe brought along his plans for the new Weider office, plans that would have made anyone jealous.

"I want to give something to bodybuilding and bodybuilders they can be proud of," said Joe, as he rolled the plans out on the floor for all of us to look at. Believe me, you feel the pride that comes with knowing you're a part of all this muscle madness.

After dinner I took everyone to my chiropractic office. It was the first time Joe or Rick had seen it. Would you believe the doctor next door complained we were making too much noise laughing?

We just got back to the house when Larry Scott arrived. He had been to a Hawaiian luau and stopped by for a visit. Larry no sooner got in the door before Art was trying to roll up Rick's sleeve for an arm shot. After some coaxing, Rick let fly with a biceps that made me wonder if the dinner we had earlier had been spiked. You have to blink when you see it. The eyes can't accept everything at the first glance. First you have to believe that blood vessels can get that big in an arm, then you have to talk yourself into believing an arm can get that big and still be well defined. Once you've done that you've got to accept the idea that the arm really belongs to a human being and not a statue of Hercules. Having done all that, you might begin to understand the impressiveness of that moving club attached to the Wayne shoulder.

CARUSO

You see some bodybuilders and notice right away they brought their muscles with them. They carry them around like they were baggage or extra gear; you know, a duffle bag full of the tools of the trade, maybe contraband. Whatta ya got in the ole' sack, buddy? Laundry?

Rick Wayne's muscles go wherever he goes because they belong to him and they fit just right. They curve when they should, they emerge where they ought to and, though these fine muscles are large and rock-hard, though they are mounded on top of one another, they flow together with rhythm and rhyme.

His body is poetry, but Rick's a journalist and he sure can write.

After everyone had recovered from the sight, Scott was prevailed upon to give a demonstration of his biceps flexion. At a bodyweight of 165 pounds, he still has that fabulous Scott shape and separation. Incredible. After a while our conversation drifted from muscles to such things as religion and philosophy. It was an interesting and pleasant evening for all of us, especially me.

•

The Mr. and Miss Western America contest has just been concluded and it was a lot of fun as always. The guest posing routines by Don Peters, Reg Lewis and Rick Wayne were the highlights of the evening. Another event that kept the eyeballs working overtime was the Miss Western America contest. The second girl to pose gave a dancing routine you couldn't believe. After that it was almost anything goes. Now that's what I call a contest.

The men didn't do any dances, unless you want to call muscle-control dancing. The winner of the title was Leon Brown with Chuck Collras second, Chuck Fautz third and Eddie fourth. Brown also took every division except Best Abdominals which went to Collras.

In the afternoon we had the long-awaited power meet between Great Britain and the United States. The lifting was fantastic, especially that of George Frenn. It seems a pity more people don't support the sport. When I think of all the money and effort that was expended to get the power meet together and then look at the handful of spectators on hand for it, I get sick. Most gave the excuse that five and ten dollar seats are too high-priced. I'll bet they'd pay that much and more to go on a date or to get the car fixed or go to Disneyland. But when it comes to supporting with cold cash something you've been giving lip service to, and to get to see world-record-breaking lifting as a bonus, well, that's just not done. In spite of the crowd, or lack of it, the whole contest was good, with plans already made for next year's event.

•

Bits of chalk...The rumor has it some new European gorillas are training at Vince's, but it's so secret only the weights and Vince know their names and Vince isn't talking...Thought of another name for Ricky Wayne. How does Wonder Wayne sound? Incidentally he is one of the few bodybuilders whose arm you can touch without it going into a muscle spasm. He's relaxed all the time and doesn't take but a few minutes to pump up before posing...Reg Lewis posed for me in my living room the other day and looked in great form...Frank Zane also posed for me recently. This time it was in my office. I understand he got the greatest reception of anyone in London in September.

•

About twenty years ago Monty Wolford was a pretty active bodybuilder around Southern California. Suddenly—and I do mean suddenly—he was gone. I don't mean that he drifted away or anything like that, I mean he disappeared. Once in a while I'd hear his name mentioned as if someone was talking about a ghost. Last I heard, he was living with his family in the wilderness near Yosemite National Park in California. Suddenly, a few months ago, he sprung up on the sand dune of Muscle Beach like a pop bottle. (I don't know what I mean either.)

More recently, Monty and his beard journeyed with a group of us down Mexico way for the Mr. International contest. During the ride he kept us all entertained with some pretty great stories. For instance, didja know Monty was known as the Mahatma of Mash—long before the movie came out? He could mash his arms into his sides so they looked like they measured twenty inches while he was posing. Actually Monty's arm only measured a cold fifteen-and-a-half inches, but he could pump them to a massive eighteen inches. In case you're too lazy to count, that's a pump of two and a half! The only problem was he said it would suck all the blood from his face. Another good one was the pump he could get on his calves. He had fantastic legs, as some of you gray beards out there might remember. He could pump his calves until they would meet with his feet four inches apart and his knees two inches apart. Why, I know some guys whose calves don't meet unless they cross their legs.

•

In order to be a champion, a man must subject himself to rigid discipline and a degree of torture. What is most important is he must be willing to sacrifice certain comforts for pain. The rewards are obscure to some, but not to the real bodybuilding enthusiast.

I personally used to include something I called punishment reps. That's where I'd punish myself with extra reps if I didn't do as well in a particular set as I had planned. One day while I was doing chins I dropped off the bar because I was sick that day...even vomited. As soon as I was through—vomiting, that is—I climbed back on the bar and did extra reps because I dared to fall off before the set was through. Insanity!

The other day, however, Arnold Schwarzenegger came pretty close to my kind of nuttiness. He was too sick to work out one day and the following day he had to make up for what he missed in addition to that day's training. So the Oak gets Franco Columbu and Dave Draper to train with him by doing twenty-five sets each for the lats, chest and shoulders. That's seventy-five sets (I know, you can count), all done in an hour and forty minutes...seventy-five sets in a hundred minutes. Wonder what he'd do if he were sick for a week!

ZELLER

It's dark down here. He'd have to dig a hole to go any deeper. Full range of motion—providing no body part is compromised—is important for power and ultimate development. It's also a discipline and was the only way either of us gained approval from the other. Arnold under the iron bar and the Bomber leaning against the concrete wall.

•

There have been some great entrances in show business. John Wayne walking into a saloon, Charlton Heston descending from Mount Sinai. Mike Katz walking on stage to pose. As for Katz, he's something else again. I mean just to look at him is enough to inspire awe. That upper body of his has to rank as one of the all time great masses of blood vessels, muscles and bones. Only a fantastic entrance is worthy of its display. At the recent Mr. International contest in Tijuana, Mexico, he made such an entrance. The posing platform was made from a couple of tables in the middle of the audience with some tables placed end to end leading up to it from the stage. As each bodybuilder was called, he would separate the stage curtains and walk down the runway to the platform.

STUDIO

Eddie Silvestre had a gym in Tijuana and we went down to visit when life was loose. It was a big and open space crawling with Mexican lifters and there were no rules and regulations in particular. Lift, toss, drop, roll, throw, yell, and howl, Arriba Amigo, Aye Chihuahua, and Chiquita Banana. We always left with a pump and natural hallucinations.

When the former Mr. Universe Eddie Silvestre called Mike's name there was a long expectant pause. Suddenly Katz burst—and that's the best word for it—through the curtains. It was a startling appearance and it bowled the audience over. He walked down the runway like he owned it, and he had the muscles to back it up. He should have special curtains imported for every place he poses. It's worth it.

•

All right now here's the bet, and I suppose it's all legal since it was made in Mexico. Art Zeller and Monty Wolford were talking about great feats of strength and endurance while walking down the streets of Tijuana. Naturally they got on the subject of the mighty Marvin Eder. It wasn't long, however, until they were on the subject of one Monty Wolford. Monty is a great one for endurance. He once held the Muscle Beach chinning record with something like fifty-six chins. That's all the way up and all the way down.

"I'll bet a guy could do a hundred chins if he really trained for it." said Monty simply.

Art looked shocked. "Are you kidding? It would be impossible for any man to ever do that many chins."

"Any man?" asked Monty.

"Any man."

There was a pause.

"I'll bet I could do it," said Monty finally.

"Are you serious? No man is capable of doing that."

"I'll bet I could," insisted Monty. "In fact, I've got a thousand dollars that says I can."

"Let's make it ten thousand and I say you can't. I'll even give you three years to succeed."

Monty maintained he didn't need that much time. Only a few months would be needed. So from now until three years, ten thou should travel from Art to Monty or Monty to Art—if they decide to hold on to the bet. Do any of you reading this know of someone who can do a hundred good chins without stopping? If you do, Zeller might be in trouble.

Artie really might be in a spot with that bet because Wolford isn't too far out of condition right now. He's got Frank Zane on a leg routine you wouldn't believe. The whole routine is finished off with a run up a flight of 172 stairs several times. No, it's not Jack and the Beanstalk. The stairs actually exist. They lead from the beach to the top of Pacific Palisades. That would be 172 reps several times like a superset. Guess who holds the endurance record for the run, Zeller? That's right. Your betting buddy, Monty Wolford. He's gone up and down those 172 steps—which rise 125 feet—twenty-three-and-a-half times in an hour. The very thought of that makes me want to mortgage my home and bet on the Wonderful Wolford, but I don't bet. I haven't bet since I sunk all my money into the sheet music for the song "Welcome to the White House, Mr. Goldwater."

•

Bits of chalk...I was looking at the television the other night when on the screen comes the wrestling. Earl Maynard, the former Mr. Universe, was in the feature bout. If you haven't had a chance to see him in action you're missing one of the most exciting wrestlers in the world. The following day Schwarzenegger calls my office and says that someone wants to speak to me. You guessed it: Earl Maynard. I hadn't talked to him in a few years. I understand he plans to enter physique contests again. From the way he looked on TV, he could be winning! One of the nicest men I've ever met—great sense of humor—has to have one if he reads my junky stuff...Former Mr. America and Mr. Universe George Eiferman now has a daily show in Las Vegas TV. I hear his gym is booming like the city. Couldn't happen to a nicer guy.

•

Now be honest. Doesn't this sound like a great show? A movie all in color and sound, over an hour long and about bodybuilding and weight training in general. Huh? With such great bodybuilding stars as Hugo LaBra, Zabo, Larry Scott, and Olympic champs like Parry O'Brien, Hal Connolly and Ike Berger. How could such an enterprise be anything but a success? How? The name of the film was "Project Power" (this was the film in which Chuck Pendleton held the opening part back before he became the film star Gordon Mitchell), and it was produced by yours truly when surfing films were the big thing.

One night in 1961 it was released (some say it escaped) to the public at Hollywood High School Auditorium. The public's reaction was overwhelming apathy almost to the point of sleep. The greatest enthusiasm of the evening came at the end of the program when the captives rushed for the door. It was almost dangerous if you were caught in the aisle when the film ended. I got the feeling the picture was ahead of its time so I decided not to show it again until the audience grew up a little.

After a couple of years I gave it to a film rental agency and sat back to watch the money roll in. For five years I waited. In disgust I took my film away from them and decided to show it once again to a select audience. This time I picked carefully. Who could be a better audience than Arnold? After all, he hadn't been warned or, I mean, told about it. It would be fresh and exciting to a guy who hadn't seen or heard of the film before.

The night I chose to show the film was the night of a party at Don Peters' place. It might be the last time I'm invited there. The film served as a great conversation piece. That is, they were able to talk over the sound of the film. I looked at everyone laughing and talking and having such a good time and was happy the film wasn't interrupting.

Have I given up? No, siree. I'm looking for a world's fair to use it in a time capsule. Who knows? Two hundred years from now people may want to know how much guts we had in these days. After seeing the film they're bound to realize it took a guy with a lot of nerve to make it and fantastic guts to show it.

•

I've heard it said truth is more exciting than fiction. Over a period of years I've sometimes had cause to doubt that saying, but an incident which recently occurred at Gold's Gym makes me wonder. It all happened one night not long ago when the gym was packed with its usual muscle denizens. One of the boys really digs the incline bench and had worked his way up to quite a sizable poundage. He was able to get the poundage up rapidly because he would bring the bar to the chest with incredible force. He wouldn't just let the bar drop to the chest, he'd literally pull the weight to himself until he could almost bend the Olympic bar from the force. I suppose he felt it was some kind of a super bounce. He was warned by almost everyone that what he was doing to get the weight up might cause him a great deal of trouble as the weights got heavier. He wouldn't listen and continued pulling the bar into his chest with great force.

This particular night he finished a set and got up to walk away. Suddenly he began to sway. Before anyone could help, he tumbled to the floor as if he'd been pole-axed. His head hit the cement floor like a piece of lead shot. In fact it literally bounced. People ran over to help him up. He didn't move. His eyes were closed and his lips parted. Something's was wrong—seriously wrong.

George Frenn elbowed his way through the crowd that had gathered.

"What's wrong?" he asked.

By this time the young lifter's mouth was turning blue.

"He's not breathing," Frenn yelped as he leapt forward and started to give mouth-to-mouth resuscitation. Thus began the battle to save a human life. George worked until the sweat was pouring from his brow. Still the bodybuilder didn't respond as his face started to turn blue. George started to pound on his chest hoping to stimulate any heart action that might have ceased.

"Breathe, breathe!" he yelled frantically.

The young lifter's face was turning ranker by the second. In desperation Frenn lifted the man in his arms and started squeezing him around the chest to force his lungs to work. At last there was a gasp for air and a man's life was saved because of the efforts of George, who wouldn't let death win. The young man was taken, unconscious, to the hospital. The following week he came back to the gym. Everyone seemed astonished to see him walking around.

"How do you feel?" someone asked.

"Fine. Why shouldn't I?"

"Don't you remember what happened?"

"Yeah, I heard I got a little faint."

"A little faint! Man, you nearly cashed in your chips and went to that great gym in the sky!"

"Are you kidding?" said the young lifter.

Everyone just stared as he loaded up the bar and prepared to do his incline presses.

•

I guess most of you who know me realize I'm a Sergio man. By that I mean I admire a thick-set and rugged type of physique. This does not mean I think size is the major criterion in judging a physique. Muscularity is the key that takes in not only size, but definition, separation and shape. A lot of the mirror men, however, go for bloat. They think the only thing that matters is a twenty-two-inch arm on a five-foot, two-inch frame.

ZELLER

Here we go again. There are no adequate words. The arm is an attitude. I give it my best: Sergio Oliva playing pool in a hat and wearing a gold bracelet.

•

This may sound absurd to you who might be reading this, but it's not as farfetched as it may sound. A friend from out of town recently told me he knew of some jerks around his area who were saving their money so they could go to some doctor who could pump them full of plastic like some ladies with breast operations. This time it would be for bulging biceps and triceps.

The most unfortunate thing about all this is that some of you reading this will wonder if you, too, can get a plastic job. If you do, you're nuts. You'd be even nuttier than those who are now drugging themselves to death with steroids. In a recent editorial I mentioned with horror the specter of men so monstrous in size from steroids they would be unable to move and would have to be pushed around in wheelbarrows. I personally thought that was a disgusting idea, but Joe Weider called me the other day to tell me he was deleting the reference because he felt that too many reading the piece would want to be that big and then be inspired to take the drugs. C'mon there, say it isn't so. If any of you would take a chance on sacrificing your health for a couple of inches of biceps you need emotional help more than physical.

•

The other night I saw Chris Dickerson on television again. It was his second Johnny Carson appearance, maybe you saw it. Actually it took some determination on my part to see the thing. The previous week he had been scheduled as a guest of the substitute host Jerry Lewis. Either Lewis has a thing against muscles or there just wasn't time to get him on. Twice during the week Dickerson's appearance was announced, only to be canceled. When Carson arrived back on the scene the following week it was a different story. He had Chris on during an earlier show before he won the Mr. America title. The impression he left with that first appearance was good, so Carson wanted him on again.

The first time he was an usher and the fact that he had muscles was more of a curiosity than anything else. This time he was a guest in every sense of the word. Since Dickerson is an articulate individual, he creates a good impression. People begin to catch on that muscle doesn't sap the drain of its vitality and all that foolishness. I was a little disappointed in the audience reaction to the actual display of muscle. The first time it created a small sensation. This time his posing met with virtual silence. Of course, if Johnny had had Arnold up there, that would have blasted the most complacent person off his rocker with disbelief.

Ed Corney—The Incredible Hawaiian Transplant

WARNER

Ed Corney is a long-time friend and one of my heroes. His body is magnificent and his personality glows, but his posing can slow your mind and excite your heart, send a chill through your body and warm your soul.

A tremendous hush fell over the audience as this newcomer went through his polished performance. Few had heard of this sun-bronzed athlete, but it was obvious he was destined for stardom in the physique game.

I remember some jerk in a gym say once that all physique contests were the same.

"You see one, you've seen them all," he said in a matter of fact way, as he put down the two-pound dumbbell he was using and shuffled his skinny arms and legs into the shower. It always intrigues me the way some people will go to a muscle gym to get in shape and suddenly become authorities on everything in bodybuilding. By this particular goof's reasoning, all books are the same, so all we have to do is read one and we've read them all.

That's the great thing about bodybuilding—the contestants are as individual in their personalities as they are in their physiques. Sure, you can always find someone who reminds you of this or that person, but in the last analysis, Larry Scott is Larry Scott and Arnold Schwarzenegger is Arnold Schwarzenegger. The only similarity is that their last names begin with the letter "S."

I love going to physique contests. Bodybuilders are the wildest bunch of dedicated hard-nosed, single-purposed men you ever wanted to know. There's never a dull moment either in the audience or backstage. If you've never been to a physique contest—just try it and see.

A couple of years ago, I went to an AAU show in downtown Los Angeles. I used to enjoy waiting to see what new men would make their appearance in a local meet. No matter how great the present champs are, there is always someone climbing up the ladder to become tomorrow's hero. As the house lights darkened a hush fell over the audience and the contest began. There were the usual oldtimers who picked up fringe trophies year after year and there was a sprinkling of new boys to make the show entertaining.

Then they announced the name Ed Corney.

CARUSO

Ed Corney works hard for his trophies and he loves every uncompromising, aching, sweating and delirious minute of it. Heavy weights and big food in the off season; intense, precise training and meticulous eating as the contests approach. Living is one grand achievement. "Thanks for the trophy and the handshake, Joe, but I do it for my Rottweilers. I like that mustache."

On to the pedestal jumped a sun-bronzed athlete who made everyone sit up. It wasn't that his arms were so large or that his abs were so well defined or that his legs were so well balanced. What made most of the audience so impressed was he had so many good things placed in just the right places. To put the icing on the cake, he was able to display this in the most artisitic posing routine I had seen in years.

Often a bodybuilder will think a posing routine is great if it's weird. I've seen them get into all kinds of contorted positions and twirl around like a ballet dancer in an effort to dazzle with movements and obscure the vacuum left by the muscles they don't have.

This wasn't the case with Corney. He had the ammunition and he knew how to deliver it. Of all the men who appeared in the contest that evening, he was the one I remember. I couldn't tell you who won the event, but I sure remember Ed Corney.

Ed is one of the late starters. He didn't begin serious weight training until he was twenty-five years old, and he didn't enter his first physique contest until almost ten years after that. Fortunately he's made up for lost time. Ed is the kind of person who takes his time in deciding a course of action, but when he does decide, he clamps on and rides to the end of the line.

Born and raised in Hawaii, he eventually moved to Northern California. It was there he met Millard Williamson and the course of his life was changed. Williamson is one of the best physique men in that part of the country. It's little wonder Ed was astounded when he first saw him. One of Corney's favorite sports is volleyball. It also happens to be the favorite of Williamson. After a game they played, Ed introduced himself to the man he had been playing against just a few minutes before.

"I've never seen muscle like yours," said Ed. "Did you get it from training with weights?"

"That's right" replied Williamson. "Weights are the fastest and most complete way of developing muscle ever devised."

"I always thought that weights would slow you down, but you're one of the best volleyball players I've ever seen."

Williamson looked astonished. "Weights don't slow you down. In fact, proper weight training and nutrition only make you faster and better coordinated."

Corney couldn't argue with what he had seen with his own eyes.

In the days that followed Ed kept thinking how he too would like to have muscles like Williamson. Why couldn't he? After all he had the proper number of arms and legs. What was to keep him from building them the way he wanted to? With this idea in mind,

Ed became a man of great physical purpose. Under the tutelage of Williamson, Ed's great natural potential began to assert itself. For years it began to assert itself. In fact, it asserted itself so much that people began to wonder why this physical phenomenon didn't enter any shows.

Ed always responded that he wanted to train only for health and appearance and not for the cups he could win. Still his naturally competitive spirit kept digging on his biceps and urging him to get in there and try the waters of bodybuilding competition.

The right moment seemed to arrive. The year was 1967 and they were holding the Mr. Fremont contest in the Central California area. The pressure mounted and at last Ed Corney entered his first event. He won the title handily and the taste of victory whetted his appetite for more.

Soon he was garnering titles right and left. He won such events as Mr. Northern California, Mr. Central California, Mr. Western USA, Mr. Pacific Coast, Mr. West Coast and most recently Mr. California 1971.

With each contest his posing routine has improved along with his physique. Ed feels the presentation of his physique is almost as important as what he presents. With Clarence Ross, one of the great posers of all time, teaching him the art of physical display, he was bound to come out a winner.

Recently Ed came to another major crossroad in his life. He placed fourth in the 1971 AAU Mr. America contest. Was this to be his lot? Did a man of thirty-seven have to spend years of apprenticeship before he would be allowed to win the big title? One evening he decided to call Arnold and get his suggestions. The Oak let Ed know in no uncertain terms the wave of the future of bodybuilding rested in the hands of the IFBB. This was the deciding factor. Now he was ready to enter the big leagues. He would enter the IFBB Mr. America contest.

As one of the judges, I heard of Corney's entry and looked forward to his posing at the prejudging. I was not to be disappointed. Ed stands about five feet, five inches tall and usually tips the scales at 170 pounds. At that height and weight he sports eighteen-inch arms, a forty-four-inch chest, thirty-inch waist, sixteen-inch neck, twenty-four-inch thighs and sixteen-inch calves. He has bench pressed 400, squatted with 485 and deadlifted 500.

ZELLER

One more rep, and another. Don't stop. You can pause, my friend, but you can't stop.

This combination of power and physique, along with his fantastic posing routine, makes him one of the most formidable Mr. America contestants around. Time and again the judges asked Ed to come back and pose with others so we could get a comparison. He never suffered by this comparison with any of the contestants no matter what the height.

The evening of the show was filled with all the excitement that only a major event like this can generate. People milled around in the lobby of the Aquarius theater talking about their favorites. I was surprised to hear the name of Ed Corney so much. In the space of a very few years he had become quite well known to the bodybuilding public. He knew this and wanted to create the best impression possible. As a result he trained harder for his entry into the IFBB than he ever had for any other event. For two weeks before the show Ed trained three times a day every day of the week. He was determined to be in the best shape of his life.

The moment his name was announced and the music swelled, I knew the audience was in for a treat. He almost stole the show from some of the greatest names in the sport of bodybuilding. Before he left that night he was to claim third spot in the Mr. America contest and Most Muscular in his height class, along with the overall Most Symmetrical award and the Best Poser title.

This was a tremendous step for Ed, but he wasn't satisfied. His competitive spirit was now at full steam. The decision was made to enter the Mr. USA contest in New York City, and Ed went back into concentrated training. Ed faced a most formidable group of men in New York—Harold Poole, Charlie Fautz, Leon Brown, John Biancolli, John Maldonado.

The show was the high point of Ed's career and his hard training and polished display overwhelmed the audience and the judges. Although a relative unknown just a year before, he carried off the Mr. USA crown, the Best Arms, Best Legs and Best Power trophies.

Quite a night for the Hawaiian star, but those who have seen him in action feel it's only the beginning. Ed is destined to become one of the greats in the sport in the coming years and readers of *Muscle Builder* are indeed in for a treat.

The future? It's just getting under way for Ed Corney. Although he didn't start bodybuilding competition until he was in his mid-thirties, he's making up lost time by winning just about everything he decides to enter. A dedicated and interesting individual, his life and training methods will be most valuable to everyone interested in making improvements.

•

Not long ago a great sporting event took place which few of you know about. It was a race to end them all. Or maybe that should read, it was a race that could have ended it all. Especially the careers of Franco and Arnold. It all started when Franco decided that he couldn't live without an Italian sports car. For a month or so he looked everywhere for the car he wanted. He was just about to despair when he came across an item in the paper that offered a used Alfa Romeo for sale.

This was it. He was tired of running around in Arnold's German Volkswagen. He wanted to be behind the wheel of an Italian wonder car. Franco bought the car and immediately challenged the Oak to a race on the freeway.

"My Volkswagen against your Alfa?" asked Arnold, "I don't stand a chance."

"I know," nodded Franco. The following day was Sunday and in the morning the freeways are almost deserted. They started going along until they hit a pretty fast clip, then Franco took off, leaving the bug crawling along. A few miles later Arnold saw Franco standing at the side of the freeway hailing him.

For a moment he thought he was going to try to rub it in. Not so. Franco had to stop because the wonder car had dropped its oil and he blew the motor. Arnold still has fond memories of his little VW pushing the Alfa Romeo to the garage. He's anxious to bet on an endurance contest, but Franco doesn't believe in gambling now.

•

From the "nice to print" news department comes this one. Got a letter from a young man in New Jersey explaining that his high school had a drug problem. This young man wanted to know if I could suggest a speaker who would be willing to take the time to speak before an assembly. The first person I thought about, quite naturally, was Chuck Sipes. But Chuck lives in California while the school was in New Jersey. Still...

So, I suggested the young man contact Chuck. A few months went by and I had forgotten about the letter. Then another one arrived from the boy who sent in the original request. Chuck Sipes had gone to New Jersey and given one of his memorable exhibitions of strength and physique along with a lecture on narcotics. Naturally he wowed everyone and was the house guest of the boy who wrote the letter.

They were all tremendously impressed with Chuck the man, as well as Chuck the bodybuilder. There's nothing clever or funny about this item; it's just nice to print it.

•

Over the past few years, I've had a lot of fun at the expense of Art Zeller. All good-natured of course. Isn't that right, Artie? Art?

Anyway, you've read about Art's car and the famous doors, or how particular Art is about the way his possessions are handled, or his lust for food. I've beaten those bits into the ground. The other night, however, I went to a party at Frank Zane's apartment and Art got a boost from his lovely wife that she wanted printed. You see, Arnold was making remarks about Art's capacity to eat copious amounts of food.

"Are you counting?" said the Oak to Franco Columbu.

"Counting what?" asked Franco.

"The number of times Art goes back to the buffet table for extra helpings. I've counted three times already." We all laughed.

"The other day," continued Arnold as he glowed with the anticipation of what he was going to tell us, "Art ate fifteen meatballs. That's right, fifteen meatballs. I kept a careful count." More laughter—except from Josie.

"Yeah," said Art, "now Dick'll print it in the magazine. I'm getting a little tired of reading about my kissing the food and all that baloney."

At that point Josie leapt to Art's defense. She's beautiful when she's angry. "Why don't you mention something else?"she asked.

We all looked at her. "Like what?" I asked.

"That my Artie happens to be the greatest lover in the world." There was silence. "I mean that and I'd like it printed. Art Zeller is the greatest lover in the world."

She meant every word. So okay. What more could a guy ask for? He's undeniably one of the greatest physique photographers in history, so he's the best at his work and his wife thinks he's the greatest lover in the world. Is there anything left?

•

WARNER

We see Steve Reeves as a young man displaying his potential. Obviously, this is his first visit to the gym 'cuz he hasn't yet figured out the proper way to grasp the bar. I'd say he's spent most of his time doing calf raises in his garage. I didn't know the man, but the best tribute I can pay him is this: If I entered a "who do you want to look like" contest at the mall or on radio station WKRP, I'd have to say, "Steve Reeves." Absolute perfection is fascinating.

I know this is a gossip column, but every now and then I think it's a good idea to put in some training advice as a bonus. What made me think of it was the result of the latest popularity poll.

Steve Reeves won first place, which is pretty incredible when you think about it. Most of the people who voted for him probably never saw him in action, but he's still their favorite. One of Reeves' favorite exercises was the incline dumbbell curl.

His training partner for a long time was Gordon Scott who played Tarzan in the films. Scott was later a training partner of mine and he said that he and Reeves did a variation of the incline curl that seemed to give better results. If you have a training partner you can do it, too. It's simple. Just lie on the incline bench with a dumbbell in each hand. Have your training partner kneel behind the bench. He then places his hands slightly above your elbows and pushes forward enough to give your arms a substantial restriction. Now curl and see the difference. Have fun. Look what it did for Reeves.

•

Bits of chalk...Larry Scott told me that he likes to train in a crowded place like Vince's. Says he likes the vibrations of everyone working together closely for the same goal. Incidentally, Larry is back hitting the weights—just to keep in shape—and he's left the field of electronics and gone into selling insurance for New York Life. How about that? He's taken up bowling, too...The other evening Frank Zane was lying on the floor and pushing a small bench overhead. Said Frank, "This is the only true bench press." ... Schwarzenegger and Zane have found a great new forearm developer. They take turns churning homemade ice cream. The pump is great and the ice cream is delicious...Zane was in my chiropractic office the other day and posed in front of the mirror in the examination room. He looked thicker and better than ever. Said he weighed about 205 pounds...On that I'm sure you'll agree it's time for me to leave.

•

Well, another show of shows was just held at the Aquarius theater in Hollywood. The show was the IFBB Mr. America contest and the place was the theater that had recently been used for the West Coast production of "Hair." If the Mr. America show hadn't turned out well, I suppose they might be calling us dandruff. Luckily no scalp treatment will be needed because the producer and former Mr. America, Reg Lewis, did his usual outstanding job. The evening had some bugs in it, but not because of anything more than it being one of those zany, inspiring and wonderful muscle shows. This was the first time the Mr. America has been held in California. Now it looks like it might stay here for a while—lucky us.

•

CARUSO

What a judges' panel we had for this year's Mr. America contest: Larry Scott, Bill Pearl, Zabo Koszewski, Russ Warner, Seymour Koenig, Arnold Schwarzenegger, Eddie Sylvestre, Ernie Phillips and me. It wasn't just a list that was thrown together arbitrarily. Each man was carefully selected for his knowledge of the sport and his integrity. No one knew how the other man voted and no discussion was held between the judges. The results, I believe, were fair. No matter what the results, however, there is always someone around to claim "fix" because the judging didn't reflect his thinking.

This is especially true when you have top-grade contestants like Ken Waller and Boyer Coe. They are two great men of muscle and hardly a fiber of muscle separated the two. Waller won and the decision was popular with the audience.

Coe has spectacular bodyparts. His arms are probably the most dramatic I have ever seen and his legs are unbelievable. This sometimes tends to obscure weaknesses.

Grimek was great at that. He would conceal his lack of abdominal separation by doing incredible vacuums or his lack of pecs by showing you his phenomenal chest expansion.

Coe, unfortunately, doesn't yet have this type of showmanship. He relies on the artillery he has and drags the weak areas behind him. At this showing Boyer seemed to be smooth around the chest, and, like Grimek, he doesn't seem to have abdominal separation. These are some of the things that cost him the title.

Yes, I voted for Waller this time around. Mine may be the only vote you'll know, but I like calling my shots so everyone can hear them. Coe is a nice guy with a fantastic set of muscles. The next time Waller and Coe meet it could be another story. In the meantime all hail to the new Mr. America for a well-deserved victory.

Probably the funniest thing of the whole show was the man-eating curtain. You see, the contest was held on this tremendous stage and the curtain had to match the size in order to cover everything. Whenever the curtain would open or close, it would swing way out in an arc, like a dancer's skirt. Almost each time it opened or closed it would knock over some trophies or flowers or something.

Almost daring it to get him was Reg Lewis, who set up his lectern and little light in the path of the cloth dreadnaught. Time and time again it would make a swipe at his mighty muscles. Still he remained. The curtain got angry and then it happened. Reg called for the curtain to close while another act was being prepared. The monster started roaring down the pike. The giant folds crested like waves. The build-up was awesome. Unfortunately, Reg had his back to the impending onslaught and the curtain literally swallowed him. Just like Jonah or Pinnochio, Reg was no longer with us. He was buried deep in the heavy folds of the curtain. The creature wouldn't let go. All we could do was hear Reg over the PA system laughing about being swallowed by a curtain.

I ran onstage and tried to find him. Fortunately the light on the lectern guided me to him, so I pulled away fold after fold. This was almost as funny as the time Reg told me they decided to cut the bodybuilder's routines short by putting them on a revolving platform that was handcranked from behind the curtain. The contestant stood on the platform and was cranked on and off the stage. Something went wrong, however, and the men were cranked on too fast as they burst through the curtain in surprise and would just be hitting their first pose as they were wheeled off and back through the curtain. Ah, yes. The madness in bodybuilding. Maybe this is why we do it.

Perhaps the most inspiring moment of the evening came when Reg asked Arnold and Franco to pose together after they finished their individual posing exhibitions. The audience had already been treated to one of the most exciting muscular displays ever witnessed. They had just seen Franco Columbu dazzle them with lumps they hadn't thought existed. This was followed by the Oak, and no words can describe that. Now Reg was asking two of the greatest musclemen in the history of bodybuilding to pose together on the same platform. Reg, like everyone else, thought they would just stand behind each other and throw some poses. That would have been enough.

The music or something changed all that as they started going through a synchronized set of poses. It was like an adagio act. I've never seen anything like it. It would have been good if it were just a couple of so-so bodybuilders, but these were two of the greatest musclemen in the world. It was almost too much to accept.

Later Arnold told me he and Franco practiced this routine every so often. It helps that Franco is smaller and this allowed the Oak to see the moves Franco was going to do and then copy them. Every so often they would whisper to one another what pose they were going to do. My feeling is they will never again be able to capture the electricity of this performance. Its very impromptu nature made it unforgettable. Little did Reg know what he was doing when he asked them to pose together.

•

Bits of chalk...One of the toughest jobs of the evening was trying to find the right trophy for the right person. Every time Reg would call out a winner there was a mad scramble at the trophy table. I was almost gored by a victory wreath and again by a torch. The only thing I could get out of giving out awards was blood poisoning...funny (boo hoo), but no one asked me to kiss one of the girls when I handed out an award. Most of the time they yell out "Kiss her! Kiss her!" This time all there was were yawns. Maybe I'm just getting old...The night after the show Don Peters, Franco Columbu, Michelle Matisse (Miss Americana) and Reg Lewis appeared on local television. I still say TV is missing the boat by not televising the actual show. Some day someone with a little imagination at some station will get the idea and then everyone will discover what you and I already know...Ed Giuliani came to the contest wearing a tremendous split in his biceps. It looked great...The great physique photographer, Russ Warner, handled the lighting for the show and his magic worked. Later Arnold asked Russ if he would do him a favor by photographing him. That's quite a compliment, but one that's been earned through years of experience... On that somber note I must fade away into the pool of posing oil and no more nonsense.

A Day in the Life of the Oak

"Listen, Dick," said Arnold Schwarzenegger, "why don't you come out here tomorrow and I'll give you my forearm routine?"

"You mean to your place?" I asked.

"Ya. You've never been here before."

He was right. I'd yet to visit the Oak's pad and I was curious to see where he had taken root. (I know that's a lousy joke, but have mercy anyway.)

"Well, can't you give me the exercises over the phone?" I asked.

"Why?" asked the big one.

"Because I know once I'm at your place we'll never get any work done. Between you and Franco, who can get any work done?"

"But, Dick," replied Arnold, "Franco and I are a story without the exercises."

Dummy that I am, I was passing up a good story without realizing it. It finally dawned on me that what Arnold and his roommate, Franco, did during the day might be interesting to those of you thumbing through these pages.

We set it up to get together early Sunday morning. The next logical step was to get a capable photographer to record the historic events. Who could that be? Right. Lovable Artie Zeller. Who else?

"Does Arnold have any trunks?" he asked.

"You don't understand. We're not doing any muscle shots. It's just gonna be a story of a day in the life of Arnold Schwarzenegger."

"Does Arnold have any trunks?"

"Look," I insisted, "we're just gonna take some shots around the apartment. You know—looking at TV, eating..."

"Arnold still doesn't have any trunks, right?"

There was a pause.

"Right," I said finally. You may not believe this but Mr. Universe, Arnold Schwarzenegger, usually has to borrow posing trunks for pictures and this drives Zeller nuts.

"The beast of the earth!" exclaimed Art.

"Easy now," I cautioned, "remember your blood pressure."

"That makes as much sense as a baseball player trying to hit the ball without a bat," said Art, his voice rising. "Or going spearfishing without a spear or..."

"Aw, shaddup!"

Sunday was a good day. It was sunny and warm. I had the feeling this would be a good story.

Arnold and Franco live on a palm-lined street in Santa Monica just a few minutes from Zeller's place. The apartment is on the third floor and we had to climb a picturesque stairway to get there.

"Hello, Art!" boomed Arnold's familiar voice as Zeller reached the already open door. Inside it was bright and airy, almost like being in a solarium.

"I took you at your word," he said, as he stood there in his pajamas. "You want to do a story on my entire day so I decided to stay in bed and sleep until you came."

With that he turned around and went back into his bedroom. We followed and noticed a giant stuffed bear by his bed. "Is dat oos?" I asked.

"Ya," thundered the Oak as he tossed it on the bed.

We could hear rock music coming from the living room. "Do you have any Kaye Kayser records?" I asked. Maybe they couldn't hear me.

"How about Lawrence Welk? Wayne Kink?"

"How about Johnny Cash?" asked Arnold. "He's my favorite."

No sooner was Cash telling us how he planned to walk the line than the doorbell rang. It was Frank Zane. We all sat around and talked on this typical lazy Sunday morning.

"Dick," Arnold bellowed. He seems to get his ideas in sudden bursts. "Have you seen my Bible?"

"Huh?" He went over to the bookshelf and pulled down an aging leather-covered Bible that was dated 1811.

Its pages were yellow and brittle. In one section it listed the births, deaths, and marriages of the family who owned it. The last entry was written by an obviously elderly person. It was dated 1955. The family had originally come from New Hampshire and then settled in Michigan. The final entry was written from West Los Angeles. And now this holy work that had been cherished for over 150 years by one family was in the hands of Arnold Schwarzenegger from Austria. I looked up at Arnold. His face was wreathed in pleasure. I felt it was in good hands.

We sat around eating and watching TV for a while. Eventually the sun got to be too much for Arnold.

"Look at that beautiful weather out there. Let's go to Muscle Beach," he said.

I was nearly trampled in the rush to the door. My Super Pro 101 nearly went down my throat, can and all. Art and I scrambled for the car and we almost peeled rubber in our dash for the golden sands.

ZELLER

Muscle and cool bikes go together like lightning and thunder. Arnold and Franco are checking out a pair of racy customized beasts, their alter egos of roaring steel.

Everyone must have been there. Athletes, hippies, motorcyclists and squares like us were all mingling under the paternal eye of the Santa Monica police. Even though they tore down the adagio platform and removed the weights, it was still Muscle Beach. The gymnasts had just moved a few feet away to a grassy area. Once again the crowds gathered as in the days of old.

Gypsy Boots was there cavorting with the tumblers. Russ

Saunders, the world-famous Hollywood stuntman, was teaching some youngsters the finer points of gymnastics as he's been doing for years, while the world-famous adagio team of David and Goliath thrilled the spectators.

ZELLER

Somehow Muscle Beach is magically revived for a day as if to please our Italian and Austrian brothers. Artie and Dick must be having a ball in this flurry of nostalgia. Long live Muscle Beach in the hearts of real men and women.

Zeller couldn't stand it. Too much was happening that he wanted to photograph. Arnold and Franco got carried away and started practicing some tricks. They were pretty good. One can only imagine how good they would be with a little practice.

"I've got to take a picture of all this," said Artie, scurrying.

With that he mounted a big cement sign and started doing his Cecil B. De Mille bit. It was amazing how everyone quieted down and listened.

"You move in a little closer. Russ, I want you to jump on the board at the count of three so Pavia will be in the air when I take the picture. Gypsy, I want you to perform a pyramid with the girls. Gypsy? Gypsy!"

Boots was busy handing out posters for his next health show. Finally everything was organized.

"Ready?" yelled Art, "one, two, three!"

There was an explosion of activity. When the dust had settled, there was applause.

"Let's do that once more," said Art. "It wasn't just what I wanted."

The athletes groaned. Once again Gypsy formed the base of a pyramid for the girls. I thought I detected a blood vessel in his forehead begin to throb.

"Ready? One, two, three."

Again people went flying in all directions.

"Beautiful!" exclaimed Art. "Now, just once more."

The audience groaned this time. Even Gypsy Boots let out a moan. Again the scene was loaded. This time I was sure I saw that blood vessel throbbing on Gypsy's forehead. Again Art barked out his commands and this time it was a print.

After an hour or two we wandered to the chess tables nearby.

"Come!" said Arnold to Franco. "I beat you in a game of chess."

The game progressed, and so did the sun until it was kissing the horizon. Art and I said goodbye, but Arnold and Franco were so deeply involved in their game they didn't answer.

ZELLER

Chess is a game of deep concentration and long-term strategy. It is not undertaken by lightweight minds or the frivolous. These guys aren't pretending to play to impress an audience; they're playing to win...or lose.

Champions are forever.

We started to walk up the street. As we got to the top of the hill I heard a shout, "Goodbye, Dick!"

I turned around and shaded my eyes from the sun. Arnold was waving from the chess table. As we got in the car I looked up at the approaching evening sky with its frame of palm trees.

"That was fun wasn't it?" said Art.

I nodded and we drove away.

Afterword

For some reason I decided to go to a movie, a Saturday matinee. The theater was packed with screaming kids there to see the first "Superman" film with Christopher Reeve. The first part of the film was pure fun with everyone laughing and enjoying the man of steel's legendary feats of strength. Then he takes the lovely Lois Lane for a flying trip around the New York skyline. The kids in the theater were jumping up and down, some pretending they were flying.

At last Superman brings Lois back to her apartment. Dazzled by her flying experience Lois asks just what he stands for. His answer, "Truth, justice and the American way."

"Oh, come on," says Lois sarcastically. This mirrored the great laughter of the reaction of the audience.

Now the camera came to a close shot of Superman's face. His eyes narrowed and he replied very simply, "Lois, I never lie."

The theater sudden went silent. I could almost hear a pin drop. At that point a completely different perception took place. With the simplicity and sincerity of the statement—Lois, I never lie—the movie was transformed from a large production of a cartoon character to an epic journey in the battle of good against evil. It was the turning point of the film.

Another such example was the first "Rocky" film. Poor Rocky was out of shape for his upcoming championship fight and his wife, who was always after him to quit fighting, was in a coma in the hospital. To the great frustration of the audience, Rocky sits by her bed mumbling how much he loves her, when her eyes flutter open.

"Rocky," she whispers.

"Oh, honey, you're awake!" he says excitedly.

She motions for him to come closer and whispers one simple word, "Win."

With that, the famous Rocky theme thundered throughout the theater and the audience was electrified. With a single word, what was a corny fight film became a classic. It was that film's turning point.

I have often felt most successful endeavors revolve around a turning point that makes the common become uncommon and even great. This happened in bodybuilding with the advent of the first Mr. Olympia contest in New York.

It was not, however, the contest itself but what led up to it. For years bodybuilding contests were treated as little more than a freak show tacked to the end of a weightlifting meet, which might not end until the early morning hours.

When Steve Reeves starred in a film about Hercules in the late fifties, the public perception of bodybuilders began to change. While more and more gyms began to open, the world of bodybuilding was still a world unto itself. The public might look in wonder at the massive muscles of those who wore them, but they essentially had no concept of what it took to get them. They knew nothing of the hours and years of the smell of sweat, the clanging of heavy plates, the yells of the training partners or the grunts of agony and pain to get out one more rep. They knew nothing of sacrifices in a bodybuilder's personal life or the hours of sleep required or the diet and nutritional supplementation needed to get the most out of training. Only the true bodybuilder knew that. The money has not been minted that would be sufficient to equal the value of the sacrifices needed to become a bodybuilding champion.

It wasn't until the early '60s when Joe Weider came up with the idea of having a competition to pit only the winners of major contests against each other that the bodybuilders themselves began to realize the importance and financial value of their enterprise. This was the birth of the first Mr. Olympia.

Little did anyone realize at the time, however, the real beginning of bodybuilding's turning point would be not in the Olympia contest itself, but in the Mr. America competition that was to precede it the same night.

For over a year Weider had been extolling the wonders of a young bodybuilder named Dave Draper. He was a big kid with big muscles and had just won the Mr. New Jersey title. The problem was he was just that, a kid with big muscles. All the photos we had of his training gave the perception of a muscular Pillsbury Doughboy. There was only a small amount of muscular separation and little, if any, definition. To make things even more difficult, he had no tan. He made a white sheet look grey.

This is who Joe sent to California. One of my jobs at the time was to chronicle the bodybuilding scene in Southern California. It was virtually dumped on me to build up this Blond Bomber to hero status as part of this job.

Fortunately Dave turned out to be a nice guy and easy to talk with. Unfortunately he never wanted to talk about himself. Since my job was to write about and build up the image of the Bomber, I was in trouble as I was able to learn little about his training, and worse, just what on earth he looked like.

He always wore a baggy shirt with the sleeves turned to just above the wrists. From that I was at least sure he had the most muscular wrists I'd ever seen. He trained at the then-Muscle Beach Gym, known to everyone as the Dungeon, always away from others, at times when few others were there...and always in heavy sweats. In other words he was the best known unknown in bodybuilding and wasn't about to be any help in changing that image.

For a while he hosted a local television station's show that played all the gladiator-type movies of the time. While we could see he was big, he never flexed or posed in any way, so it was no help to me at all.

I was beginning to panic. How could I write anything that was more myth that substance? However, my job was not so much to think as to do. So, I expanded on the things I knew: He was a great person to be around and he was very strong.

In the meantime Weider came up with the idea of the Mr. Olympia contest to determine the champion of champions. It was to be held at the Brooklyn Academy of Music along with the Mr. America, Mr. Universe and Miss Americana competitions. And guess what? Dave Draper was to be an entrant in the Mr. America, his first competition since winning the Mr. New Jersey two years before.

To me and to everyone else, for Dave to enter the Mr. America competition was something of a joke. This was to be the greatest bodybuilding extravaganza every presented. To take a virtually untested bodybuilder, build him into almost mythical proportions and then offer him as some kind of freakish sacrifice was the height of cruelty. I felt sorry for Dave and the anxiety he must have been feeling.

Finally it was the day of the contest. In New York, with Weider driving, we picked up Rick Wayne and Earl Maynard from their hotel. They had just arrived from England and were quite excited about competing that night. Soon the conversation turned to the contestants and, of course, to Dave Draper.

Rick, with his biting wit, began to ridicule Dave in not a very gentle way. "Oh, yes," he said, "The great Dave Draper, otherwise known in England as the great white whale." I started to laugh. Ooops.

Joe glanced over at me, "Wait till they see him, eh, Dick?"

I gulped. "Yeah, right," I replied weakly. "Just you wait."

That didn't slow Rick or Earl down a bit; they were on that proverbial roll. I only wish I'd had a tape recorder—this was funny stuff. Joe, however, was not amused.

The Brooklyn Academy is an enormous opera house. Just off the main stage was a dressing room that had been turned into a warm-up area, and in it, preparing for the prejudging, were just about all the great bodybuilders of that time. They were all either pumping like mad or practicing their posing in front of the mirrors. It was a writhing pit of muscles in the truest sense.

But where was the vaunted Blond Bomber? He was in a corner, lifting in a robe. Still, no one knew what he looked like. The moment of truth was fast approaching.

A few minutes before Dave was to go before the judges, Wayne approached him. "Look, Dave," he said, taunting. "I do believe you plan to pose with your robe on. Is that right?"

Dave didn't answer as others began to gather around. I watched and could tell the pain he was feeling. The others started kidding and telling him to take off the robe.

What happened next is hard to describe. It's one of those rare times when words fail to carry the message of what the eyes see.

Dave dropped his robe and for the first time we could see what he had been so carefully hiding. There was an audible gasp from those who gathered around. Rick Wayne took a step backwards and his jaw dropped.

I have personally never seen such a combination of raw power sculptured on such bronzed, separated and defined muscles in my life.

Dave Draper went on to win the Mr. America, which began the turning point that culminated with Larry Scott winning the evening's Mr. Olympia contest. That night set the benchmark for all that would follow in the pages you just read, and the years that came after.

Almost like Rocky, the audience leaned forward as Joe Weider whispered "Dave Draper," and the individuals were electrified. And, dear reader, as in "Superman" what I've told you is true because…I never lie.

Dick Tyler
January 2004

To the lensmasters

Many years ago I was a child actor and worked in the films a great deal. What the cameramen did with the lighting directors always fascinated me. While others might be drinking coffee and eating donuts, I would sit and watch them produce their magic. They would take what seemed a bland mixture of chairs and tables and would paint their "canvas" with deft strokes of light and filters. While it was the actors who got most of the attention, it was the cameramen and the lighting directors who made what might look plain and turned it into the rare.

Those of us who write about bodybuilding know all too well that no one would read what we put down without first being inspired to do so by seeing a great photo. I might never have started weight training had I not seen pictures of Eric Pedersen's big arms, or the powerful physique of John Grimek. This, then, is a tribute to those who stood behind the lenses and created the images that inspired us all. The Lanzas, Carusos, Warners, Urbans, Zellers and so many other led. Those of us who wrote only followed.

Dick Tyler

About the Author

Dick Tyler was an actor for twenty-six years. During that time he starred on Broadway and later in a television series winning numerous acting awards. His abiding love of strength and well-developed muscles led him into writing for Joe Weider. It was this enterprise that helped put him through chiropractic college. Dick has been a practicing chiropractic doctor for the last thirty-five years; he presently lives and practices in Rocklin, California.

About the Photographers

The reader will have by now discovered the great affection Dick Tyler and the rest of the characters of the Golden Era felt for the photographers recording their history. Thanks to the following artists for their contributions to this book, and to our knowledge and memories of bodybuilding.

Bruce Bellas, Jimmy Caruso, Pat Casey, Cecil Charles, Steve Downs, Lon Hanigan, George Kaye, Don Leomazzi, Gene Mozee, Bill Pearl, Ray Raridon, Anita Santangelo, Wolf Schramm, Leo Stern, Dick Tyler, Al Urban, Russ Warner, Art Zeller

Index